Greek Pedagogy in Crisis

Greek Pedagogy in Crisis

A Pedagogical Analysis and Assessment of New Testament Greek in Twenty-First-Century Theological Education

David R. Miller

FOREWORD BY
David Alan Black

WIPF & STOCK · Eugene, Oregon

GREEK PEDAGOGY IN CRISIS
A Pedagogical Analysis and Assessment of New Testament Greek in Twenty-First-Century Theological Education

Copyright © 2019 David R. Miller. All rights reserved. Except for brief quotations in critical publications or reviews, no part of this book may be reproduced in any manner without prior written permission from the publisher. Write: Permissions, Wipf and Stock Publishers, 199 W. 8th Ave., Suite 3, Eugene, OR 97401.

Wipf & Stock
An Imprint of Wipf and Stock Publishers
199 W. 8th Ave., Suite 3
Eugene, OR 97401

www.wipfandstock.com

PAPERBACK ISBN: 978-1-5326-9093-8
HARDCOVER ISBN: 978-1-5326-9094-5
EBOOK ISBN: 978-1-5326-9095-2

This Dissertation is prepared and presented to the Faculty as a part of the requirements for the Doctor of Education Degree at Southeastern Baptist Theological Seminary, Wake Forest, North Carolina. All rights and privileges normally reserved by the author as a copyright holder are waived for the Seminary. The Seminary Library may catalog, display, and use this Dissertation in all normal ways such materials are used, for reference, and for other purposes, including electronic and other means of preservation and circulation, including on-line access and other means by which library materials are or in the future may be made available to researchers and library users.

Scripture quotations taken from the New American Standard Bible® (NASB), Copyright © 1960, 1962, 1963, 1968, 1971, 1972, 1973, 1975, 1977, 1995 by The Lockman Foundation Used by permission. www.Lockman.org

Manufactured in the U.S.A.

To my father, Ricky Lee Miller
(who passed away just a few weeks before this work was finished):
You inspired me with your work ethic and
displayed to me that anything is possible.
I love you and miss you greatly.

Also to my beautiful wife Alayna Miller:
Your patience and love have supported me
every day of this process. I love you more than
words can express.

Contents

Foreword by David Alan Black | ix
Preface | xi
Abbreviations | xiii

Chapter 1
    Research Concern | 1
    Research Purpose | 3
    Research Questions | 4
    Delimitations of the Study | 5
    Terminology | 5
    Research Assumptions | 6
    Precedent Literature | 7
    Methodological Design | 9
    Chapter Summary | 13

Chapter 2
    Literature Review | 14
    Theory | 21
        A Brief History of the Greek Language | 22
        Grammar–Translation Method | 23
        Unique Models | 28
        Non–Greek–Specific Approaches | 38
    Chapter Summary | 66

Chapter 3
    Research Methodology | 67
    Research Questions | 67
    Research Design | 67
    Description of the Sample | 68

Description of the Instruments Used, and
the Procedures Followed | 69
Internal Validity | 71
External Validity | 73
Chapter Summary | 74

Chapter 4
Research Findings | 75
Expert Survey | 75
Chapter Summary | 115

Chapter 5
Summary and Conclusions | 116
Summary of Research and Procedure | 116
S.W.O.T. Analysis | 117
Language Teaching Methodology Comparison | 122
Final Thoughts on the Survey | 123
Implications of the Findings | 127
A Proposal for a Pedagogical Solution: Exegetical Greek | 128
Instructional Design for Exegetical Greek | 129
Structural Elements of Exegetical Greek | 135
The Resulting Product: Exegetical Greek | 140
Application of Exegetical Greek | 146
Limitations | 151
Suggestions for Further Research | 151
Chapter Summary | 152

Appendix 1
List of Experts | 153

Appendix 2
GTM Expert Survey Transcript | 155

Appendix 3
GTM Expert Survey Response Transcripts | 159

Bibliography | 239

Foreword

David Alan Black

When David Miller asked me to write a foreword to his book, I immediately agreed. This was for two reasons. In the first place, David wrote his dissertation under my supervision, and I knew him to be one of the finest students I've had the opportunity to work with. In the second place, my own journey as a Greek teacher has been a combination of academic and practionioner and has bred certain convictions in me, not least that a revolution in Greek pedagogy is long overdue.

I began teaching Greek at Biola University in 1976. I was still years away from getting my doctorate in New Testament. But I had developed a deep love for Koine Greek, a love that has never left me. Verbs, nouns, paradigms—I was fascinated by them all. Several years later, a big change occurred. B & H Academic asked me to produce my own beginning Greek grammar. I declined. I did not regard my approach as sufficiently different from that of the textbook I was using in my classes. They asked me again. This time I said I would commit the matter to prayer. Four months later they had a completed manuscript on their desk.

Now, at that time I knew a good deal about Greek but very little about pedagogy. Thankfully, God gave me the good sense to recognize this shortcoming. In fact, the year I began teaching at Biola I also enrolled in two classes in the Christian Education Department—College Teaching Procedures, and Tests and Measurements. Both classes proved invaluable to me as I embarked on what is now a 43-year career of teaching Greek. These courses set me to thinking. I had unwittingly stumbled upon one of the most important discoveries of my academic career. Elton Trueblood, the great American Quaker scholar, put it this way in one of the books I read that semester: "Holy shoddy is still shoddy." This quote would prove to be a mantra I would follow throughout the course of my career, although I have never lived up to it. I was now convinced that pedagogy played an essential role in becoming a Greek teacher. And I realized that it all had to do with outcomes. If our students are not using what they learn, what earthly good was their instruction?

That was not all. My searchings over the next few years had convinced me that the goal of Greek instruction was exegesis, not grammar. "What are you going to *do* with this information?" I began asking my students. Although there was still much about Greek pedagogy I didn't understand, the heart of the matter was now plain to me. The study of Greek would require of us far more than getting an A on the final exam. What I had discovered was that Greek needed to be applied if it was to justify its existence in our curriculum. An old Scottish proverb puts it like this: "Greek, Hebrew, and Latin all have their proper place, but it's not at the head of the cross where Pilate put them, but at the foot of the cross in humble service to Jesus." The imagery of the cross was lucid and compelling, so much so that I decided to produce a practical book called *Using New Testament Greek in Ministry* that outlined reasons and a methodology for using our knowledge of Greek for the edification of Christ's church. It is not knowledge but application that matters. Curiously enough, many Greek teachers had enunciated this truth, but few had ever done any scientific research into the effectiveness (or lack thereof) of our methodologies.

Enter David Miller's book. When I took David under my wings several years ago, I had no idea that he would produce such a helpful work. This book occupied a great deal of his time, and when it was finished I strongly encouraged him to have it published. As you will see, the book is lively, contemporary, and has a somewhat racy style. The author writes compellingly about the evidence for exegesis-focused Greek instruction on the one hand, and equally compellingly about the significance that sound pedagogy has for our churches and our individual lives. Nowadays Greek teachers are wondering (some out loud) if their approach to Greek instruction could stand up to critical examination. This book has the answer to that question. It is a tract for our times, and it is being published at just the right time, combining as it does competent scholarship with a reverent attitude toward the biblical text. This book is in no sense a dogmatic manual, but sets out to start a conversation about Greek pedagogy, a conversation that, as I said above, is long overdue. I have found the book to be both provocative and edifying. After all, sound pedagogy has always been a central concern of mine. How can we teach Greek if we don't question our methodologies? The book, therefore, has a real place in the whole of Christian education.

I do not suggest that this book will resolve all of the nagging issues that Greek teachers face. But it will go a long way toward doing that. As Greek instructors, we must be willing to submit our own preferences to what will best serve the community in which we worship and serve. This book has helped me to do just that, and I trust you will come away from reading it with the same result.

Preface

IN THE FALL SEMESTER of 2005 I took my first biblical language course. My degree at Moody Bible Institute only required two vague "foreign language" courses, which meant German, Spanish, Greek, Hebrew, etc. qualified. I wanted to learn more about God's word and almost every professor at Moody strongly encouraged original languages, so I signed up for New Testament Greek. I did not do well. My professor, Dr. Michael Vanlaningham, did an excellent job making the class entertaining and the language easy to grasp, but I had never learned another language and was struggling with dyslexia, making my learning process considerably different from most others. Even though I struggled, I enjoyed it immensely. Being able to read the Bible in its original language was exciting and, in many ways, fulfilling as well. Ultimately, I went on to take graduate level Hebrew courses, in addition to Greek courses all the way up to the doctoral level. Throughout all those courses and study groups and late-night discussions, an honest confession kept surfacing from fellow students. The confession was that many of the students, dare I say the vast majority, had lost or forgotten their language proficiency.

Again and again, I have heard professors (gently) chastise their first-year students about practicing and retaining their language skills after the coursework is finished, and yet, the struggle remained. The students I have known, myself included, really wanted to attain proficiency and use their biblical language abilities for personal and professional Bible studies and sermons. They did not lack the motivation to learn and retain the language, the skills simply were pushed out by too many other necessary skills for ministry. In the end, a tradesman can obtain every tool ever made and not use the majority of them. The tools used are the tools needed. A carpenter does not need plumbing or electrical tools just as a plumber does not need masonry tools. Unused tools become clutter, and still other, more practical tools, may never get used because proper training has not been attained. So, does theological higher education in America today understand the value, the scope and sequence, the volume, or the demands that are needed to prepare ministry students in modern Christian vocations?

I have met too many students and pastors who have confessed to these same struggles with humility and even some disappointment. Every one of these Christian leaders want to understand the Word of God better and they deeply desire to proclaim the Word well. Original languages are a key component to these goals, but it cannot be a coincidence that so many students from various backgrounds and institutions lack the ability to retain their language proficiency. I wanted to dig deeper into this dilemma and discover the root of the issue. I wanted to know if the culprit was the professors, the institutions, or the students. On the other hand, what if the problem that has caused so many students to falter in their noble desire was not an active agent at all? What if the contributing factor to this matter was a "tool" that had become dull, laborious, and/or inefficient? Maybe it started as a sharp and effective tool that made learning languages easy, but time weakened its ability to be useful. This is precisely where I decided to begin my research. I wanted to assess the way original languages are taught (pedagogy) and discover why the results have been so inconsistent. Additionally, in an effort to initiate a conversation on the subject, I wanted to design a new approach (methodology), from the ground up, beginning with cutting-edge educational research and didactic best practices. My genuine desire is to find a better way to teach biblical languages to the benefit of the students who take the courses, the churches where those students will serve, and the awesome God whom we proclaim.

Abbreviations

BCE	Before Common Era
CE	Common Era
GTM	Grammar–Translation Method
M.A.	Master of Arts
M.Div.	Master of Divinity
NT	New Testament
OT	Old Testament
Ph.D.	Doctor of Philosophy
SLA	Second Language Acquisition
TBLT	Task–Based Language Teaching

Chapter 1

Research Concern

THE PROCESS OF LEARNING and the results of using biblical languages are immeasurably valuable to the theological student regardless of age, gender, geographical location, or professional vocation.[1] New Testament Greek, the principal focus of this work, can certainly be a daunting task to learn and a precarious effort to apply properly, but it is not without intrinsic motivation. Benjamin Merkle and Robert Plummer express that "the goal of learning Greek is first and foremost born out of a desire to behold unhindered the grandest sight: God himself."[2] On the same note, David Alan Black states that learning Greek is done to "glorify God."[3] The sixteenth-century reformer, Martin Luther wrote, "Although the gospel came and still comes to us through the Holy Spirit alone, we cannot deny that it came through the medium of languages, was spread abroad by that means, and must be preserved by the same means."[4] The study and application of Greek hold such richness and reward that A. T. Robertson once wrote that "the minute study called for by the Greek opens up unexpected treasures that surprise and delight the soul."[5] With these quotes in mind, it is clear that the church needs men and women who can properly exegete Scripture through the use of biblical languages to better understand God and his plan. And, based on this necessity, it is vital that the theological institutions and related authors

---

1. Although New Testament Greek will be the primary example in this study, the concepts and applications can be easily adapted to other ancient languages such as Hebrew, Aramaic, and Latin.
2. Merkle and Plummer, *Greek for Life*, 2.
3. Black, *Using New Testament Greek in Ministry*, 9.
4. Luther, *To the Councilmen of All Cities in Germany That They Establish and Maintain Christian Schools*, 358. Luther later added (on p. 364), "It is . . . a stupid undertaking to attempt to gain an understanding of Scripture by laboring through the commentaries of the fathers and a multitude of books and glosses. Instead of this, men should have devoted themselves to the languages. . . . If you knew the languages, you could get further with the passage than they whom you are following. As sunshine is to shadow, so is the language itself compared to all the glosses of the fathers."
5. Robertson, *The Minister and His Greek New Testament*, 21.

who train and equip pastors and missionaries worldwide search continuously for improvements in teaching these language skills.

Many theological institutions today faithfully teach New Testament Greek through a centuries-old method which, although it has its benefits, may be severely outdated. The current, majority-used method of teaching New Testament (NT) Greek is called the Grammar-Translation Method (GTM) or Classical/Traditional Method.[6] The name, GTM is derived from its core model of teaching a language through building the student's knowledge of the basic rules of grammar, paradigms, and key vocabulary words to lead toward the ability to translate and, in some cases, read the target language for use in research.[7] The name, "Classical/Traditional" came from the use of this model in the teaching of classical Greek and Latin. This instructional tool originated in the early sixteenth century, shortly after Erasmus published his major updates of the Latin Vulgate and the Greek New Testament (1516 CE). He then placed a major emphasis on the "classical" pronunciation of these languages (c. 400 BCE–500 CE) as opposed to the "modern" pronunciation (c. 500 CE–modern day).

Erasmus's work was monumental for its time and allowed the Scriptures to be translated into dozens of common languages, which would later eliminate lay people's need to learn Hebrew, Aramaic, Greek, or Latin to read the Word of God for themselves. But the foundation Erasmus laid, which helped produce Luther's German translation (1522) and William Tyndale's English Bible (1526), has seen little change over the last 500 years. This is not to say that the GTM is obsolete and completely ineffective. On the contrary, it is quite helpful for many aspects of learning classical languages for research, but it is also highly antiquated for modern theological Greek students who seek to use its fruits in their weekly ministry. Therefore, this dissertation seeks to analyze and assess the pedagogical approach to NT Greek through a twenty-first-century educational mindset focused on usability and practical application for hundreds of theological students that will begin this indispensable portion of their training in the coming years.

---

6. This statement is a result of sales numbers for New Testament Greek textbooks sold through Amazon.com and Christian Book Distributors (CBD) from 2000–2016. The list of top selling books includes those by William Mounce, David Alan Black, N. Clayton Croy, S. M. Baugh, all of whom employ the GTM in differing forms based on their lesson content and exercises.

7. McManis, Stollenwerk, and Zhang, *Language Files*, 259–62. Et al.

CHAPTER 1

Research Purpose

The purpose of this research is twofold: (1) to discover the strengths, weaknesses, opportunities, and threats (S.W.O.T.) of the GTM; and (2) to begin the process of developing a more modern, innovative, and purposeful NT Greek pedagogy for modern theological students that are called into non-academic ministry. These two aspects of the research purpose will be explored later, but suffice it to say that the goal is not to modernize the 500-year-old method. Rather, the intention will be to find a language learning model that may best complement GTM while also creating a sustainable design beneficial to learners today as well as those who follow them.

Aspect One: Grammar–Translation S.W.O.T.

Although the quality of architecture and craftsmanship has waned over the last few centuries, building costs, design quality, and efficiency have greatly improved. Gone are the drafty castles and rickety shanties replaced with precision cut doors, double-paned windows, and fiberglass insulation. Similarly, gone are the days of hand-written copies of books and manuscripts; they have been replaced by copy machines and digital PDFs. The best and worst aspects of a stone-built dwelling in England provided innumerable lessons for current construction practices just as hand-copied papyri drafts helped expose the need for and determine the process of press printing and later digital reproduction. Most advances do not occur in a vacuum; they are built upon numerous changes and adjustments in the past. Therefore, it is important to remember that GTM has been and still is quite helpful in many ways (e.g., morphology). However, it is also important to identify what those helpful aspects have been and in what manner GTM can still be useful and beneficial to the modern student. It is also quite imperative to recognize the weaknesses of such approaches (e.g., rote memorization) to improve upon deficiencies and work toward modernization. That is why this study will explore the strengths, weaknesses, opportunities, and threats that exist when using GTM for teaching NT Greek.

Aspect Two: Innovative Instructional Methodology

The danger of approaching a comparison of methodologies today, where one is old and one is modern, is that a teacher or institution can carelessly assume nothing that is 500 years old has any use today. Newer is not always better, which is why a methodology comparison cannot function properly until a full analysis has been performed on the existing pedagogy in question. Without analyzing the S.W.O.T. of GTM first, it is not possible to understand what changes, adjustments, or adaptations need to be made to improve the instruction of NT Greek in theological institutions. After completing the S.W.O.T. analysis, researching how languages are best learned today can provide excellent insight into how to improve instruction as needed. This process will be done through dissecting the procedures of the most-used modern-day language teaching methods of Second Language Acquisition (SLA), Task-Based Language Teaching (TBLT), Scaffolding, and Learning Target practices.[8] The details gleaned from these three popular methods will then be compared to and contrasted against GTM to help build a more useful and beneficial model for teaching Greek for non-academic students. This study will focus primarily on non-academic students because the majority of Bible college and seminary students go on to serve in churches, on the mission field, or in the secular industry. Additionally, this delimitation allows the researcher to concentrate on a ministry-oriented direction, which would result in more specific changes and therefore have a more immediate impact.

Research Questions

1. What, if any, are the current benefits and detriments of the Grammar-Translation Method on New Testament Greek instruction in the twenty-first century?

2. To what extent, if any, can current, unique pedagogical methods help improve New Testament Greek instruction in the twenty-first century?

3. To what extent, if any, can the research and practices of Second Language Acquisition, Task-Based Language Teaching, and Educational Scaffolding help improve New Testament Greek instruction in the twenty-first century?

4. What would a modern, non-academically focused Greek pedagogy look like in today's theological educational setting?

---

8. Many educational authors relate Learning Targets to Scaffolding; the only identifiable differences are (1) cosmetic: where Scaffolding is explained as a vertical process of learning, Learning Targets are described as a bullseye approach that works its way inward instead of upward, and (2) applicability: Scaffolding is most often applied to an overall structure whereas Learning Targets can be applied to daily instruction as easily as it can be to an entire semester.

Delimitations of the Study

This study will be delimited in the following ways:

1. The subject matter of this dissertation is New Testament Greek.
2. The setting of the of this study is intended for theological institutions of higher education.
3. The use GTM in teaching NT Greek will be assessed as the primary model of teaching in theological education.
4. An emphasis is placed on non–academically focused students of theological education (e.g., pastoral, evangelical, or lay ministry).

Terminology

1. Grammar–Translation Method—The classical method of teaching primarily Greek and Latin that focuses on a target language's grammatical concepts to help the student gain the ability to translate the target language.
2. Grammar—The basic system and structure of any language (including vocabulary, parts of speech, declensions, tense structure, etc.).
3. Translation—The practice of carrying the meaning of one language into another language (spoken or written).
4. Method—A particular style of doing something (e.g., teaching, exercise, etc.).
5. Second Language Acquisition—The process of learning a second language after establishing a first language.
6. Task–Based Language Teaching—An aspect of SLA that emphasizes the use of language through asking students to do meaningful tasks using the target language in and outside of the classroom.
7. Task—An objective goal the teacher sets for the student to accomplish.
8. Scaffolding—This process of teaching starts at the bottom of a learning process and works its way to the top. The bottom level of information is the most basic facts and rudimentary pieces of the course. The top of the process includes the most detailed and refined pieces of information. Similar to Bloom's Taxonomy, this process begins with easy memorization and context building while requiring the student using

critical thinking and problem solving to better understand the intricate details of the course work.

9. Learning Targets—Similar to Scaffolding, this method of teaching/learning new information within various, intentionally-designed levels of engagement (i.e., basic facts → detailed information → interactive engagement → critical assessment). The primary difference between these two procedures is that Scaffolding is an upward process and Learning Targets are an inward process.

10. Theological Education—A Christian education is specifically aimed at teaching each student the moral virtues, historical principles, and systematic practices of the Christian religion. This can be done in an undergraduate, graduate, or seminary context.

11. Koine Greek—The form of "common" Greek spoken and written in and around the first-century CE within the western portion of the Roman Empire. This is the specific dialect of Greek in which the New Testament of the Bible was written.

12. New Testament Greek—The specific application of Koine Greek in the original and reproduced documents of the New Testament of the Bible.

13. Modern Greek—This is the current form of the Greek language predominantly spoken in modern-day Greece.

14. Erasmian Pronunciation—A demarcation of the Greek language that refers to the "proper" pronunciation of the Greek before the sixteenth century as opposed to modern Greek.

15. Instructional Methodology—An intentional and specifically designed process of teaching the educational material.

16. Pedagogy—The method and practice of teaching, especially as an academic subject or theoretical concept.

Research Assumptions

1. That there is a need for an in-depth analysis of the current model of teaching NT Greek (i.e., GTM). This assumption will be better explained through the S.W.O.T. process and the expert survey, but little to no previous work has been done to produce any longitudinal studies regarding the use and retention of biblical languages after theological education using this approach.

2. That theological students should be required to learn both biblical languages to complete a Master of Divinity degree.
3. That biblical languages are necessary in the non-academic world today.
4. That Greek should still be taught using the Erasmian method of pronunciation rather than switching to an all-modern approach, which other researchers have suggested.
5. That NT Greek ought to be taught as a research language rather than a spoken language due to Erasmus's time frame distinction and the lack of modern-day fluent Koine Greek speakers.
6. That accurate and theologically sound biblical interpretation is the purpose of theological education (i.e., knowing the Word of God as it was intended to be known).

Precedent Literature

The History of the Greek Language

This portion of the paper will focus on the history and development of the Greek language regarding its maturation and development. Much of this portion will narrow in on the dialect of Koine Greek, which was prominent in the first-century CE and the written form used in the New Testament of the Bible. Some of the included sources are listed below:

- Adrados, Francisco Rodríguez. A History of the Greek Language: From Its Origins to the Present. Leiden; Boston: Brill, 2005.
- Christidēs, A.-F., Maria Arapopoulou, Maria Chritē, and Centre for the Greek Language. A History of Ancient Greek: From the Beginnings to Late Antiquity. Rev. & expanded translation of the Greek text. Cambridge, UK; New York: Cambridge University Press, 2007.

The Grammar-Translation Method

The majority of Greek professors in theological education have used the Grammar-Translation Method of teaching Greek. This segment of the research will consider the use and history of this practice. A few of the rich publications existing for this portion of the study include:

- Caragounis, Chrys C. The Development of Greek and the New Testament: Morphology, Syntax, Phonology, and Textual Transmission. 1st pbk. ed., with corrections. Grand Rapids: Baker, 2006.
- Fasold, Ralph W., and Jeff Connor-Linton. An Introduction to Language and Linguistics. 2nd ed. Cambridge: Cambridge, 2014.
- Richards, Jack, and Theodore Rodgers. Approaches and Methods in Language Teaching. 2nd ed. Cambridge: Cambridge University, 2001.

Second Language Acquisition and Task–Based Language Teaching

SLA and TBLT are both modern adaptations of language learning methodologies that have been developed through countless hours of research and practice. Some aspects of these methods will be highly beneficial for Greek pedagogy, but some facets do not apply to this and other classical languages. Some sources included are:

- Doughty, Catherine., and Michael H. Long. The Handbook of Second Language Acquisition. Malden, MA: Blackwell, 2003.
- Ellis, Rod. Task–Based Language Learning and Teaching. Oxford; New York: Oxford Applied Linguistics, 2003.
- Larsen-Freeman, Diane, and Marti Anderson. Techniques and Principles in Language Teaching. 3rd ed. Oxford; New York: Oxford University Press, 2011.
- Long, Mike. Second Language Acquisition and Task–Based Language Teaching. Oxford: Wiley-Blackwell, 2014.
- McManis, Carolyn, Deborah Stollenwerk, Zheng-sheng Zhang, and Ohio State University Dept. of Linguistics. Language Files: Materials for an Introduction to Language. 4th ed. Reynoldsburg, OH: Advocate, 1988.
- Nunan, David. Task–Based Language Teaching. Cambridge: Cambridge Language Teaching Library, 2004.

CHAPTER 1

Methodological Design

Population and Sample

Thirty-two professional Greek professors and prominent subject-matter authors participated in this study. These experts teach in the United States, Canada, and Israel while representing multiple denominations, institutions, and educational backgrounds.

Accessible Population

Thousands of professors teach NT Greek. The goal in participant selection was to procure the most notable names and the most experienced teachers in the study. When some of those most notable names were not available, recommendations were sought from the participating experts.

Sample and Sampling Procedure

These experts include authors of New Testament Greek textbooks, NT professors at accredited theological institutions (both undergraduate and graduate), and directly recommended experts in the field who are not currently writing or teaching the subject but are still highly esteemed.

Limitations of Generalization

- At this point, no long-term studies addressing student retention or post-graduation use of languages in ministry have been conducted. Some studies concerning the idea of perception exist, but these are limited in their scope, use too many generalizations, and are not focused on biblical language learning.
- GTM does not currently compare to any other methodology used because no one-to-one comparison is available. A study exposing two groups of beginning Greek students, with no prior knowledge of the language, to two different methodologies would certainly help, but it would also require additional follow-up contact to display retention and usefulness in subsequent years.
- Very few schools are attempting new or unique instructional strategies in this field and therefore applying modern strategies to a classical language learning process would be somewhat theoretical in nature.

- Many schools do not have a unified institutional approach to teaching biblical languages regarding textbooks, didactic practices, and assessment standards. Therefore, contacting schools, deans, and/or department heads would likely not result in conclusive data. Due to this reality, each professor must be contacted individually to ascertain his or her personal methodology and experience–based thoughts regarding Greek pedagogy.

Research Method

This research was built upon a survey of a hand–picked expert group of thirty–two men and women from a broad array of backgrounds, using these survey results for the basis of a S.W.O.T. analysis, and comparing the most common biblical language learning methodology with modern practices. This information was then assessed and employed to develop informed conclusions regarding the modern approach to a biblical language pedagogy.

Instrumentation

An expert survey best fits this research as the project focused on teaching methodology and not students' retention rates or perception of effectiveness. The experts provided rich data and a professional perspective on this subject matter that others could not. Additionally, a content analysis of language learning publications helps assess the strengths and weaknesses of multiple methodologies to best amalgamize a useful and beneficial solution to the stated problem.

Research Procedures

The research procedure for this dissertation was designed and oriented in specific steps that utilized the experts' views to produce research continuity and professional coherence. The survey results, therefore, function as the foundation for the rest of the analysis and the conclusions. But in order to properly begin this procedure, there needed to be an analysis of the history and current practices of NT Greek in theological education and a comparison to other unique practices of instruction. Next, an evaluation of the best practices of language teaching/learning through SLA, TBLT, and any other, similar methods needed to be conducted. After these steps have been completed, the survey of NT Greek experts was brought in to accumulate measurable data to better understand the current state of Greek instruction in theological education. The survey included a voluntary follow-up portion in which the experts were asked to expound on their thoughts about the current practices of Greek pedagogy. These experts' experience and opinions, a S.W.O.T. analysis of GTM, and the best practices of SLA will help to shape the direction of how theological Greek pedagogy ought to proceed. An intentional and detailed suggestion for a modern instructional design has been formulated from the data and research gathered through this process.

Statistical Measures

The statistical measures in this dissertation have been derived from the expert's survey responses. Their lists of strengths and weaknesses and their specific answers to the ten survey questions were tallied, where applicable, and displayed in figures per each section. These statistical measurements provided rich data that informed the S.W.O.T. analysis and the conclusions portion of the research.

Contribution of the Research

The researcher believes a need exists to analyze current biblical language pedagogy through an educational lens and, if deemed necessary, overhaul it for the sake of the theological institution and its students. Education today is changing so quickly with the innovations of technology and didactic research, but many theological institutions do not appear to be advancing along with the larger educational community. With so many schools moving toward online degrees, flipped classrooms, unique degree programming structures, and shortened curricula durations, pedagogy must fight to keep up. If one considers the enormous growth of information dispensing technologies like Google, Wikipedia, Siri, Alexa, and similar avenues, higher education is becoming less and less necessary in the modern student's mind. This research will address such shortfalls in one of the oldest practices in theological education: the teaching of New Testament Greek.

Because teaching NT Greek has changed very little over the last 500 years, Greek pedagogy needs to be assessed and likely updated. Many students today fall into one or more of the following mentalities when faced with taking a required Greek course:

- Fear—the subject is too difficult

- Apathy—there will not be enough time to use this in ministry
- Frustration—the subject has no use in modern ministry
- Disappointment—it is a waste of money if not used in later ministry

Although the above list is not exhaustive, each of these perceptions can become a reality if they are not addressed well in the actual Greek class. For instance, if a Greek professor simply hands each student a textbook and requires them to learn its contents without providing any illustrations or explanations, this expectation will most likely confirm the student's fear of difficulty. Similarly, if a professor simply points out the vocabulary, diagrams, and paradigms but fails to provide useful context for those grammatical aspects, then apathy and frustration will set in. These hurdles can be greatly limited if not avoided with proper intentional instruction.

The objective of this dissertation is to find ways to (1) make Greek more attainable for those who do not seek an academic vocation, (2) draw upon modern language learning strategies and recent educational practices to improve the learning process, and (3) provide ministry–focused methods of teaching the language that will aid the student for the entirety of their ministry service. Although some research exists into the strengths and weaknesses of GTM and some exists on the need for modernization of biblical language pedagogy, most of it appears in short articles or resulted in a simplistic adjustment of teaching style. Conversely, this study will focus on the newest research regarding instructional methodology and objective–focused course structuring. While teaching style is important, it may not be the sole solution in this case. The material being taught might be the most import aspect of Greek pedagogy because it is what the professor instructs from and what the student learns from at the most basic level. Therefore, the curriculum and the instructional methodology is addressed from an educational standpoint and not the teaching style from an academic perspective.[9]

---

9. It is vital to this research that the professor remain the professional in his or her content area. Therefore, this dissertation only focuses on the overall methodology and its functional application and not the specific application of the content as far as it pertains to the daily dissemination of the material. This researcher does not feel that it is appropriate to instill a rigid teaching structure on the instructor, but rather believes that it is better to provide a detailed structure with applicational guidelines that allows the professional to determine the specific content, trajectory, and tempo of the subject matter material.

Chapter Summary

This research is designed to analyze and assess the current model of NT Greek pedagogy: GTM. Some people have suggested that this model is failing, but no research can be found to confirm whether or not this assumption is true. This dissertation addresses that very assumption.

Chapter 2

Literature Review

Theological Foundation

THE PURPOSE OF THIS research is to analyze the current pedagogical practices of New Testament Greek in theological institutions and to determine if that process is beneficial for the body of Christ. This research is not aimed at undermining the practice of teaching or the use of biblical languages. On the contrary, the objective is to ensure the practice of teaching and the use of biblical languages are faithfully preserved through a system and methodology that will produce a strong and consistent use of these original languages among alumni in pastoral, evangelistic, or lay ministry positions. By itself, the diligent and patient process of learning a biblical language can produce a richer and more intimate understanding of God through the judicious study of his Word. Beyond that, the regular and pertinent use of Greek and Hebrew can greatly enrich sermons, group studies, evangelical conversations, and personal Bible study. Philipp Melanchthon once told his students, "Only if we have clearly understood the language will we clearly understand the content. . . . If we put our minds to the [Hebrew and Greek] sources, we will begin to understand Christ rightly."[1] Although learning biblical languages is not a requirement for all men and women who choose to seek God, it can certainly help reveal copious details of intentional literary and linguistic devices used by the original authors. Although other resources are a great blessing, commentaries or study Bible notes cannot replace the benefits of learning a biblical language; these tools are intended to be supplementary. The true benefits of this practice take place in the heart of the student as he or she reads God's Word in its original languages and discovers the nuanced truths within its pages.

The apostle Paul understood the importance of a true and accurate portrayal of the message of God in the world. His letters were replete with

---

1. Philipp Melanchthon, "The Reform of the Education of Youth," as cited in *The Reformation: A Narrative History Related by Contemporary Observers and Participants*, ed. Joachim Hillerbrand (Grand Rapids: Baker, 1987), 59–60.

reminders for followers to preserve the nature of the gospel (cf., 2 Corinthians 10; Galatians 5; 2 Timothy 4; Philippians 1) as well as warnings about the results of distorting the Good News (cf., Galatians 1; Colossians 2; 1 Timothy 1; Titus 1). Paul addressed this matter to the church at Colossae, challenging them to teach and exhort the people through the Word of God.

> He whom we proclaim, exhorting every man and teaching every man with all wisdom, so that we may present every man complete in Christ. To this end I labor, striving according to his power, which works mightily in me. (Colossians 1:28–29, personal translation)

The proclamation at the end of Colossians 1 sits in direct reference to the previous fifteen verses that painted a remarkable picture of Jesus Christ. He is the one who is proclaimed (καταγγέλλομεν), and He is also the one who provides the very power by which the proclamation goes out.

As Paul describes the "incomparable Christ" in Colossians 1:13–27, he portrays a Savior who rescued (ἐρρύσατο) humanity from darkness and transferred (μετέστησεν) people's eternal souls to heaven through redemption (ἀπολύτρωσιν) and forgiveness (ἄφεσιν). These verses also proclaim Christ as the very image of God and the instigator of all creation. As awe-inspiring as the apostle's words are, they cannot do justice to the reality of the long-awaited Messiah. Paul continues to rhapsodize about Christ as the supreme head of heaven and earth who chose to be humbled and humiliated on a cross for the sake of his own creation. He wanted to remind his audience in Colossae why they had left their foreign gods for this crucified Jew from Nazareth. He also wanted to sharpen their memory about who they were being pressed to proclaim to the world.

With this in mind, it is easy to understand why the first chapter of Colossians stands as one of the most Christ-honoring passages of Paul's epistles. It is at the end of this first chapter of Colossians that the author chose to issue the challenge in Colossians 1:28. Three major didactic aspects to this pericope (objective, methodology, and motivation) are important to a pedagogical study like this one because they form the foundation for why a detailed analysis and evaluation of theological education practices are necessary.

Objective

The objective of any proclamation, at its core, is to pass along information, but it is also to declare something that may not be known with the "implication of broad dissemination."[2] This is, in reality, the goal of every teacher to some degree: to proclaim. Proclamation ought to be the goal of every Christian believer as well. In this case, every person needs to hear the message of Jesus Christ and his glory. All Christ-followers have been charged with the task of spreading the word about what they have heard, read, and experienced in relation to Christ and his message to the world (Matthew 28:18–20). The problem, in relation to this study, is whether or not the message that has been heard or read is accurate and reliable. A pastor, missionary, or layperson cannot effectively proclaim a biblical message without first understanding the subject matter that they are called to communicate. This is the precise reason for theological schools requiring, or at least strongly encouraging, their students to study the original languages of Scripture. They believe the student needs to have a solid grasp on the meaning of the text and therefore should study the text in its original form.

Every theological school that boasts a proclamation-focused objective will likely provide a structured biblical language program for its students and typically requires a minimal amount of languages for ministry-oriented students. Fuller Theological Seminary's statement on studying biblical languages says:

> If you are looking for serious growth in your understanding of Scripture and theology, we're glad you're looking at the emphasis in Biblical Languages. Cultivating faithful interpreters of the Bible is foundational not only to this emphasis, but all we do at Fuller. Whether you plan on further doctoral study or just want to be more informed in your reading of Scripture, you'll learn foundational tools to engage the Hebrew Bible and the Greek New Testament in their original languages.[3]

Reformed Theological Seminary states:

> Do you love the gospel? Then come study the biblical languages in Jackson, MS this summer. If God has called you to gospel ministry, then he has called you to study the biblical languages—all of them—not to simply get by and use the tools, but to know God's Word better and be transformed by that Word into a minister of God's gospel! Martin Luther once said, "Without the languages, the gospel will surely perish!"[4]

---

2. Arndt, Danker, and Bauer, *A Greek-English Lexicon of the New Testament and Other Early Christian Literature*, 515. Et al.

3. Fuller Theological Seminary, "Biblical Languages," http://www.fuller.global/biblicalstudies/ (26 March 2018).

4. Reformed Theological Seminary, "Summer Institute for Biblical Languages,"

CHAPTER 2   17

Wheaton College boasts:

> You will gain the academic skills necessary for advanced study and service in the church and society through formation in three interrelated areas: biblical and theological knowledge; academic skills and critical reflection; and Christian life and service. Our graduate programs are committed to stimulating learning that bears fruit in lives of faithful thinking and witness for Christ and his kingdom.[5]

Many other schools and publishing companies offer rich and well-promoted language programs for everyone from linguistic scholars to laypeople in the church. Ultimately, biblical languages should lead to promoting and proclaiming the Word of God with accuracy and confidence.

Methodology

Paul states in Colossians 1:28 that he and others were proclaiming Christ and then he clarified what this proclamation included: admonition and education. Both of these words are descriptive present active participles.[6] In other words, Paul stated that the believer's responsibility of proclaiming Christ is fulfilled through the two-pronged approach of admonition and teaching, both of which are tempered by wisdom. The Greek word νουθετοῦντες ("admonishing") conveys the idea "to counsel about avoidance or cessation of an improper course of conduct, admonish, warn, instruct."[7] Louw and Nida clarify this sentiment further when they write "to provide instruction as to correct behavior and belief" referring to wrong thinking.[8] Along with that same line of thinking, Robert Beekes and Lucien van Beek point out that the root word νουθετέω is etymologically connected to νοός, which translates as "mind, intellect, or reason" and suggests that this is a cognitive

---

http://www.rts.edu/site/rtsnearyou/jackson/mdiv/summerinstitute.aspx (26 March 2018).

5. Wheaton College Graduate School, "M.A. in Biblical Exegesis," https://www.wheaton.edu/graduate-school/degrees/ma-in-biblical-exegesis/ (26 March 2018).

6. Although some debate exists concerning the use of these two participles here (i.e., means or accompanying circumstances), the context does not provide a clear indication of which was intended or if a distinction is even relevant here. Due to the author's ambiguity and commentator's lack of agreement, it will be used as "means" for this study.

7. Arndt, Danker, and Bauer, *A Greek-English Lexicon of the New Testament and Other Early Christian Literature*, 679.

8. Louw and Nida, *Greek-English Lexicon of the New Testament*, 415.

approach to wrong beliefs.[9] It appears that Paul's point is that the people needed to be corrected in their thinking of faith and theology within the process of proclaiming Christ as Lord. Later in Colossians 3:16a, Paul writes, "Let the word of Christ richly dwell within you, with all wisdom teaching and admonishing one another." With his use of almost identical language, this is another example of Paul's emphasis on the dual aspect of teaching and admonishing, but among believers. Paul knew that the process of providing new and unique ideas and philosophies in the immediate Roman context (as well as later societies) must be preceded or accompanied by the correction and/or demolition of previously held, heretical mindsets.[10] Just as John the Baptist baptized Jews to prepare their hearts for the coming Lamb of God (Matthew 3:1–3), Paul stresses the need for preparing the heart and mind before building a new foundation.

The second aspect of Paul's call for proclamation is to teach. Paul uses διδάσκω, or one of its cognates, fifteen times in nine different letters,[11] but his use of the word in Colossians 1:28 and 3:16 is most important here. Although teaching is a simple concept, it is a complex process to complete effectively. At its core, teaching is simply the act of transferring knowledge. The Merriam–Webster dictionary defines teaching as "to cause to know, to guide the studies of, and to impart the knowledge of" something to someone.[12] But this does not address the purpose of the action, the methodology of the process, or the intention of the resulting knowledge. In other words, the why, how, and so what of teaching is missing from the definition. How can a believer go about "teaching" something to someone without an understanding of why they are engaging this person, how to engage them properly, or to what end? Fortunately, Paul provides all of this necessary information.

First, Paul begins verse 28 with the subject matter of "teaching" when he writes, "We proclaim him," referring to Jesus, whom the apostle had spent the previous twenty-seven verses discussing. Furthermore, the apostle provides the identity of the intended audience twice, "all men" or "every man," implying that this "teaching" should never come to an end. Then Paul explained the why, how, and so what.

9. Beekes and van Beek, *Etymological Dictionary of Greek*, 1025, 1023.

10. Pao, *Colossians & Philemon*, 132.

11. Romans 2:21 (part. and verb); 12:7 (part.); 1 Corinthians 4:17 (verb); 11:14 (verb); Galatians 1:12 (verb); Ephesians 4:21 (verb); Colossians 1:28 (part.); 2:7 (verb); 3:16 (part.); 2 Thessalonians 2:15 (verb); 1 Timothy 2:12 (verb); 4:11 (verb); 6:2 (verb); 2 Timothy 2:22 (verb); and Titus 1:11 (part.).

12. Merriam–Webster, "Teach," https://www.merriam-webster.com/dictionary/teach (26 March 2018).

- Why—"so that we may present every man complete in Christ"—Paul places the responsibility of the eternal destination of "every man" squarely on the shoulders of believers.
- How—"admonishing every man and teaching every man with all wisdom"—This is to be done through admonition and teaching.
- So What—"so that we may present every man complete in Christ"—This responsibility is not simply to tell them, rather it is to "labor and strive" (v. 29) with them toward the goal of presenting "every man complete in Christ."

In other words, teaching establishes the basis of the Christian faith. James Dunn explains that "νουθετέω and διδάσκω are near synonyms, both meaning 'instruct.'"[13] He distinguishes the two by saying, "The former carries the implication of exhortation, warning, and correction" and "the latter . . . more characteristically refers to the skill of the teacher in imparting practical and theoretical knowledge to the pupil."[14] In other words, admonishing seems to refer to the tone of the content while teaching refers to the application of the content.

The content and application of the message of Scripture are precisely why a study of this nature is necessary; what is being taught is so important that it must be taught well. If a Greek professor simply teaches the basic functions of the language, how will the students learn to apply those basic functions? A skilled carpenter can give his apprentice a top-of-the-line drill, but it is no more than a paperweight to the young man until he is taught how to put it to use. Similarly, a parent does not give the keys of a two-ton vehicle to a sixteen-year-old young woman; rather they require driver training classes, parent-monitored driving hours, and restricted freedom until the person can drive safely. The weight of the objective (proclamation) and the subject matter (Christ crucified) need to be taken seriously and attended to regularly to ensure the quality of the methodology (admonition and teaching) is upheld.

Motivation

The motivation for Colossians 1:28, like this research, is simply to glorify the living Savior. The message is 2,000 years old and stronger than ever,

---

13. Dunn, *The Epistles to the Colossians and to Philemon*, 124.

14. Dunn, *The Epistles to the Colossians and to Philemon*, 124. Dunn also points out that this idea is exemplified through Romans 2:21; 12:7; 1 Corinthians 11:14; Galatians 1:12.

but the messengers are fallible and fragile men and women who will pass from this life in the blink of an eye (1 Corinthians 15). Paul's motivation in this passage is to promote Christ to the world, and considering Colossians 3:16, that audience includes the church as well. Paul uses the words "that we may present every man complete in Christ" as if the act of admonishing and teaching is a gift to the Son of God whereby men are made complete. τέλειος is often translated as "perfect" or "one who reaches a goal."[15] Unfortunately, the semantic range of this word is quite wide and spans from "meeting a high standard" to "being a cult initiate."[16] A. T. Robertson argues that Paul directly intended to refer to a believer who is "mature . . . fully developed," but that the apostle might have also used the word to draw the attention of the Gnostics who used τέλειος for their ideological initiates.[17] Douglas Moo clarifies the use of this word well when he writes, "Similar to the Hebrew word tamim (which is translated by teleios five times in the LXX), teleios connotes the quality of being so wholehearted in one's devotion to the Lord that one can be said to be blameless in conduct (see esp. Matthew 5:48; 19:21; Ephesians 4:13; Hebrews 5:14; James. 1:4b)."[18] This use of τέλειος suggests not perfection or maturity, but instead an idea of someone wholly devoted to Christ and his kingdom. What better motivation for someone to proclaim Christ through admonishment and teaching than to develop men and women who have committed solely to their Savior?

As noted previously, the goal of learning a biblical language is to understand and glorify God to the best of one's abilities. While this researcher could not agree with that sentiment more, that idea could infer that the understanding and glorification of God is limited in the life of a believer without the acquisition of original languages. Of course, the authors and professors who espouse that belief do not suggest this, but it is important to note that not everyone is gifted with the ability to learn or retain a foreign language (especially a dead one). Therefore, the motivation for learning a language needs to be more application–driven and less focused on the implication of glorifying God. In other words, biblical languages may be better understood as tools for "admonishing and teaching" just as they are tools for "proclaiming." This simple shift would place emphasis on how the languages are taught (as specific tools) rather than that they are being taught as a perfunctory requirement. Ultimately, the motivation is to bless Christ with the

---

15. Zodhiates, *The Complete Word Study Dictionary*, 1373.

16. Arndt, Danker, and Bauer, *A Greek–English Lexicon of the New Testament and Other Early Christian Literature*, 995–96.

17. Robertson, *Word Pictures in the New Testament*, 485–86.

18. Moo, *The Letters to the Colossians and to Philemon*, 161.

gift of "wholly devoted" followers instead of sinful people who are constantly seeking to be "perfect" (as the word is often translated). This impetus would be lost without men and women dedicated to the study of New Testament Greek and their ability to apply it to the lives of believers.

Theory

The Bible is a unique collection of books, primarily because it was originally written in three languages: Hebrew, Aramaic, and Greek. Although this may not appear to be a strong differentiating quality from other ancient documents, Scripture is a binding document that has governed the morals and convictions of millions of people throughout history. Due to this fact, the Bible must be carefully preserved, even thousands of years after its writing, for the glory of its divine Architect and those who desire to commit their lives to its message. Therefore, these three languages must be translated and the content made available to those people who seek the history, wisdom, and guidance included in its pages. Even though this dissertation will focus solely on the biblical language of New Testament Greek, its concepts are easily transferable to Hebrew and Aramaic.

The Word of God stands at the core of the Judeo–Christian faith. It is the basis on which missionaries introduce Jesus Christ to reclusive tribes and the platform from which thousands of pastors preach each week all around the world. It was a major contributing element to the re-establishment of the Roman Empire under Constantine as well as one of the key founding documents for the constitution of the United States of America. The Bible's advocates apply its words to their architectural cornerstones, home décor, and personal memories, while its antagonists fight to ban its use in schools, public venues, and politics. The Bible is a powerful book that polarizes the masses, but it can just as easily bring them together. The uses and abuses of Scripture have caused severe divides between countries and family members alike. All this havoc and harmony derives from a patchwork collection of letters and events written down thousands of years ago. Scripture should never be taken lightly and neither should the teaching and learning of its original languages.

A Brief History of the Greek Language

The Greek language has gone through many changes and adaptations throughout its existence.[19] According to the Encyclopedia Britannica, Greek has a "long and well-documented history—the longest of any Indo-European language—spanning 34 centuries."[20] Francisco Adrados adds that Greek and Chinese are the only 3,500-year-old languages that still have a spoken version today. Adrados goes on to write that, "There is no doubt that, if judged by the influence it has had on all of the European languages, and continues to have today on all languages, Greek can be regarded as the most important languages in the world. The direct or indirect influence of its alphabet, lexicon, syntax and literature has been and is immense."[21] Since the Scriptures were written in three ancient forms of culturally marginalized languages, the global spread of its message was highly unlikely. That was until the unparalleled conquest of Alexander the Great.[22] Alexander was best known for his rapid and mostly unchallengeable military land acquisitions over his thirteen-year reign of Greece, but along with Greek/Macedonian rule came the spread of the Greek dialect. He took the Greek language "to the whole of the 'inhabited earth' (οἰκουμένη)."[23] Without Alexander's relatively short conquest, it is unclear if the Bible would have had the necessary political, cultural, and linguistic climate to emerged from its humble beginnings.

Additionally, throughout its thousands of years of existence, Greek has undergone five major periods of classification:

1. Mycenaean period (14th–13th century BCE)
2. Archaic and Classical periods (8th–4th century BCE)
3. Hellenistic and Roman periods (4th century BCE–4th century CE)
4. Byzantine period (5th–15th century CE)
5. Modern period (15th century CE–present day)[24]

---

19. This will be a brief yet important review of the origins of the Greek language; a much more detailed account of the history of Greek can be found in Christidēs's 1,600-page tome listed in the reference section of this paper.

20. Ruijgh, Newton, Malikouti-Drachman, and Lejeune, *Greek Language*.

21. Adrados, *A History of the Greek Language*, xiii.

22. Christidēs, Arapopoulou, Chritē, and Centre for the Greek Language. *A History of Ancient Greek: From the Beginnings to Late Antiquity*, 325–28.

23. Christidēs, Arapopoulou, Chritē, and Centre for the Greek Language. *A History of Ancient Greek: From the Beginnings to Late Antiquity*, 160.

24. Ruijgh et al., "Greek Language."

A. N. Jannaris claims that a clear history of Greek is difficult to compile due to many of its stages being based on "vague speculation" or some periods being "overshadowed" by others.[25] Christidēs proves otherwise when he argues that the Hellenistic Koine dialect "[led] to the disappearance of the ancient dialects and was to become the linguistic organ . . . of the Hellenized populations of the East" which then ultimately led to the New Testament Koine Greek in the Hellenistic/Roman period.[26]

Due to the changes and transitions explained above, Koine (common) Greek became one of the most well-documented classical languages in philology. Classical and biblical scholars alike analyzed certain forms of Ancient Greek literature from the writings of Homer to the Septuagint, and the New Testament. This linguistic effort unearthed copious amounts of historical and cultural discoveries that better shaped the modern understanding of these classical periods. Concerning this study, these efforts are carefully laying the theological foundation for the moral standards the inspired authors of the biblical texts prescribed. In other words, the detailed study of New Testament Greek has helped explain the narrow road of salvation for non-believers (Matthew 7) and provided biblical Christians with an accurate and clearly-defined path that leads them toward godly sanctification (Romans 6).

Grammar-Translation Method

The study of the biblical Scriptures has been a religious endeavor since Moses began recording the history and laws of the Israelite people in the Torah. Jews and Christians alike are commanded to memorize and apply these words as a regular part of their daily activities (Deuteronomy 6:4–9). In order to fulfill this command, one must first understand the text, thus the need for translating the original and now defunct languages into modern ones. Obviously, this was not originally a need because the basic written forms of the Septuagint and the New Testament were still in use until at least the fourth or sixth century CE. But as Greek vocabulary, morphemes, and pronunciation changed, translation practices became necessary.[27] These minor rudimentary translation practices continued to take shape until the end of the Byzantium period (1500 CE) when Erasmus changed the way Greek would be understood for the next 500 years.

---

25. Jannaris, *An Historical Greek Grammar*, v.
26. Christidēs et al., *History of Ancient Greek*, 160.
27. Adrados, *A History of the Greek Language*, 226–29.

Desiderius Erasmus of Rotterdam was a famous Catholic theologian and grammarian who provided invaluable work on modern New Testament translations in both Latin and Greek.[28] Erasmus published his Dialogus in 1528 CE, which supposedly explained the "proper" pronunciations of Greek and Latin words in antiquity. Chrys Caragounis explains that "the line he struck out would determine not only the pronunciation but also the approach to the study of the Greek language and its literature for almost five centuries."[29] Greek was, from that point forward, distinctly divided between ancient and modern dialects. Erasmus's single publication set the stage for several resounding events in Christian history. First, his work on the Latin New Testament (first translated in 1514 CE from his superior Greek update) addressed several translation errors in St. Jerome's revered Vulgate that exposed theological misunderstandings held by the Roman Catholic Church.[30] Erasmus explains his reasoning for this effort when he writes:

> But one thing the facts cry out, and it can be clear, as they say, even to a blind man, that often through the translator's clumsiness or inattention the Greek has been wrongly rendered; often the true and genuine reading has been corrupted by ignorant scribes, which we see happen every day, or altered by scribes who are half-taught and half-asleep.[31]

Unfortunately, by updating the Greek text and bringing these Latin errors to the surface, Erasmus caused many Vulgate-faithful Catholics to call for his condemnation as a heretic.

The second history-making event that resulted from Erasmus's translations was the Protestant Reformation. Martin Luther and other devout Catholics realized the severity of Erasmus's work and called for Rome to address multiple issues that strained church relations at the time. Luther believed these issues could be addressed and adjusted through an accurate and honest return to the original texts of the Bible.[32] In the end, the church refused the notion that there was a serious problem and proceeded on a Counter-Reformation or Catholic Revival (1545-1648 CE) to improve church relations.

The third and maybe most significant effect that Erasmus had on Christian history was that he (and the reformers) introduced a renewed focus upon the original languages for biblical translation. His Greek New

---

28. Christidēs et al., *History of Ancient Greek*, 1239-40.
29. Caragounis, *The Development of Greek and the New Testament*, 3.
30. Christidēs et al., *History of Ancient Greek*, 1239-40.
31. Erasmus, *Collected Works of Erasmus*, 134.
32. Christidēs et al., *History of Ancient Greek*, 1240.

Testament allowed many people, most of whom were products of the Protestant Reformation, to begin work on translations in modern languages such as German and English. Gone were the days of searching for limited Byzantine Greek manuscripts or relying on a copy of the Vulgate to study the Scriptures. Now scholars and students alike were able to find a fresh copy of Erasmus's text to study and, thanks to the invention of Gutenberg's printing press (c. 1439 CE), the populous could access this scribal tool with the right knowledge. Ultimately, what Erasmus accomplished was likely not his intended goal, but his effect was indelible as he may be the very reason that Greek is so heavily studied today as well as his setting the stage for how Greek is being translated still today.

How a language is taught is often a reflection of its intended use. For example, if a student planned to travel to Mexico on a short-term class mission trip, her teacher would impart common terms and phrases that would allow for easy communication in repeated settings (e.g., greetings, polite responses, restroom locations, etc.). On the other hand, if the student planned to move to Mexico for schooling, she would need to learn more complex conversational speech for an academic setting through highly intentional methods (e.g., emersion, language partnerships, tutoring, etc.). This is also true for teaching/learning New Testament Greek. Erasmus did not just produce a Greek New Testament; it was a tool for future scholars to use in creating more accurate translations.

As already noted, the Grammar-Translation Method (GTM) of teaching languages stretches back to Erasmus in the sixteenth century.[33] The GTM is also sometimes called the "classical" method because it was primarily used to teach classical Greek and Latin. Richards and Rodgers describe the GTM process when writing that the students "were initially given a rigorous introduction to Latin grammar, which was taught through rote learning of grammar rules, the study of declensions and conjugations, translation, and practice in writing sample sentences, sometimes with the use of parallel bilingual texts and dialogue."[34] GTM is based on the idea that learning the details of the grammar of a given language aids the student in using classical languages for translation and research.[35] To put it another way, the objective is not to communicate; rather it is to "develop explicit knowledge of language structure with constant reference to the L1 (the

---

33. Richards and Rodgers, *Approaches and Methods in Language Teaching*, 3.
34. Richards and Rodgers, *Approaches and Methods in Language Teaching*, 4–5.
35. Fasold and Connor-Linton, *An Introduction to Language and Linguistics*, 476.

learner's primary language)."³⁶ Larsen-Freeman and Anderson expound on the core characteristics of GTM as summarized below:

1. Designed for the purpose of reading the classical text through the memorization of grammar rules and vocabulary
2. The teacher is typically the authority in the classroom
3. Students practice by translating sentences, studying grammar deductively, and memorizing paradigms
4. Little student–student interaction
5. Student feelings are not accounted for
6. Literary language is considered superior to spoken language
7. Vocabulary and grammar are emphasized
8. Student's native language is both the result of the translation and the language most used verbally in class
9. Assessments typically consist of translating from target language to native language or vice versa as well as questions about grammar rules
10. If the student errs, the teacher typically corrects them³⁷

The GTM process had become prominent for many languages, including in the United States. In fact, until World War II, the United States government practiced GTM for French, German, Russian, and other languages before largely abandoning it to adopt a more fluid and "painless" method for learning foreign languages focused on spoken fluency.³⁸ Due to the United States government's decision to emphasize the ability to speak foreign languages in the 1940s and not simply reading them, GTM was once again relegated to classical practices.

GTM for teaching NT Greek is prominent throughout theological education and is fairly easy to identify. This can be done by either looking through the Table of Contents of an introductory Greek grammar/primer or sitting through a NT Greek course. Prominent linguist and language professor Stephen Krashen identifies the key components of GTM this way:

> While there is some variation, grammar-translation usually consists of the following activities:
>
> 1. Explanation of a grammar rule, with example sentences.

36. Fasold and Connor-Linton, *An Introduction to Language and Linguistics*, 476.
37. Larsen-Freeman and Anderson, *Techniques and Principles in Language Teaching*, 19–20.
38. McManis, Stollenwerk, and Zhang, *Language Files*, 259.

2. Vocabulary, presented in the form of a bilingual list.

3. A reading selection, emphasizing the rule presented in (1) above and the vocabulary presented in (2).

4. Exercises designed to provide practice on the grammar and vocabulary of the lesson. These exercises emphasize the conscious control of structure . . . and include translation in both directions, from L1 to L2 and L2 to L1.[39]

The four indicators above clearly identify GTM in a similar manner as Larsen–Freeman and Anderson and also describe the typical NT Greek textbook found during a simple browsing through internet bookstores or theological libraries.

Some of the most popular Greek textbooks that employ GTM include William Mounce's Basics of Biblical Greek Grammar (2009 and earlier iterations); David Alan Black's Learn to Read New Testament Greek (2009); S. M. Baugh's A New Testament Primer (2012); and N. Clayton Croy's A Primer of Biblical Greek (2011). These books and many others are designed around the concept of introducing the student to Greek through the alphabet, pronunciation, accent marks, punctuation, and other fundamental aspects of the language. These works then introduce parts of the linguistic structure through nouns, verbs, conjunctions, participles, etc. for the purpose of teaching the student to translate verses from the Greek New Testament into English (or vice versa). Once the student is able to translate rudimentary sentences, he is then led through another second–level set of books that cover basics of syntax, verbal aspect, and other deeper elements of the language for the sake of reading and interpreting the Greek New Testament. A few examples of these second–level books include Daniel Wallace's Greek Grammar Beyond the Basics (1997); David Alan Black's It's Still Greek to Me (1998); Stanley Porter's Idioms of the Greek New Testament (1992); and the recent addition of Köstenberger, Merkle, and Plummer's Going Deeper with New Testament Greek (2016). A slew of other resources direct students from basic syntax to in–depth Greek exegesis, but they reside outside the scope of this research.

The most recent GTM–based Greek grammar is by Richard Gibson and Constantine Campbell titled Reading Biblical Greek: A Grammar for Students.[40] This book is listed separately for two primary reasons: (1) the authors made a concerted effort to slim down the grammar content, and (2) they have incorporated an intentional pedagogy. Although neither of

---

39. Krashen, *Principles and Practice in Second Language Acquisition*, 127.
40. Gibson and Campbell, *Reading Biblical Greek*.

these elements appear revolutionary at first, they are both quite rare in a NT Greek grammar. In the preface of the book, the authors write about their motivation toward the student, saying, "The effort put in over decades to redesign, reorganize, and refine has been motivated by these students in attempts to reduce the hours of the pain required to start translating the New Testament." They continue, "The goals have been clarity, convenience, and currency."[41] The objective is to equip the student with the skills to read and translate a portion of the Gospel according to Mark. With this purpose in mind, the grammar is minimalistic to produce quicker reading ability and the vocabulary lists are Mark-centered, which should also speed up this process.[42] The book's methodology is explained overtly on page 1 when it outlines the six steps that make up the page-by-page format: Engage, Rehearse, Observe, Learn, Memorize, and Complete & Check. The authors have laid this strategy out in three columns that follow the Present-Practice-Produce (PPP) methodology without identifying it as such. This book represents a large step forward for GTM grammars with its slim 129-page layout and its obvious PPP methodology. Because, although it remains a basic NT Greek grammar, it presents a clear end-goal for the user and provides a well-thought out model for achieving said goal. Anyone would be hard-pressed to find another textbook that so clearly and overtly works to design a goal-driven textbook like this one. It is still fixated on translation and it still requires rote memorization to accomplish many of the tasks within the eighty-three lessons, but, it is still a step forward based on its reduction of required grammar details and its intentional strategy.

Unique Models

Although GTM is the most widely used technique of teaching NT Greek, several other methods are available to the modern ministry student. The following list of alternative strategies is not meant to be exhaustive; rather it is intended to display a few of the more creative or well-known approaches offered. Some are still founded on GTM but add a unique spin that results in creative objectives.

---

41. Gibson and Campbell, *Reading Biblical Greek*, vii.
42. Gibson and Campbell, *Reading Biblical Greek*, xiii.

Communicative Greek

This particular process of teaching a foreign language is formally known as Communicative Language Teaching (CLT). CLT is an aspect of the linguistic methodology called Second Language Acquisition (SLA).[43] The fundamental idea of this methodology is to immerse the student in the language through "everyday" conversations and phrases such as greetings, questions, directions, and small talk. Even though this educational tactic is growing in its use, little published material exists on its use with NT Greek, which means the primary medium for instruction is the internet through blogs and video streaming sites. Some of the proponents of this technique include Michael Palmer, an Ethics and Philosophy professor with Regent University; Paul Overland, an Old Testament professor at Ashland Theological Seminary; Donald Cobb, a professor of New Testament and Greek at Faculté Jean Calvin, Institut de théologie protestante et évangélique in Aix-en-Provence, France; Paul Nitz, a Greek and Andragogy professor at Lutheran Bible Institute; and Daniel Streett, a professor of Theology at Houston Baptist University. All of these men have either written online articles or host websites promoting the practice of actively speaking Koine Greek just as one might speak Spanish or French while working to acquire the language. Dozens of videos and tutorials are available for students to experience these professors speaking Koine Greek with their friends, colleagues, and even pets.

Michael Palmer is a well-published author and university professor in ancient Greek culture, literature, and linguistics. He and Jonathan Robie presented on CLT and its application to Koine Greek at the Society of Biblical Literature annual meeting in November 2016, but they have yet to publish anything on the topic to this point. Along these same lines, Paul Overland wrote the 2014 article, "Can Communitive Methods Enhance Ancient Language Acquisition?" for Teaching Theology and Religion about the benefits of using CLT within theological education for both Greek and Hebrew. After analyzing the aspects of CLT within SLA, Overland concluded that "Ancient Language Acquisition students will benefit from Second

---

43. Second Language Acquisition (SLA) is both a general description and an official term for a methodology. In general, SLA is the process of learning an additional language to one's native tongue. As an official term, SLA is a research-based systematized methodology for teaching and learning a language that includes various techniques with specific steps and processes designed to lead the learner through the acquisition of an additional language. Due to this dual definition, this paper will only use the term to refer to the official practice of Second Language Acquisition upon which there is a large amount of writing and research.

Language Acquisition discoveries."[44] He followed this statement with four pointed suggestions for language professors from the SLA method: "(1) teach to the learning styles of our students with particular attention to visual and experiential modes, (2) use interactive CD tutorials and music, (3) devise oral presentations to consolidate learning, and (4) create small group projects and games to foster relaxation."[45] Overland's ideas may not be as poignant today as they were in 2004, but they certainly add a level of creativity to the teaching of NT Greek.

Among the plethora of videos that can be found on YouTube and similar websites that display the CLT method of teaching New Testament Greek, Donald Cobb and Daniel Streett star in several. They use mostly conversational efforts. They have not published on this topic yet, but they contribute to blogs frequently about this topic. Another contributor of these popular blogs is Paul Nitz, who specifically applies this communicative procedure through an approach called Total Physical Response (TPR), in which he gives his students physical commands to follow (e.g., sit down, pick up the book, walk to the door, etc.).[46] Nitz believes that this method aids language acquisition rather than simply understanding.

Lastly, Apostolos Koutropoulos is a professor of Linguistics at the University of Massachusetts Boston and authored the 2011 article "Modernizing Classical Language Education: Communicative Language Teaching & Educational Technology Integration in Classical Greek." Koutropoulos has a lengthy background in both information technology and linguistics; this provides him with a unique platform from which he can address the topic. Although his article deals exclusively with Classical Greek as opposed to Koine Greek, his input is none the less valuable when it comes to teaching the language. Koutropoulos is a native (modern) Greek speaker, but he wanted to see how Classical Greek was being taught in the classrooms in the United States. What he found was a "massive difference" between the teaching of modern Greek and Classical.[47] He ultimately argues that classical languages ought to be taught using the CLT method for the sake of the student's acquisition and the professor's ease of use.[48]

---

44. Overland, *Can Communicative Methods*, 55–56.

45. Overland, *Can Communicative Methods*, 56.

46. Nitz, "Communicative Greek.old," *Youtube.com*, 14 June 2015, https://www.youtube.com/playlist?list=PLpxcmJ23ymcWixPoZUqggk-IztqZb57hG (26 March 2018).

47. Koutropoulos, *Modernizing Classical Language Education*, 55.

48. Koutropoulos, *Modernizing Classical Language Education*, 55–56, 66.

Usage–Based Greek

This style of teaching NT Greek is primarily utilized by Stanley Porter, Jeffery Reed, and Matthew O'Donnell in their book titled Fundamentals of New Testament Greek (2010). Porter explains and defends this approach in a later (2014) article published in Biblical and Ancient Greek Linguistics titled "The Usage–Based Approach to Teaching New Testament Greek." He begins this article by stating that there is and likely will never be a "perfect approach" to teaching Greek because "there will always be disagreement about the best ways to teach and to learn Greek."[49] Porter later defines his methodology this way, "This usage–based approach essentially states that—so far as it is possible within certain constraints—the various phenomena of the language, including both its grammar and its vocabulary, are introduced to the student according to frequency of usage, with the most frequent introduced first."[50] Porter goes on to explain his approach in further detail and posits his rationale for producing such a book among so many other beginning grammar books. Although Porter wrote that he found few NT Greek textbooks that "have an explicit methodology," his anecdotal assessment is based on a simple misunderstanding.[51] In all actuality, most NT Greek textbooks apply GTM, which has a very clear methodology and which was also the methodology Porter used in his own 2010 book. The primary difference between GTM and Usage–Based pedagogy is that Porter rearranged his grammar elements based on usage instead of the traditional format. This is not too different from David Alan Black's (2009) decision to address verbs first, then nouns, and so on, based on his objective of leading the student toward the ability to read the text in short order. Porter ultimately believes that this Usage–Based strategy provides "the kind of language learning and knowledge that students of Greek in seminaries and colleges need and deserve so as to develop into competent interpreters of the Greek New Testament."[52] Whether a usage–based approach accomplishes this task or not is still to be determined.

Singing Greek

When most professors decide to write their own Greek textbooks or design their own curricula, they typically do so by following GTM and then adapt

---

49. Porter, *The Usage–Based Approach to Teaching New Testament Greek*, 120.
50. Porter, *The Usage–Based Approach to Teaching New Testament Greek*, 126.
51. Porter, *The Usage–Based Approach to Teaching New Testament Greek*, 123.
52. Porter, *The Usage–Based Approach to Teaching New Testament Greek*, 139.

their classroom teaching style to fit a more modern setting. This is how several professors have come to the practice of singing Greek. They tend to use traditional textbooks and curricula, but they adjust their pedagogy to infuse the Greek grammar elements into songs and jingles which the students then memorize. Many of the proponents of this method have found that it is easier to memorize limericks and nursery rhymes than straight lists and paradigms and thus they attempt to marry the two.

Ken Berding's 2008 *Sing and Learn New Testament Greek: The Easiest Way to Learn Greek Grammar* is a great example of this methodology. Berding has recorded many of his class sessions and places them on YouTube and other sites to promote this style of teaching and learning Greek. He explained his original motivation in a 2008 interview with Zondervan Academic when he told a story about having to re–learn Greek after learning modern Turkish: "I decided that I wanted to re–learn Greek in such a way that I would never again forget it. That's when I started putting grammar patterns to music. I've been putting Greek grammar to songs since 1994." Berding continues, "The most difficult part of the project was organizing complex grammar patterns into learnable structures and finding simple songs that worked well with those patterns."[53] In a parting morsel of wisdom, Berding says, "Memorize grammar using songs! Do you want to learn Greek just so you can pass a class, or do you want to remember what you learn over the long haul? If you want to remember your grammar forms, learn them to music."[54] Berding is obviously passionate about this pedagogy and promotes it to the public well.

Another such musically inclined Greek professor is Dr. John Nordling, who authored "Teaching Greek at the Seminary" for Logia in 2012. Nordling has two main points in his article. The first is that he believes seminary courses should be shortened due to the success he has found with the ten–week system Concordia Theological Seminary in Fort Wayne, Indiana instituted.[55] His second and more related point was that singing songs in Greek reinforces what the students learned and brings unity to the class. Nordling writes that "singing hackneyed Greek songs together is a very good way of keeping all the students together."[56] Regardless of whether the student sings

---

53. ZA Blogs, "Interview with Ken Berding part 1—'Sing and Learn New Testament Greek,'" *Zondervan Academic*, 16 September 2008, http://zondervanacademic.com/blog/interview-with/ (26 March 2018).

54. ZA Blogs, "Interview with Ken Berding part 2—'Sing and Learn New Testament Greek,'" *Zondervan Academic*, 17 September 2008, http://zondervanacademic.com/blog/5-with-all-that/ (26 March 2018).

55. Nordling, *Teaching Greek at the Seminary*, 70.

56. Nordling, *Teaching Greek at the Seminary*, 70.

ditties comprised of Greek grammar or songs with Greek lyrics, both Berding and Nordling believe that songs are the best way to learn and retain the elements of the Greek language.

Tools–Based Greek

The reality that learning New Testament Greek is a difficult venture has not changed in the last 500 years, but several major advances have been made in the areas of teaching and learning the language. From scholars publishing their research more widely to regularly updating New Testament Greek texts, the world of New Testament Greek has become more accessible. In fact, just ten years ago most students were still hand–writing vocabulary cards and recreating endless paradigm charts to prepare for quizzes and tests. Today, students can simply "borrow" pre–made, interactive vocabulary and paradigm cards from other Quizlet users and review them on their smartphones as they wait in lines or eat their breakfast each morning. A rapidly growing number of websites and smartphone applications greatly simplify the process of learning and using Greek. Add to this the many user–friendly Bible software programs like Logos, BibleWorks, Accordance, and WORDsearch, and the typical sermon preparation time quickly dwindles and messages become significantly more robust.

Although language professors often discourage using Bible software, these tools can provide access to thousands of books and resources at the click of a mouse.[57] Two of the more recent proponents of utilizing Bible software and other digital tools in theological language learning are James Coakley and David Woodall. Both professors at Moody Theological Seminary, they co-authored a chapter titled "Using Bible Software to Exegete the Text" in The Moody Handbook of Preaching. They wrote this chapter for the following reason:

> A recent survey of pastors attending the Pastor's Conference at Moody Bible Institute revealed that although the pastors had a high regard for the use of Hebrew and Greek in the exegetical process, they had not internalized the languages, almost never used them for personal devotions, and were highly unsatisfied with their level of biblical language use.[58]

Coakley and Woodall point to four main reasons pastors do not use their languages: (1) language difficulty, (2) lack of retention, (3) too time–consuming,

---

57. This will be addressed more specifically later.
58. Coakley and Woodall, *Using Bible Software to Exegete the Text*, 389–90.

and (4) too technical. Coakley and Woodall then argue that "digital technology, however, allows pastors to overcome these barriers and offer ways to redeem the use of biblical languages in effective sermon preparation."[59] Coakley and Woodall do not promote a specific software, but argue for the use of any Bible software in the process of sermon preparations.

Coakley and Woodall are not alone in this belief. Professor Carl Sanders of Capital Seminary and Graduate School presented a similar viewpoint at the 2016 annual meeting of the Evangelical Theological Society (ETS). Sanders presented a preview of his now-published article "Biblical Language Instruction by the Book: Rethinking the Status Quaestionis," in which he strongly supports the use of Bible software and other technologies in modern educational settings. Sanders writes, "The availability of a large set of resources for immediate access across multiple devices, with special linking, indexing, and electronic search capabilities likewise enhances the value of these resources. Even in a more traditional seminary language approach, these electronic resources make great sense."[60] In the end, Coakley, Woodall, and Sanders argue that software and other "tools" ought to be not only accepted as useful, but taught and utilized by the professor to promote their rich benefits. In fact, several theological institutions are adopting a "Tools-Based" approach to the biblical languages for both online and traditional students. Seminaries such as Moody, Liberty, Indiana Wesleyan, and Capital have begun using a Tools-Based approach of some sort to help their students learn and retain their biblical language skills in their post-graduation ministry.

Practically-Based Greek

Many of the methods explained above aim at either grammar-focused knowledge or acquisition-focused outcomes, but this practical approach is more closely tied to the Tools-Based style due to their shared goal of reaching the non-academic Greek student. The authors of these books began with different objectives and therefore assume different outcomes from their audiences. These books do not attempt to teach translation skills to a large degree; rather, they teach recognition abilities so that the reader can identify many aspects of Greek and possibly even use some of the tools and "helps" that exist on the market ("helps" will be addressed later).

Two of the primary resources in this area of writing are David Alan Black's Using New Testament Greek in Ministry (1993) and William

---

59. Coakley and Woodall, *Using Bible Software to Exegete the Text*, 390.
60. Sanders, *Biblical Language Instruction by the Book*, 218.

Mounce's Greek for the Rest of Us (2003). Both books are aimed at filling the role of a practical tool for Christians who desire to learn Greek but lack the ability to attend Bible college or seminary for various reasons. Black states he intended his book to "prepare you to use Greek in your ministry."[61] Similarly, Mounce expresses his desire for Greek to be used in ministry while explaining his reluctance and motivation for writing the book:

> You will not be learning the full language, and my concern is that you will forget that you know only a little. I'm going to give you the ability to sound authoritative by citing Greek and Hebrew words and grammar, and perhaps be completely wrong. I actually put off writing this book for several years because of this concern, but I finally came to the conclusion that it's not a little Greek that proves dangerous. It's a little bit of pride that proves dangerous.[62]

Each of these books provides differing methods: Mounce addresses the fundamental aspects of biblical Greek to lay-people while Black speaks to the use of proper exegesis from behind the pulpit. Both are useful, and neither are out-of-reach for the typical pastor or Sunday school teacher.

Along a similar vein, Joseph Webb and Robert Kysar's 2002 book, *Greek for Preachers*, is built upon ten "principles" that assist the pastor in using languages in sermon preparation. Additionally, L. William Countryman's *The New Testament is in Greek: A Short Course for Exegetes* (1993) contains twenty-four lessons and is infused with lengthy examples and practical lessons specifically designed to help pastors. Two other resources available are Found and Olson's *Basic Greek in 30 Minutes a Day: A Self-Study Introduction to New Testament Greek* (2012) and Edward Goodrick's *Do It Yourself Hebrew and Greek* (1980). Both of these texts are aimed at allowing the learner to pace his or her own language learning progress and dictate the use and application of the ability gained.

The newest addition to this category is an innovative book from A. Chadwick Thornhill titled *Greek for Everyone: Introductory Greek for Bible Study and Application* (2016). Thornhill admits early on that "this book will not make you a master of the Greek language, but it will enable you to understand its basics, interact with quality commentaries and research on the New Testament, and gain more confidence in rightly interpreting the Bible."[63] With his inclusion of such topics as useful resources, comparing English translations, word study instructions, and a big picture emphasis,

---

61. Black, *Using New Testament Greek in Ministry*, 14.
62. Mounce, *Greek for the Rest of Us*, xviii.
63. Thornhill, *Greek for Everyone*, xi.

this text creates a very helpful bridge for a pastor or Sunday school teacher to decide on further, formal language study. Few texts dive this deep into Greek study without losing focus on the everyday believer, and as the title infers, Thornhill has done just that. This book is aimed at equipping "the reader with a working knowledge of Greek" rather than those who seek a deeper, theological education.[64]

Greek Helps

This final category of Greek-specific approaches includes the books and articles that have been published to assist NT Greek students in their retention and use of the language that they spent so many hours learning during their theological education. Many terms are used to describe such publications of this nature such as helps, tutors, tools, and so on. In the end, each of these products is designed to reinforce the former student's already-learned skills. For the sake of this paper, they will be referred to as "helps" because that is their innate function and because "tools" is often used to refer to lexicons, exegetical guides, software, and other forms of assistance that are typically used during the original learning process, whereas these sources are designed to be used after the original learning process has taken place (i.e., post-coursework).

The biblical language market is saturated with resources aimed at helping Greek and Hebrew students retain their skills for later use. Some of these helps are preemptive in nature like Samuel Lamerson's English Grammar to Ace New Testament Greek (2004); Harvey Bluedorn's A Review of English Grammar for Students of Biblical Greek (2008); and Peter Perry's Brushing Up English to Learn Greek (2014). All three focus on laying a familiar grammatical foundation for native English speakers who desire to learn Greek. When approaching a language through GTM, it is vital to know and understand proper grammar usage.

Another popular purpose of Greek helps is to provide practical aids for post-classroom Greek students, such as in Constantine Campbell's Keep Your Greek (2010) and the more recent addition from Benjamin Merkle and Robert Plummer: Greek for Life (2017). Both books aspire to provide advice and guidance for struggling students during and after the formal learning process. Merkle and Plummer designed their text to work as a companion to their Going Deeper (with Andreas Köstenberger, 2016) book, while Campbell's book is essentially a collection of related excerpts from his online blog. Robert Plummer has also spearheaded a very helpful website and mobile

---

64. Thornhill, *Greek for Everyone*, xii.

application, "Daily Dose of Greek," that produces six short videos each week; five that translate and exegete a single verse of the New Testament (around two minutes each) and one that focuses on a specific topic (lengths vary).[65] This innovative "help" was designed for current or former Greek students around the world to assist their retention and improve their skills at the same time. Along these same lines are vocabulary builders like Robert Van Voorst's 1990 print of Building Your New Testament Greek Vocabulary, which targets the largest aspect of GTM, vocabulary memorization. Additionally, some professors have provided practical hands-on workbooks similar to that from William Mounce's A Graded Reader of Biblical Greek (1996), which dovetails well with his textbooks and Richard Goodrich and David Diewert's 2001 book, A Summer Greek Reader. Goodrich and Diewert's workbook provides a well-structured twelve-week program for students who desire to retain their Greek from the Spring semester to the Fall, a gap when courses may not be available. Goodrich and Diewert laid out their intentions in the preface of this resource:

1. To help students retain Greek skills over a summer.
2. To allow the student, working independently, to translate lengthy selections from the Greek New Testament.
3. To allow students to continue building a vocabulary of New Testament Greek.
4. To help students enjoy reading the Greek New Testament.[66]

Many students struggle after finishing their language course and it is encouraging to know that there are many resources, like those listed above, to aid their ongoing studies. Although these "helps" are designed to guide and support the student's education, they will never replace the classroom professor, which is not their objective. These "helps" are resources to assist a student in their understanding, retention, and application, but not to teach in and of themselves.

The final and more ministry-focused Greek "help" is a set of books aimed at providing devotional material based on NT Greek passages and exegetic insights. These two essay-based volumes are edited by J. Scott Duvall and Verlyn Verbrugge, and Paul Jackson respectively.[67] The goal of these

---

65. Robert Plummer, "Daily Dose of Greek," https://dailydoseofgreek.com/ (26 March 2018).

66. Goodrich and Diewert, *A Summer Greek Reader*, 7–8.

67. Duvall and Verbrugge, *Devotions on the Greek New Testament: 52 Reflections to Inspire and Instruct* (Grand Rapids: Zondervan, 2012); Paul Norman Jackson, *Devotions on the Greek New Testament*, vol. 2, *52 Reflections to Inspire and Instruct* (Grand

books is to (1) incorporate Greek into devotional thoughts, (2) review grammatical and syntactical Greek elements, and (3) concentrate on the spiritual side of the language application. This type of publication can be incredibly helpful for the student who struggles to see the practical side of biblical languages and the student who desires a somewhat in–depth resource to keep their skills sharp after completing their language work.

Non–Greek–Specific Approaches

This final category of approaches includes examples of language learning methods from a secular, non–Greek perspective that will broaden the topic to multiple subject matters, methodologies, and analytical techniques. Many of these approaches have not been applied to the teaching or learning of a biblical language in any public, formal manner. Therefore, each of these will be solely explored as a pedagogical language learning methodology first, and for what it may be able to offer to the theological language setting second.

Distinctions: Living Language vs. Research Language

It is important to distinguish the differences between a "living" language, a "dead" language, and a "research" language before addressing some of the methodologies that follow due to their focus on living language learning. First, a few terms need to be defined:

- Living Language—"is imperfect, i.e., it is badly adapted to reality—which can be seen in the abandonment of inflections (Flemish, Dutch)—but open to the conquering life."[68]
- Dead Language—"one that is complete. Insofar as it is complete, it can no longer evolve, and whatever is external to it in the linguistic field is the fruit of an illogical derivation."[69]
- Research Language—This is a language that can be "living" or "dead," but it is being studied for the purpose of reading and translating rather than being spoken fluently.

As an example, English is a living, active language even if Anglo–Saxon, an early form of English, is no longer used or understood. Conversely, Latin

---

Rapids: Zondervan, 2017).

68. Philonenko, *Langue morte et langue vivante*, 157.

69. Philonenko, *Langue morte et langue vivante*, 157.

is a dead, unused language that is often relegated to High Church liturgy and professional terminology (e.g., medical field, legal jargon, etc.). On the other hand, modern-day French and German are often employed as research languages to be studied by Doctorate of Philosophy students who typically do not learn them for speaking purposes.

Consequently, for the purposes of this study, Greek is a living, active language which is spoken in Greece, but Erasmus created an era-distinction between Ancient Greek and Modern Greek which caused a divide in use and evolution that allowed ancient forms of Greek to be isolated for study without confusing them with the modern iteration of the language. Donald Fairbairn makes an argument against the idea that languages like Greek and Latin are "dead," holding to the belief that "Greek has had a continuous history as both a spoken and written language" and that Latin "is still the primary language used in writing by Roman Catholic ecclesiastical officials."[70] Fairbairn further clarifies his view:

> Therefore, the only way one can refer to Greek and Latin as "dead" languages is to claim that Latin is dead because it is not an everyday language of the people any longer, and that the Greek spoken today is different enough from the Greek of Plato and Paul that it hardly qualifies as the same language. Students of Greek or Latin in schools, universities, and seminaries today are primarily (but not exclusively) interested in the ancient versions of Greek and Latin, not the modern Greek or in Latin as it is used by the Vatican today. As a result, study of these languages usually focuses on reading, not speaking or writing, and this focus adds to the misleading impression that these are dead languages.[71]

With Philonenko's definitions and Fairbairn's explanation in mind, it is easy to see why a debate exists regarding language classification for New Testament Greek. Although Erasmus's historical evolutionary distinction is often described as artificial (and it is), it has helped many Greek language educators isolate the specific distinction which they intend to teach.

Additionally, Matthew O'Donnell argues there are innate hurtles with using an ancient language as a research language when he writes, "The fundamental problems for the linguistic analysis of Hellenistic Greek are (1) the lack of native speakers, excluding an introspective rule-based analysis of language structure, and (2) the lack of complete and certain

---

70. Fairbairn, *Understanding Language*, 14–15.
71. Fairbairn, *Understanding Language*, 15.

situational data, which hinders a social approach to language study."[72] Several scholars, some outlined above, argue research languages ought to be learned as an actively spoken language if mastery is the goal of the learner. Both of these views bring to light a certain amount of introspection for the language instructor and remind students and teachers alike that purpose is the key to a strong pedagogy.

Whether one categorizes NT Greek as a "dead" language or a "research" language, it is important to clarify that this researcher follows the Erasmian distinction for NT Greek with both pronunciation and segregation of grammar. This means that NT Greek will not be considered as a living, spoken language to be practiced, nor will it be relinquished to a literary relic with no contextual/social, interpretive value. On the contrary, NT Greek will be considered as a classical, research language which contains interpretive value rather than simply historical value (cf., Virgil and Plato) as well as intended meaning rather than a one–dimensional, translatable text (cf., legal or instructional document).[73]

Second Language Acquisition (SLA)

The basic concept of SLA is quite simple: the learning of a new language (second, third, etc.) in addition to the learner's native language; the new language is typically referred to as a "target" language. Gass and Selinker break SLA down into multiple categories to assist the learner in their motivation by identifying the targets as multilingualism, Heritage, bilingual, and first language acquisition.[74] They go on to explain the intricate details of learning and understanding a new language from various aspects. Similarly, Stephen Krashen offers his five hypotheses for the SLA process in which he explains several important aspects discussed below.[75]

---

72. O'Donnell, *Corpus Linguistics and the Greek of the New Testament*, 4.

73. This distinction is vital because many, this researcher included, believe there is a considerable difference in intent and value between the Word of God and Greek legal documents or semi–fictional historical records.

74. Gass, and Selinker, *Second Language Acquisition*, 20–39.

75. These five SLA aspects are an intricate part of SLA literature. Whether other authors agree with them or not, they are regularly discussed in the field. Krashen is a key figure in this area of research and his theories have been widely discussed and debated.

Acquisition–Learning Distinction Hypothesis

First is the Acquisition–Learning Distinction, which will be key to the discussion of biblical language teaching. Krashen explains acquisition is similar to the process of a child learning their first language as it is "a subconscious process; language acquirers are not usually aware of the fact that they are acquiring language, but are only aware of the fact that they are using the language for communication."[76] This process does not result in an acute sense of proper grammar or systematic linguistics; rather it "sounds" or "feels" right as a method of communicating.[77] This idea of acquisition has also been referred to as implicit, informal, and natural learning due to its non-systematized progression.

Whereas Krashen defines acquisition as "informal," he views learning a language as quite the opposite. Learning, in this approach, is thought of as "formal" in the sense that it is strict and rigid in its methodology and use, as opposed to being fluid and conversational. While some argue that true acquisition is only attainable by children (i.e., native language), many linguists believe differently. Regardless, Krashen describes learning as "knowing about a language" with a focus on the rules and grammar.[78] Krashen posits that the gap between acquisition and learning is insurmountable and that only one of these goals can be attained in a given process. But he is not in the majority when he argues there is an unbridgeable gap between learning and acquisition; in fact, many linguists disagree.[79] The prevailing view of this separation is that the terms are merely a didactic preference and most likely just different stages of one process.

In this distinction, it is important to note that, when speaking about biblical languages, there is a strong debate growing between language professors. Some, like Streett, Buth, and Nitz, argue GTM only helps students in the learning process rather than the acquisition process. These proponents maintain that this limitation does not allow the learner to really grasp the language and therefore hinders their later ability to use it in ministry. Paul Nitz says as much when he states, "If we are serious about learning Greek, and want to be able to help people read and understand the Greek Bible and other Ancient Greek literature, treating Greek as a real language and using methods that help people acquire it as a real language is the way to

---

76. Krashen, *Principles and Practice*, 10.
77. Krashen, *Principles and Practice*, 10.
78. Krashen, *Principles and Practice*, 10.
79. E.g., DeKeyser, 1997; McLaughlin, 1990; Schmidt, 1994; Swain, 1985, 1995. These authors hold that learning and acquiring are both attainable and bridgeable depending on the method and the desired goal.

go."[80] Many others echo this sentiment, including Randall Buth and Brian Schultz in popular blog posts related to the subject.[81] They firmly believe that NT Greek ought to be learned as a "living" language rather than the dead or research variety if the student desires to acquire the language instead of simply learning it. In a recent example of this philosophy, Daniel Streett attempted to prove that language professors at the 2008 meeting of the Evangelical Theological Society had not really acquired the NT Greek language by giving them a quiz that asked for the Greek translation of words such as ball, chair, cat, etc. Although Streett proved these professional Greek teachers could not pass the simple test, he did not explain why those words are necessary for biblical Greek research or weekly exegetical sermon preparation. In reality, the difference in philosophies is based on a difference of intended use of the language in question. To explain it another way, Streett and others believe NT Greek needs to be acquired through fluent speech for proper use while others defend the process of learning the language to be used for research rather than speaking.

With the above thoughts in mind, a logical question arises: could one use acquisition methods to develop a better learning process? This is an important question because many teachers may desire to teach and use NT Greek as a research language without the limitations the learning process places on the language. This will be explored more later, but SLA research and practices have seen great success in language learning and development, which might apply to dead/research language students. The distinction between acquisition and learning is important, but their respective resources might be helpful to each other when their objectives overlap.

Natural Order Hypothesis

For his theoretical basis, Krashen summarizes several language–focused authors and researchers regarding the Natural Order Hypothesis. His basic argument is that people learn certain parts of a language before they learn others. This natural order is borne out through research that explains that children pick up on and use different morphemes of a language quicker and earlier than others. For instance, in English, children learn "–ing" endings and simple plural endings (–s) before they understand articles, progressive

---

80. Randall Buth, "Eureka! I Found a New Approach to Greek," *Biblical Language Center*, 29 April 2012, https://www.biblicallanguagecenter.com/eureka-approach-greek/ (26 March 2018).

81. Brian Shultz, "Why Fluency Workshops," *Biblical Language Center*, 22 April 2012, https://www.biblicallanguagecenter.com/fluency-workshops/ (26 March 2018).

statements, and irregular past tense.[82] And, interestingly, they typically learn irregular past tense verbs before they learn regular past tense verbs. Although there is some variation in the research between levels of acquisition and certain aspects of the language, much of language acquisition is not necessarily logical in its order or use. Krashen does provide a caveat about this grammatical sequencing: "I do not recommend teaching -ing early and the third person singular /s/ late."[83] He ultimately argues that grammatical sequencing is not ideal for language acquisition, and although it is "natural," that does not make it pedagogically sound.[84] On the other hand, Ellis and Shintani point out that Krashen's view of "natural" language learning sees the process as strictly implicit and incidental with no formal grammatical explanations.[85] Some have argued that this is a simplistic understanding of the process and needs to be broadened to grasp the more active role of the learner when interacting with the linguistic forms and input material.[86] The differences in these philosophies can be boiled down to their position on learning versus acquisition.

The Natural Order Hypothesis is helpful for NT Greek courses since they focus strongly on grammar (GTM) in the first two semesters. Should the grammar be structured in a frequency pattern, as Porter suggests, or in a proportionate pattern, as Mounce puts forth? Does it help the student when the focus of the grammar is placed on the ability to be able to read more quickly, as Black has designed his book, or strictly for translation, as Croy lays out in his book? These are just a few of the considerations that need to be made.

Monitor Hypothesis

Monitor hypothesis states that one must acquire a language to a large degree and then the "monitor" comes into play as a sort of grammatical filter for output.[87] Essentially, Krashen's research suggests acquisition is required before the monitor is useful, and the monitor is integral to the speaking process to avoid simple grammatical mistakes. An example would be the difference between someone saying "I [himself] needs to take a shower" rather than "you need to take a shower." This monitor assists the speaker in their

82. Krashen, *Principles and Practices*, 12–13.
83. Krashen, *Principles and Practices*, 14.
84. Krashen, *Principles and Practices*, 14–15.
85. Ellis and Shintani, *Exploring Language Pedagogy*, 119.
86. Ellis and Shintani, *Exploring Language Pedagogy*, 119.
87. Krashen, *Principles and Practices*, 15–16.

use of proper word order, vocabulary, verbal tenses, appropriate articles, etc. as they communicate with others. This is much more easily done through writing than it is through speaking due to the additional amount of time, focus, and resources allotted in the writing process as opposed to a face-to-face conversation.[88]

When this hypothesis is applied to NT Greek pedagogy, it can be instrumental in several ways depending on the teacher's approach. First, it can be used with the communicative process easily because the objective is to speak NT Greek as a modern, living language. Second, it is practically synonymous with the foundation of GTM, which focuses almost solely on proper word order, vocabulary, verbal tenses, appropriate articles, etc. In either case, the monitor hypothesis applies strongly to this research because of its practical and instrumental effect on the use of a new language.

Input Hypothesis

Input hypothesis is slightly more complex than the previous three concepts. The complexity comes from the fact that the input hypothesis runs counter to many established theories and is a relatively new area of research. At its core, input hypothesis suggests that for the learner to progress from one stage of acquiring a language to another, he or she must understand the forthcoming concepts before learning them.[89] Kashen clarifies this idea when he writes, "[The hypothesis] says we acquire by 'going to meaning' first, and as a result, we acquire structure!"[90] This is the exact opposite of the traditional view, which asserts that students learn structures first and then practice using those structures in conversation.[91] Krashen further contends:

> We may thus state parts (1) and (2) of the input hypothesis as follows:
>
> (1) The input hypothesis relates to acquisition, not learning.
>
> (2) We acquire by understanding language that contains structure a bit beyond our current level of competence (i + 1). This is done with the help of context or extra-linguistic information.[92]

---

88. Krashen, *Principles and Practices*, 16–17.
89. Krashen, *Principles and Practices*, 20–21.
90. Krashen, *Principles and Practices*, 21.
91. Hatch, *Second Language Acquisition*, 1–18.
92. Krashen, *Principles and Practices*, 21.

This philological approach is not completely new. James Asher wrote about it as a theory in the 1960s called the Total Physical Response (TPR) approach, as did Tracy Terrell in the 1970s.[93] Krashen later came to support this approach alongside Terrell. Additionally, Krashen believes that this process is very well-suited for the classroom setting because it can provide regular, consistent, comprehensible input for the learner.[94]

The field of NT Greek pedagogy is filled with new and unique ideas of how to apply GTM, but few truly diverse approaches to teaching the language. NT Greek seems to be viewed as either a dead language (GTM) or a living language (Communicative). In the case of the input hypothesis, some, like The Jerusalem Institute of Language and Humanities, have adopted Total Physical Response methodology, called Polis, for their Greek and Hebrew courses.[95] They are certainly not alone in this TPR movement; as mentioned earlier, Paul Nitz and Randall Buth both support this concept to various degrees.[96] It is grounded in the theory that SLA should be tailored after the first language process that all people experience. And learning a language is just that, an experience rather than a systematically structured methodology. Although it is growing in popularity, TPR in NT Greek has not rendered enough steam to have caught the attention of major academic programs in the United States.[97] Therefore, it has not been fully vetted or applied on a large, controlled scale as GTM has been over the last few hundred years.

Finally, Gass and Selinker did an excellent job of explaining the research behind the basis for the input hypothesis, called Universal Grammar. Universal Grammar (UG) is a philosophy that argues that learning a second language should look the same as learning one's first language.[98] By this, the authors argue that a common or "universal" grammar exists between every

---

93. Asher, "The Learning Strategy of the Total Physical Response: A Review," *Modern Language Journal* 50 (1966): 79–84; Asher, "The Total Physical Response Approach to Second Language Leaning," *Modern Language Journal* 53 (1969): 3–17; and Terrell, "A Natural Approach to Second Language Acquisition and Learning," *Modern Language Journal* 6 (1977): 325–37.

94. Krashen, *Principles and Practices*, 30.

95. Christophe Rico, *Polis: Speaking Ancient Greek as a Living Language* (Jerusalem: Polis Institute Press, 2015);, idem, http://www.polisjerusalem.org/polis-method (26 March 2018).

96. Buth, "Erika!"

97. Gerald Peterman of Moody Bible Institute presented on his recent experience with CLT and TPR at the 2017 meeting of ETS. He found it exciting and saw a big difference in the students, but ultimately had to revert back to GTM because he could not find a bridge to the traditional syntax course that would follow.

98. Gass and Selinker, *Second Language Acquisition*, 164.

language, which allows a new language to be acquired more quickly and effectively. But, it is important to note that when speaking of UG, certain areas of difference ought to be addressed. First, when children learn their native language, they attain a state of "completeness" fairly quickly and easily, whereas adult learners of a second language will struggle mightily or may never reach that state of completeness.[99] Second, adult learners have already internalized a linguistic system and understand that changing social contexts may also require adjustments in communication style, but children must learn this while building their language skills.[100] This provides an obvious benefit when learning a new language since the process can be streamlined by eliminating many of the social and context related adjustments that are often shared by all cultures. Third, although children are able to learn any native language equally well, SLA is not as equally universal based on the "association" significance mentioned above.[101] Thus universal grammar research is helpful, but UG not a sure-fire method of learning a second language, especially an ancient one. And, for example, since the TPR method is based on the first language acquisition process, it is therefore subject to the weaknesses of UG as well as the unique difficulties of the adult learner.

Affective Filter Hypothesis

An affective filter motivates an individual to acquire a second language and thus produces better learning results. Krashen puts forth a compelling case for three main categories of affective filters that summarize many variables in the hypothesis.

> (1) Motivation. Performers with high motivation generally do better in second language acquisition (usually, but not always, "integrative").
>
> (2) Self-Confidence. Performers with self-confidence and a good self-image tend to do better in second language acquisition.
>
> (3) Anxiety. Low anxiety appears to be conducive to second language acquisition, whether measured as personal or classroom anxiety.[102]

---

99. Gass and Selinker, *Second Language Acquisition*, 164.
100. Gass and Selinker, *Second Language Acquisition*, 164.
101. Gass and Selinker, *Second Language Acquisition*, 165.
102. Krashen, *Principles and Practices*, 31.

Krashen goes a step further to explain that he believes these factors pertain solely to acquisition and not learning because situational comprehensive input is available in the testing of acquisition, but he is clear that this is a belief and not a research–based conclusion.[103]

Additionally, it is important to note that these affective filters are typically considered to function outside of the acquisition device or pedagogical methodology. That means that each learner can have a completely different experience and varying results based on their attitude throughout the process. Someone who is eager, confident, and relaxed will typically do better than someone who lacks any or all of these descriptors in the same exact classroom. So, does the pedagogy even matter? Yes, of course! The pedagogy could, if designed properly, act as the affective filter that provides the motivation, builds the learner's confidence, and reduces overall course–wide anxiety for the students, thereby improving the success rate for everyone.[104]

NT Greek is no different when it comes to who might be successful and who will struggle the most. The three affective filters listed above play a role in any new language acquisition or learning process just as they play a role in any educational setting. Motivation has been shown to be the single biggest contributor to educational performance for both the teacher and the learner.[105] In the same way, self–confidence has been seen to affect the student's contribution to the learning process dramatically and therefore develop greater success in learning and test–taking.[106] And finally, as every professor already knows to some extent, anxiety can make or break a student's learning process at every level; from reading outside of class to taking a final exam, reduced anxiety equals improved performance.[107] If these factors play a role in acquisition, why would they not play a similar role in learning?

According to the affective filter hypothesis, if a NT Greek professor were to provide the appropriate motivation, develop the student's self–confidence, and reduce the amount of anxiety in the lesson plan and on assessments, the difference could be palpable. This could be done in a variety of ways, but in the end, any teacher, in any course, could improve their

103. Krashen, *Principles and Practices*, 31.

104. Krashen, *Principles and Practices*, 32.

105. Kusurkar, Cate, Vos, Westers, and Croiset, How Motivation Affects Academic Performance: A Structural Equation Modelling Analysis," *Advances in Health Science Education*, 22 February 2012, https://www.ncbi.nlm.nih.gov/pmc/articles/PMC3569579/ (26 March 2018).

106. Booth and Gerard, *Self-Esteem and Academic Achievement*, 629–48.

107. Carla Reiter, "Anxiety Affects Test Scores Even Among Students Who Excel at Math," *UChicago News*, 10 March 2017, https://news.uchicago.edu/article/2017/03/10/anxiety-affects-test-scores-even-among-students-who-excel-math (26 March 2018).

students' learning success if they are able to properly design a lesson plan and implement it through a pedagogy that allows for such creativity. Without making provisions for such didactic elements, it is up to the student to draw such motivators from themselves or the text provided. The problem is that the text cannot provide motivation, self-confidence, or reduced anxiety, and if the student were able to do so, they could successfully learn biblical languages on their own. It must be the teacher's burden to ensure successful education as far as they are able. The teacher cannot force a student to study or do their homework, but they can provide a learning environment that provides specific assistance and alleviates hurdles.

Task–Based Language Teaching (TBLT)

Task–Based Language Teaching, at its core, is most often traced back to N.S. Prabhu in the early 1980s in India and is part of the Communicative Language Teaching (CLT) methodology. Prabhu saw a broken and ineffective language system (Structure–Oral–Situational) in India and wanted to find a solution.[108] This situation led him to design a learning device called the Procedural Syllabus.[109] The Procedural Syllabus was originated to provide the learner with a new and more innovative method focused on communicative practices and situational language skills. Prabhu designed his educational philosophy around tasks that function this way: the teacher gives the student an instruction, and then the student follows the instruction and provides a verbal summary, with all of this being accomplished in the target language.[110] Although this is the origin of TBLT, the methodology has been subject to numerous changes in the last 30 or more years. Rod Ellis, David Nunan, and Mike Long have been at the forefront of this practice for the last several years, but there is a growing number of supporters who are noticing the effects of TBLT.

The first thing to address is the definition of a "task." Although this may seem like a relatively simple introductory step, it is not. Whereas Prabhu began by using what he called "pedagogical" tasks, many linguists today prefer what are called "target" tasks. By way of a general definition, "'Task' is the unit of analysis throughout the design, implementation, and evaluation of

---

108. Structure–Oral–Situational (SOS) is also known as Present–Practice–Produce (PPP).

109. Long, *Second Language Acquisition and Task-Based Language Teaching*, 216–19.

110. Long, *Second Language Acquisition and Task-Based Language Teaching*, 216–17.

the TBLT program, including the way student achievement is assessed—by task-based, criterion-referenced performance tests."[111] That is, a task in TBLT is a building block which makes up the functioning whole of the program. David Nunan takes this process a step further when he explains the difference between a targeted task and a pedagogical task: "Targeted tasks, as the name implies, refer to uses of language in the world beyond the classroom; pedagogical tasks are those that occur in the classroom."[112] If Nunan's "clarification" seems somewhat murky, it is. Rod Ellis provides an excellent illustration of the inherent problem of defining a task when he lists nine prominent publications, including ones by Prabhu, Long, and Nunan, over a span of sixteen years which all give slightly different definitions of a "task."[113] Webster's Dictionary defines a task simply as, "a usually assigned piece of work often to be finished within a certain time; duty or function."[114] But, as it pertains to TBLT, a task is a very specific idea that has specific features. Rod Ellis lists six features of a task in language learning:

1. A task is a workplan
2. A task involves a primary focus on meaning
3. A task involves real-world processes of language use
4. A task can involve any of the four language skills
5. A task engages cognitive processes
6. A task has a clearly defined communicative outcome[115]

This list is also helpful to distinguish the difference between a "task" and an "exercise," which is a debate that is often mentioned in TBLT books. On a larger scale, the topic of which type of task is to be used is addressed in every book on the subject with no clear consensus.

TARGET TASKS

Some examples of a target task include asking for the location of a restroom, giving driving directions to a store, providing feedback on a project

---

111. Long, *Second Language Acquisition and Task-Based Language Teaching*, 216–17. (Italics original)

112. Nunan, *Task-Based Language Teaching*, 1.

113. Ellis, *Task-Based Language Learning and Teaching*, 4–5.

114. Merriam-Webster, "Task," 15 March 2018, https://www.merriam-webster.com/dictionary/task?src=search-dict-box (26 March 2018).

115. Ellis, *Task-Based*, 9–10.

at a place of employment, or engaging in a simple exchange of pleasantries. Nunan adds, "It is non-technical and non-linguistic. It describes the sorts of things that the person in the street would say if asked what they were doing."[116] Richards and Rodgers explain them as "tasks that require them [the learner] to negotiate meaning and engage in naturalistic and meaningful communication."[117] In other words, these are tasks that result in understanding.

Pedagogical Tasks

Long described pedagogical tasks as "the activities and the materials that teachers and/or students work on in the classroom or other instructional environment."[118] David Nunan broadens the scope of a pedagogical task when he defines it as "a piece of classroom work that involves learners in comprehending, manipulating, producing or interacting in the target language while their attention is focused on meaning rather than grammatical form."[119] This is where things can become confusing. Richards and Rodgers say the target task aims toward meaning, while Nunan suggests that it is the pedagogical task that is meaning-centered. Similarly, Nunan states a pedagogical task is an interaction with the language, but Long clearly states that it is a non-linguistic effort.[120] Herein lies a major problem with Task-Based Language Teaching: there is little agreement on terms, functionality, or direct methodology. Tasks become flexible in nature because there is no concise definition among theorists/authors, which has resulted in an unclear path for methodology due to the lack of distinct differences between target and pedagogical tasks.

Synthetic Tasks (Task Supported Language Teaching—TSLT)

Long holds to a particular view of tasks that other authors seldom address; he believes there is a distinct difference between proper TBLT (uppercase) and tblt (lowercase). He holds that "genuine" TBLT consists solely of target

---

116. Nunan, *Task-Based*, 2.

117. Richards and Rodgers, *Approaches and Methods in Language Teaching*, 223–24.

118. Long, *Second Language*, 6. Long clarifies that these types of tasks have often been mistakenly identified as Target Tasks based on pedagogical benefit rather than real-world application benefits. He refers to these ill-applied tasks as "counterfeit."

119. Nunan, *Task-Based*, 4.

120. Long, *Second Language*, 6–7.

tasks to advance the language, and pedagogical tasks are solely non-linguistic in nature.[121] At TBLT's origin, Prabhu used pedagogical tasks as real-world language lessons and a classroom structure, while today's version has adjusted away from the early model. As mentioned already, this pool of information is somewhat dark, which has produced a type of blended TBLT among experts. Rod Ellis has been a key figure in providing a general understanding of this synthetic division, which blends the two previous models into a methodology and goes by many names (e.g., task-supported, synthetic).[122] It is considered unique because it does not hold to the general definition of a task in that it can be both linguistic and non-linguistic in use and is typically applied through the Present-Practice-Produce (PPP) didactic methodology.[123] In general, this synthetic process is easier for teachers to apply and students to pick up on because of its fluidity of use and lack of debated terminology. A course of study can more easily be broken down into classroom tasks and real-world tasks that would be presented by the teacher, practiced by the students under the teacher's supervision, and produced either verbally or on paper as a sign of retention.

Scaffolding and Learning Targets

Scaffolding can be traced back to Jerome Bruner in a co-authored 1976 article.[124] The article addressed many aspects of educational tutoring that were later applied to childhood language development.[125] Bruner likely gleaned some of his concept from Benjamin Bloom's 1956 educational theory, later enshrined as Bloom's Taxonomy.[126] Bloom staggered educational concepts into a multi-leveled scheme that, he believed, would lead the student from a basic level of knowledge toward a more engaged and creative level of knowledge. Both Bloom's and Bruner's research would later dovetail well with Lev

---

121. Long, *Second Language*, 6–7.
122. Ellis, *Task-Based*, 27–30.
123. Ellis, *Task-Based*, 27–30.
124. Wood, Bruner, and Ross, *The Role of Tutoring in Problem Solving*, 89–100.
125. Bruner, The Role of Dialogue in Language Acquisition," in *The Child's Concept of Language*, ed. A. Sinclair, J. Jarvelle, and W.J. M. Levelt (New York: Springer-Verlag, 1978).
126. Bloom, Engelhart, Furst, Hill, and Krathwohl, *Taxonomy of Educational Objectives: The Classification of Educational Goals, Handbook I: Cognitive Domain* (New York: David McKay Company, 1956). This work was later revised and redacted to better fit the modern educational landscape: Lorin Anderson, *A Taxonomy for Learning, Teaching, and Assessing: A Revision of Bloom's Taxonomy of Educational Objectives* (New York: Longman, 2001).

Vygotsky's 1978 theory of the Zone of Proximal Development, which explains the gap in a child's cognitive development in which he or she needs knowledgeable guidance and assistance to progress.[127] With a basic understanding of these three cognitive approaches to learning, it is easy to see why strategic educational structures became such a publishing juggernaut in the 1980s and continues today. The basic theory for scaffolding is that knowledge must be strategically introduced to the student to (1) improve retention and (2) allow for new information to be effectively added to the process. If this process is followed, the student would be able to relate each level of information to the previous and following levels of information and result in better engagement with the material and longer-term retention.

In his 1978 chapter on language learning, Bruner explains scaffolding as "the steps taken to reduce the degrees of freedom in carrying out some task so that the child can concentrate on the difficult skill she is in the process of acquiring."[128] Based on this premise, Bruner says, "We begin with the hypothesis that any subject can be taught effectively in some intellectually honest form to any child at any stage of development."[129] Without stating it, Bruner and those who apply scaffolding ultimately utilize the PPP methodology for each level of knowledge being taught.

The most recent adaptation of this learning theory is titled Learning Targets by Connie Moss and Susan Brookhart.[130] Their theory, in essence, is to turn Bloom's Taxonomy and Bruner's Scaffolding models on their side to redirect the educational approach. Instead of starting the learner at the bottom of a pyramid and working them up to the top, Learning Targets begins the students on the outer-most ring of a bullseye and directs them inward toward the center of a target. This concept can be tailored to structure a course in many ways, such as a one-day class lesson or a semester-long scope of the educational goals for the course. The authors encourage both options and a variety of creative applications that can benefit almost any classroom or learning setting. Although the concepts of Scaffolding and Learning Targets are not very different in their ultimate objectives, it is worth noting that former is aimed at overall knowledge while the latter is designed to be applied in various, overlapping areas of the scope and sequence of the learning system in an individual classroom lesson or an entire school. And, where scaffolding acts more like the unseen support beams that hold up a bridge, learning

---

127. Vygotsky, *Mind in Society: The Development of Higher Psychological Processes* (Cambridge, MA: Harvard University Press, 1978).

128. Bruner, *The Role of Dialogue*, 19.

129. Bruner, *The Process of Education*, 33.

130. Moss and Brookhart, *Learning Targets: Helping Students Aim for Understanding in Today's Lesson* (Alexandria, VA: ASCD, 2012).

targets are intended to be the brightly painted lines, arrows, and signage that visually direct those on the bridge about where to go.

Scaffolding is essentially a didactic structure that almost any subject matter could be adapted to for better results, and biblical languages are no different. NT Greek is already using this basic concept when GTM breaks down the grammatical aspects of the language into separate parts and staggers them according to the professor's learning goals. For example, William Mounce designed his book to teach the steps leading to translation proficiency, while David Black arranges these levels for reading ease, and Stanley Porter applies his methodology to a usage model. Regardless of the desired outcome is, scaffolding can help the teacher lay out an easy-to-follow structure and help the student to stay on track with the teacher's educational goals. But, of course, this implies that the professor begins with a clear end-goal in mind rather than a vague idea of success in one's class.

Technology in Language Education

One rapidly growing aspect of learning biblical languages often gets overlooked or ignored: technology. Coakley and Woodall address this oversight when they write, "The digital revolution now underway has the potential to transform our culture in the same way that the printing press transformed society in Gutenberg's day."[131] Technology is an ever-expanding part of modern society that will not likely experience a slow-down anytime soon. With desktop computers now considered too expensive and cumbersome to be useful and laptops falling close behind them, the world is more connected and transient than ever. Digital books, magazines, and newspaper sales are on the rise with Amazon, Google, and other third-party apps for smartphones and tablets all heavily promoting their convenient digital services, leaving traditional publishing companies trying frantically to figure out their new roles. Although digital sales have not exceeded print sales to date, the proportions are changing, and the shrinking of the coming generation's attention span may push the scales further away from physical media.[132] Many schools of higher education claim to fully embrace the technological revolution taking place by offering campus-wide internet connectivity, digital library resources, and a Learning Management System (LMS) such as Moodle or Blackboard to their students. The question remains whether these efforts are enough.

---

131. Coakley, *Using Bible Software*, 389.

132. Weinreich, Obendorf, Herder, and Mayer, "Not Quite the Average: An Empirical Study of Web Use," *ACM Transactions on the Web* 2.1 (February 2008).

It is important to note early on that "the use of technology is not to be regarded as a pedagogical panacea."[133] Technological involvement in language learning is not a new concept; Rosetta Stone, Rocket Language, and Babbel are just a few of the growing number of software programs available on the market today. These methodologies work by integrating audio, visual, and strategic language learning principles through many of the SLA theories outlined above, like Input Hypothesis and Universal Grammar. But, ultimately, they are designed to be customizable in their delivery and, most importantly, mobile in their platform. The student can take these language learning tools everywhere they go, on or offline, and the learner can even form communities with other online learners all over the world to build relationships while they develop their language skills. Would a tool with these same functions benefit biblical language learning? Facebook pages and web-based community forums are available, but those are passive and not directed at teaching. Examined below are the areas of software use and optimizing online education for NT Greek in modern higher education.

Although websites and blogs are considered a passive form of language learning, they aid and supplement the process for those who seek them out. Hundreds of these digitally-formatted sites and communities exist around the world and are not limited by time, location, or face-to-face interaction. Some of the more prominent online communities found on Facebook are:

- Nerdy Language Majors by William Varner (4,000+ members)
- New Testament Greek Study by Joseph Greer (1,600+ members)
- NT Textual Criticism by James Snapp Jr. (1,500+ members)
- Biblical Language Coaching Forum by Anthony Cummings (500+ members)

Some of the more eminent blog sites and forums are:

- daveblackonline.com and newtestamentgreekportal.blogspot.com by David Alan Black
- centerforlearningbiblicalgreek.com/blog by Alan E. Kurschner
- ibiblio.org/bgreek/forum by Jonathan Robie

133. Porter and Brook O'Donnell, *The Linguist as Pedagogue*, 27. In his chapter on "Adapting Technology to Teach Koine Greek," Rodney Decker does a good job of outlining the benefits and pitfalls of technological tools while teaching and learning Greek. But, unfortunately, as with any technology-focused publication, the chapter is now quite dated. Published in its final form in this 2009 edition, his recourses were limited and have changed drastically by today's standards. Thus, although his thoughts and concerns are insightful, they are also limited in scope.

- ntgreekgeek.blogspot.com by Joshua Covert
- dailydoseofgreek.com by Robert Plummer
- billmounce.com/blog by William Mounce
- ntgateway.com by Mark Goodacre

Resources like these can be an excellent tool for the student who is currently learning Greek, trying to retain their Greek, or for those working to deepen their language and exegetical skills.

Software

In the past, and in some classrooms today, theological professors have been cautious to promote Bible software. In fact, several have called them a crutch or a hindrance to the learning of biblical languages. Constantine Campbell writes, "In much the same way that an interlinear can be a crutch and shortcut the learning process, so software tools can be used such that your Greek will suffer—and probably die."[134] Similarly, in a publication focused on academic counsel, Nijay Gupta says this:

> On the one hand, many students who study the biblical languages in graduate school find it difficult to work efficiently or quickly with the Greek or Hebrew text for the benefit of academic study or pastoral ministry (i.e., preaching preparation). Learning how to use software programs could encourage such students to maintain an active use of their grammatical knowledge. On the other hand, it is entirely possible that graduate training in language software could become a crutch and communicate (however wrongly) to the student that facility with the software is a sufficient replacement for critical knowledge of paradigms, syntactical relationships, and significant aggregate of vocabulary words.[135]

In fact, many professors openly promote this sentiment to their students while regularly using the very same software that they demean. Professors use Bible software specifically because of its efficiency and speed to improve their research and grading. Gone are the days of digging through a Greek NT for the number of times Paul used a specific word or looking for a particular morpheme in Revelation. Parsing, diagramming, and lemma searches can be done instantly. So, why do so many professional NT Greek

---

134. Campbell, *Keep your Greek*, 28.
135. Gupta, *Prepare, Succeed, Advance*, 126.

teachers scoff at Bible software? Partly because it can be a shortcut to avoid the hard work of thinking, deliberating, and wrestling with the text in one's heart and mind.

Some NT Greek teachers are looking for alternative methods on how to incorporate software into the language learning process. In the promotional material for his NT Greek Stripped Down resource, Danny Zacharias writes, "New Testament Greek Stripped Down is a unique introductory Greek grammar which seeks to provide students with an understanding of the essentials of Greek grammar while equipping them to make immediate use of Greek for exegesis using Logos Bible Software."[136] He focuses on using Logos Bible Software to speed up the students' progress as well as build their self-confidence. Each lesson is taught through the lens of software to make the entire process digitally integrated.

In their contribution to Keossler's *The Moody Handbook of Preaching*, James Coakley and David Woodall outline four primary roadblocks for biblical language students and four benefits that will come to the students who choose to utilize software in their linguistic journey. Because the four roadblocks were mentioned earlier in the Tools-Based section, they will simply be listed here to serve as a reminder before expounding on the four benefits.

Road Blocks to Hebrew and Greek Language Study

- Languages are hard to grasp
- Languages are fleeting
- Languages are time-consuming
- Languages are technical[137]

These "roadblocks" were derived from a Moody Bible Institute Pastor's Conference survey taken in the mid-2000s. They reveal a pastor's priorities from week to week if their biblical language training did not ultimately show the benefit of overcoming these fears in their sermon preparation. The four benefits Coakley and Woodall list are not all directly correlated with the roadblocks, but they provide an alleviation for much of a pastor's trepidation in this area of study.

---

136. Zacharias, *NT Greek Stripped Down: Mastering Greek Essentials in Conjunction with Bible Software* (Scholar's Publisher, 2012).

137. Coakley, *Using Bible Software*, 390.

Space

The foundational point by Coakley and Woodall here is that proper exegetical work requires vast bookshelves for resources, a workspace cluttered with open books, and tethering oneself to one's office to access those resources. They explain that "in contrast, with the use of Bible software, the study resources are neatly organized in the condensed space of the computer screen."[138] They go on to state, "Through the use of a laptop, the workspace can actually travel with the pastor. Bring your library with you to study at home or on the mission field. Pack thousands of volumes on the hard drive. Space is no longer an issue in the new digital age."[139] Such a benefit is useful when a pastor does regular, in-depth Bible studies which require multiple resources.

Functionality

Space is important, but only if the software can get the job done week in and week out for a pastor, Bible study leader, or missionary. Coakley and Woodall explain that Bible software is easily capable of digging into the languages by providing more than morphological short-cuts; it can now outline and diagram a passage while displaying syntactical aspects of the text. Through screenshots and textual examples, the authors display the powerful exegetical capabilities of several Bible software packages for the reader. Bible software can be an enormous blessing through space, but, as with functionality, that is based on the quality of the resources in the software. This assertion is contingent on the software offering useful resources at a reasonable price; otherwise, space and functionality are quite limited in their effectiveness.

Time

Time might be the greatest benefit of using software to explore Scripture. Coakley and Woodall say, "A recent time management survey concluded that 70 percent of the time a pastor spends in Bible study is actually spent in searching for resources, paper flipping, page turning, looking for information in hard-copy resources, or arranging the resources on the desk."[140] They

---

138. Coakley, *Using Bible Software*, 391.

139. Coakley, *Using Bible Software*, 393.

140. Coakley, *Using Bible Software*, 399. They cited Dennis Rainy's interview with Scott Lindsey from Logos Software on June 19, 2006. The interview is no longer available at the cited location.

continue to explain that these software-based resources are so easily available that, "a clicking frenzy can take one quickly from a Greek word to the Greek lexicon BDAG to the unabridged works of Josephus to the Pseudepigrapha book Enoch and then to the internet for an advanced search."[141] In this way, a pastor can use his time more efficiently and prioritize better.

Availability

Availability is the simplest benefit of software, but it must be stated again that it is only a blessing if the resources are included in one's package. Ultimately, Coakley and Woodall propose that, with software, "students who were not able to retain the paradigms necessary to sight-read the Bible in the biblical languages are still able to work with the text in a meaningful way."[142] Is this not is the goal of so many professors, that their students would be able to dig into the sacred text with meaning and discover God's truth for themselves?

Coakley and Woodall do a wonderful job outlining the use and benefit of a Bible software for professional and lay believers alike. Many beginning NT Greek grammars relegate the idea of "technology" to web-based tools like blogs and memory devises while others ignore the use of technology completely. With so much accessibility at the minister's fingertips today, it seems unfortunate that so few NT Greek resources introduce students to a software-integrated approach even if the software's role is limited.

Most recently, Carl Sanders II published an article strongly promoting the use of technology, and specifically Bible software, in theological education. Sanders states, "We have been preparing students to minister using methods developed with old tools when new tools are in the process of transforming education and biblical research."[143] He makes a strong point that may be true at many levels and in many disciplines within high education.

Online Education

Technology has opened many new doors for education, including the massive advancement that is online or distance education. Unfortunately, many schools take a minimalist approach to online education. They know that it brings the greatest financial benefit for the least amount of investment, but

---

141. Coakley, *Using Bible Software*, 399.
142. Coakley, *Using Bible Software*, 399.
143. Sanders II, *Biblical Language Instruction by the Book*, 218.

CHAPTER 2   59

it is possible that a small investment attitude could result in a diminished product and poor returns now or in the future. This section will outline the ideal and logical path forward for online pedagogy and structurization from a variety of angles and will then tie in its application to biblical languages. This process will be done in four steps:[144]

1. Philosophy—The underlying mental and didactic objectives of the task in question with an intentional concentration on the question of "why."

2. Methodology—The process of theoretically organizing and arranging the philosophical objectives into a manageable progression—"how."

3. Application—The actual steps of producing a product which applies the philosophy to the methodology in a tangible form as the "what."

4. Assessment—The final stage of reviewing the results of the application to determine its effectiveness in accomplishing the three previous aspects and making adjustments as needed.

The above four sections of this process should lead each course, on-site or online, toward a more intentional and effective educational product which would, in turn, lead to a better-educated student and stronger curricula.

Philosophy

The philosophy of an educational course should always be the beginning point, even if one desires to use the Backward Design method.[145] Why is this course being designed and taught in the first place? What are the learning objectives of the course? Is the information of this course new and unique or built upon other courses or even an entire degree program? Questions like these form the foundation of how one will ultimately design and teach any given amount of information. Due to the unique nature of online education, a lack of forethought and philosophical due diligence is more easily exposed in a virtual setting.[146] Sanders explains this importance well when he writes:

---

144. These steps are an adaptation of two premiant theories of instructional-design models: ADDIE, which derived from, Walter Dick and Lou Carey, *The Systematic Design of Instruction* (New York: Harper Collins, 1996) and Backward Design, which was proposed by Grant Wiggins and Jay McTighe, *Understanding by Design* (Alexandria, VA: ASCD, 2005).

145. Wiggins and McTighe, *Understanding by Design*. Although the authors support this, many third party summaries of their approach neglect to mention this step.

146. Major, *Teaching Online*, 9–11.

New methods of delivering courses, such as online and blended (part on-line, part face-to-face), are part of that new reality. These new options make courses more accessible and affordable, extending the reach and impact of institutions using them effectively. Teaching our students with online collaboration, exposing them to the vast resources of the Internet (along with the skills to critically evaluate those resources), and introducing them to the immense new world of electronic databases and other new tools fundamentally transforms the delivery of education.[147]

One of the primary goals of a teacher is to provide quality information in an effective method that results in the student's acquisition of knowledge. Unfortunately, many times that goal is not achieved due to a few simple and avoidable mistakes.

Educational Approach

Many professors underestimate the significance of the learning process, which results in missed objectives and underachieving students. Quality education is difficult to provide and doing it at a distance is even more difficult. For example, where Bloom's Taxonomy can assist in the educational process, some suggest that it is fundamentally flawed and in need of complete reversal.[148] It is important for a professor to know what he or she believes in instances like this to help dictate their course trajectory.

Similarly, it is important to determine what defines good education. Are final exam grades an accurate measurement of the success or failure of the course? What about end-of-course surveys or professor popularity? In the end, the teacher must understand the educational process to measure and identify achieved and failed objectives.

In the field of biblical languages, the professor must know what he wants the students to know when the course is complete. For instance, he would need to determine whether the main objective is vocabulary retention, translation proficiency, phonetical acumen, etc. and how to measure for that objective.[149] By way of a specific example, if the professor's goal is that his students can read their NT Greek Bible, then there are several questions that need to be answered:

---

147. Sanders, *Biblical Language*, 218.

148. E.g., Robert Marzono, Ronald Case, Brenda Surgue, Donald Clark.

149. Harlow, *Successfully Teaching Biblical Languages Online at the Seminary Level*, 18.

CHAPTER 2

1. How does the professor define reading? What does reading look like?
2. What information does the student need to know in order to read?
3. Does the order of the information matter in this process?
4. How long would the process take to produce a proficient reader?
5. How does the professor intend to measure the student's reading proficiency?
6. How can this process be done when the student is not in the same classroom as the professor?
7. How can cheating be prevented in this process?

Not only does a pedagogical approach need to be sound and demonstrable, but it needs to be adaptable to the growing online format of education. Regardless of the teacher's learning objectives, the new asynchronoustic reality of learning has to be considered when designing a pedagogy.

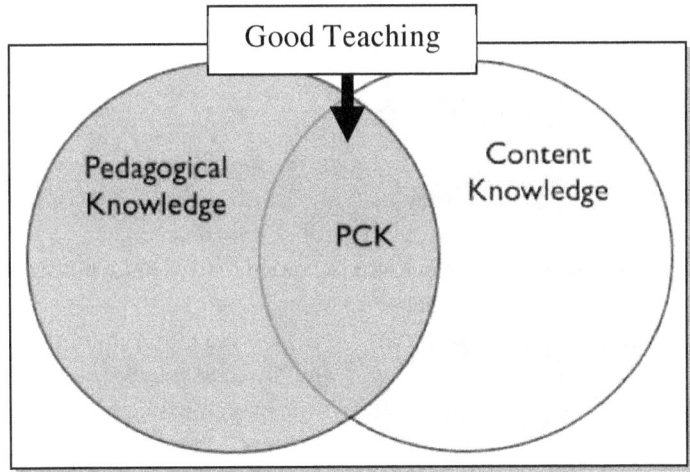

Figure 1: Pedagogical/Content Knowledge

Didactic Approach

Every teacher and professor ought to be able to understand the meaning of "good teaching," but this can be quite subjective.[150] Lee Shulman believes

---

150. Major, *Teaching Online*, 25.

the intersection between one's knowledge of a content area (CK) and one's knowledge of pedagogy (PK) is where effective teaching exists (PCK).[151] In fact, Mishra and Koehler argue that the content knowledge must be transformed to be taught better.[152] Although this concept does not appear surprising, many teachers and professors are not taught pedagogical practices and therefore severely limit their quality of teaching effectiveness.

Technology Approach

Finally, teachers need to choose what they want to do with technology when designing and teaching online courses. The question is this, is technology a passive conduit that delivers the information, or is technology an active part of the information? Claire Major believes many online teachers see technology as nothing more than a conduit and that this is the root of many educational errors.[153] Many schools today simply record the professor during her regular class meeting and then link that recording to an online portal for distance students. The students are then expected to take notes, which will aid them on quizzes and tests from the same pre-recorded class. Major argues that technology is and must be considered a key aspect of online education if success is desired. Via and Sosulski explain the bare minimum technological fluency when deciding to teach an online course: "You need to know how to use basic programs such as a word processor, spreadsheets, photo manager, and email. Understanding how to properly save, upload, and download files is critical."[154] The Technological Pedagogical Content Knowledge (TPACK) model of online education explains that not only do content and pedagogy need to be balanced, but technological knowledge must be included for good teaching. Major makes a crucial point when she writes, "TPAC advances the notion that faculty who teach online need new and different knowledge and expertise than those who teach onsite" and "discrete knowledge of any of the three main areas [i.e., PK, CK, TK] is insufficient for effective online teaching. It is the overlaps that are critical."[155] Many educational institutions would benefit from this understanding.

---

151. Shulman, *Those Who Understand: Knowledge Growth in Teaching*, 4–14.
152. Mishra and Koehler, *Technological Pedagogical Content Knowledge*, 1017–54.
153. Major, *Teaching Online*, 9–11.
154. Via and Sosulski, *Essentials of Online Course Design*, 17.
155. Major, *Teaching Online*, 30–31.

Figure 2: TPAC Illustration

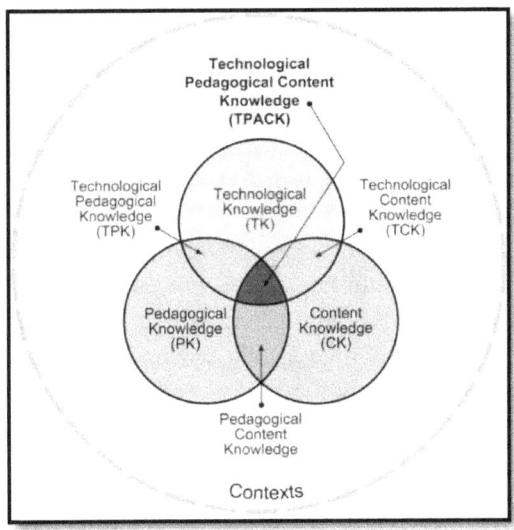

METHODOLOGY

Although most often the philosophical steps of planning and teaching a course are taken for granted, methodology also receives less attention than it should since it is the bridge between one's desire/intention (philosophy) and the product itself (application). Once learning objectives are established, and the purpose of the course is clear, the next step is to plan out what the course will look like once launched.[156] This is a very important step in online education since the course needs to use technology and creative pedagogy intentionally in its application. Without forethought and planning, an online course can become burdensome to the student and unfruitful for the institution.[157] As it is in a traditional course, the responsibility to design and implement the objectives and lesson plans for the content falls on the of the teacher of the course, but it is also that teacher's duty to understand and utilize the technological side of an online course. Many professors leave the technical side of the course to the Distance Learning department while others ignore it altogether, but this is a critical step in ensuring the success of an online class. As explained above, there are three key aspects to good teaching for an

---

156. Boettcher and Conrad, *The Online Teaching Survival Guide*, 63.

157. Via and Sosulski, *Online Course Design*, 190–205. The authors stress the importance of visual design in chapter four of this book, but they reserve structure until the final chapter. This seems unusual since as argue for its key role in the learning process.

online course: pedagogy, content, and technology, and any teacher who lacks in one or more areas will likely cause significant strain on the others.[158] Many teachers today would benefit from Ruben Puentedura's SAMR model of technology integration.[159] Puentedura proposes four levels of integration that could either slightly assist the learning process (limit paper use by posting documents online) all the way to redefining the learning process (the course and its activities are built upon advanced technologies).

Biblical language courses typically use very little technology. Although documents are often posted on a course website, they rarely go deeper into technology that the Substitution level of the SAMR model. To be fair, it would be difficult to imagine how biblical language courses could reach the Modification or Redefinition levels, but few attempts have been made in this realm at all. Since Bible software is often treated as a hindrance, many schools stay away from technology in the language classrooms.

Figure 3: The SAMR Model Illustration

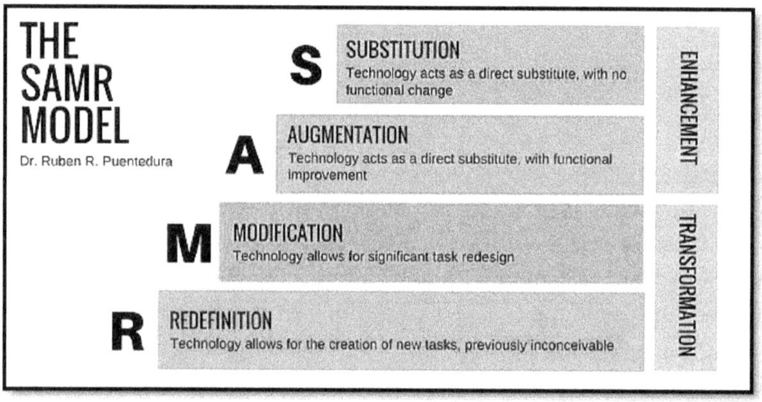

THE SAMR MODEL
Dr. Ruben R. Puentedura

S — SUBSTITUTION
Technology acts as a direct substitute, with no functional change

A — AUGMENTATION
Technology acts as a direct substitute, with functional improvement

ENHANCEMENT

M — MODIFICATION
Technology allows for significant task redesign

R — REDEFINITION
Technology allows for the creation of new tasks, previously inconceivable

TRANSFORMATION

Application

Once the ideas and goals are set and the planning stage is completed, it is time for the course to be built on the preferred Learning Management System (LMS) and opened up for students to use. One major consideration when teaching and facilitating an online course is to determine how to communicate the information to the students. Many professors have simply recorded

---

158. Major, *Teaching Online*, 31.

159. To this date, Ruben R. Puentedura has not published anything about this methodology except on his personal blog: http://hippasus.com/blog/archives/227 (26 March 2018).

on-site lectures and posted them online for a distance course to watch while others record lectures from their office desks. Since many educational scholars agree that lecture is not the most productive method of teaching, it is important to know how long a recorded lecture should be and what other means are available for content dissemination. Relevant handouts, articles, audio and video clips, and interactive discussion boards are all good examples of how to provide information without using pre-recorded fifty- to ninety-minute lecture.[160] But, if lecture is necessary in some cases (e.g., a history course) then it would behoove the teacher to use the "chunking" technique of creating units and subunits of information to assist the student in better acquisition and retention of the information.[161]

Much of biblical language curricula is already broken into "chunks" due to the emphasis on grammar elements and the progression of learning the languages through stages of increasingly greater grammatical difficulty. This means that online videos can be short and poignant while homework assignments will naturally be more lengthy. Online courses are convenient because they do not tie the student down to a particular time or location. They also allow the student to dictate, to varying degrees, their own educational pace and duration. With this in mind, it is vital for every online teacher to find creative and relevant applications for the content material through their pedagogy using modern technology.

Assessment

No course can be proven effective without an intentional and well-directed assessment of its foundational concepts, planning process, and real-life field testing. What this means is that quality and effectiveness are based on results, and results come from careful planning and the tracking of information. Therefore, if the philosophy step or the methodology step were skipped or glossed over, then the final assessment will be flawed because one or more of the key stages was not fully developed and thus could not be reviewed properly. Below is an assessment tool proposed by Debbie Morrison on the Online Learning Insights website. As a warning, Misut and Pribilova explain that "some assessments are inherently limiting with a prescriptive set of standards that may not fit all contexts."[162] With that in mind, Morrison's five-step process is designed to discover the effectiveness of a given online course by using basic elements.

---

160. Via and Sosulski, *Online Course Design*, 129–149.

161. Via and Sosulski, *Online Course Design*, 191–93.

162. Misut, and Pribilova, *Measuring Quality in Context of E-Learning*, 312–19.

> Five Steps to Assessing Online Course Quality (parentheses added)
>
> 1) Assess Using a Rubric or Other Tool to Consider Basic Course Elements (Philosophy)
>
> 2) Analyze Course from a Student Perspective (Application)
>
> 3) Assess Course Artifacts, Materials, & Feedback (Methodology)
>
> 4) Consider Level and Type of Student–to–Student and Student–to–Instructor Interactions (Application)
>
> 5) Results: Are Students Learning? (Application)[163]

If these five assessment steps reveal undesired results, then the instructor needs to go back to the beginning of the development process and find the place where the plan did not function properly. If the weak link cannot be found, then the process must begin again with the expressed purpose of producing a quality online course that meets the needs of the student and the institution.

This outline of the prevalent literature on the subject of NT Greek history, pedagogical practices, and secular language training was designed to assist the reader with a more complete understanding of where language training has been and where it currently stands today. It is not exhaustive, but it lays a foundation of what research is being used to analyze and assess GTM against modern language learning pedagogies and determine its place in the field of constantly advancing educational technology. The next chapter will provide the research methodology and data collection strategy used during the expert survey.

Chapter Summary

There are numerous approaches to teaching NT Greek, and as noted, many of them are slightly unique renditions of GTM pedagogy. New approaches and publications seem to pop up every day and that makes it difficult to stay abreast with the newest ideas in this field. This chapter aimed to capture the scope of publication available along with some of the pertinent SLA approaches as well. The next chapter will explain the research methodology and assessment tools.

---

163. Morrison, "How 'Good' is Your Online Course? Five Steps to Assess Course Quality," *Online Learning Insights*, 26 May 2015, https://onlinelearninginsights.wordpress.com/2015/05/26/how-good-is-your-online-course-five-steps-to-assess-course-quality/ (26 March 2018).

Chapter 3

Research Methodology

With previous chapter's literature review regarding relevant methodologies for language learning in mind, this section explains the research strategies that will shape the rest of this dissertation. Several of the authors and professors mentioned during the literature review have agreed to participate in the following stages of research as well as several previously unmentioned experts. Here, the names of survey participants, the instrument used, and the detailed strategy of the researcher are explained to provide the reader with a better understanding of the coming data.

Research Questions

1. What, if any, are the current benefits and detriments of the Grammar–Translation Method on New Testament Greek instruction in the twenty-first century?
2. To what extent, if any, can current, unique pedagogical methods help improve New Testament Greek instruction in the twenty-first century?
3. To what extent, if any, can the research and practices of Second Language Acquisition, Task–Based Language Teaching, and Educational Scaffolding help improve New Testament Greek instruction in the twenty-first century?
4. What would a modern, non–academically focused Greek pedagogy look like in today's theological educational setting?

Research Design

Research in the area of biblical language pedagogy has been limited. As mentioned in the previous chapter, many seasoned professors have studied ways to improve the use of GTM in a college classroom, which has led to several unique applications of the method. But, these efforts are not considered innovative because they are mostly based on one strategy of teaching. Rather, it is necessary to analyze GTM pedagogy first and then determine whether it is suitable to stand as the foundation of language teaching platforms today. In the same way that it would be ill–advised to remodel an old house without inspecting the foundation to find out if it has faltered, it is not wise to continue basing biblical language training upon an uninspected methodology. That is the intention here.

The research for this dissertation includes many levels that build upon each other to form an analysis of GTM and determine if it is sound as a structural foundation for a NT Greek pedagogy. These analytical steps are explored and applied in the following order:

1. New Testament Greek expert survey
2. S.W.O.T. analysis of the GTM
3. A comparative study of Second Language Acquisition (SLA) practices and Grammar–Translation Method (GTM) practices

The wisdom and experience of the expert group members will provide the basis for the S.W.O.T. analysis that will then inform the comparative study. These three levels of research and scrutiny ought to provide ample evidence about the health and viability of GTM as schools and institutions work to improve their didactic language approaches in modern–day education.

Description of the Sample

The expert survey sample was chosen carefully with respect to three criteria related to NT Greek. A priority was placed on selecting NT Greek professors who have significant experience teaching in the field (ten or more years). Next, authors of published NT Greek textbooks were selected to participate. And last, all survey participants were asked to suggest names of people who might be a good fit for this research, and those names were considered and contacted if applicable to the study. Consequently, all survey participants have experience teaching and/or developing scholarly material related directly to NT Greek methodology and pedagogy.

CHAPTER 3

Description of the Instruments Used, and the Procedures Followed

Stage 1: Expert Survey

The instrument for this research was an expert survey that followed a meticulous process to ensure professional accountability and academic integrity for the participants and this researcher. First, a list of professors and authors was compiled and public email addresses were collected. This list of participants and their employers can be found in Appendix 1.[1] Second, a personal "inquiry of interest" email was sent to each email address. The transcript of this email can be found in Appendix 2. The objective of this step of the research was to obtain at least thirty participants to complete the survey. This initial email was sent for two primary reasons: (1) to ensure that the email address used was correct, and (2) to present a non–invasive introduction that would allow the person to accept or decline without pressure or compulsion. This step also ensured that the participant knew the researcher's name and that the survey email that would follow would not end up in their spam or junk mail folder. This email received one of three responses: a "Yes" which was followed up with a separate email containing the survey with detailed instructions, a "No" response was sent a courteous email thanking them for their time, and some of those emailed did not respond at all. If the introductory email did not receive a response, each person was sent a second attempt about ten days later to be certain that the email did not get lost or forgotten.

The list of desired and/or suggested names that fit this research well included fifty-three names. Of those initial fifty-three names, forty-nine total email addresses were acquired and sent an inquiry of interest letter with about ten saying "no" for various reasons and four people who did not respond at all.[2] The third and final stage of this process was to write and send the survey. When the supervisors approved the survey, it was sent only to the people who reciprocated interest in participating in the survey. A transcript of the survey can be found in Appendix 2. This survey was written to be poignant, direct, and within the suggested guidelines of Simon and White's Rubric for Expert Validation of Survey or Interview, which provides excellent advice about how to conduct highly effective expert surveys.[3]

---

1. Some of the participants opted to list their answers as "Anonymous" in the results, but they were notified that they would be listed here for accountability.

2. It is not clear if those who did not respond were due to non–interest or a wrong email address.

3. Simon and White, "Survey / Interview Validation Rubric for an Expert Panel,"

The instrument was also designed to be open-ended and in an essay-format to allow the participant to speak openly and provide as much or as little information as they desired while still furnishing the researcher with valuable information and quotable material. The decision was also made to include a "Strengths and Weaknesses" portion at the beginning to allow the participant to contribute to the S.W.O.T. Analysis in the second stage of the research. The majority of the participants displayed a keen interest in the process and the results of the survey.

Stage 2: S.W.O.T. Analysis of Grammar-Translation Method

The S.W.O.T. analytical tool is often traced to Albert S. Humphrey during his time at the Stanford Research Institute in the 1960s, but Humphrey never laid personal claim as the architect. In general, this tool is used for organizational and business ventures but can be applied more widely. The acronym stands for the following:

- Strengths (internal, positive factors)
- Weaknesses (internal, negative factors)
- Opportunities (external, positive factors)
- Threats (external, negative factors)[4]

Due to the tool's ambiguous origins, a seminal text or source for its original intentions as opposed to modern uses does not exist, thus it will be utilized in its current form. For the purposes of this research, the tool will be applied in the following manner:

- Strengths—How does GTM benefit the ministry-focused student when learning NT Greek (non-academic)?
- Weaknesses—How does GTM hinder the ministry-focused student when learning NT Greek?
- Opportunities—What parts of GTM are used in everyday ministry settings?
- Threats—What parts of GTM are NOT used in everyday ministry settings?]

Dissertation Recipes, 4 February 2016, http://www.dissertationrecipes.com/surveyinterview-validation-rubric-for-an-expert-panel/ (26 March 2018).

4. Berry, "What is a SWOT Analysis," *Bplans*, https://articles.bplans.com/how-to-perform-swot-analysis/ (26 March 2018).

CHAPTER 3

Because the expert survey provides a variety of strengths and weaknesses from field-tested professionals, it is safe to say that those two categories of the S.W.O.T. analysis will be reliably supplied. The final two categories will be derived from both the other survey answers and literature on the use of GTM.

Stage 3: Comparative Study of SLA and GTM Research

This final stage of conducting a comparative study of SLA and GTM research was chosen to determine if SLA research can in any way improve twenty-first-century NT Greek pedagogy. Because it is logical to assume that all pedagogical methodologies have weaknesses and threats when critically assessed through the S.W.O.T. Analysis, it is not too much to assume that another methodology may provide strengths and opportunities to compensate where needed. Therefore, this process will compare the primary language learning strategy for NT Greek (GTM) against the newest and most effective strategies of modern language learning (SLA). Included in this stage will be the application of modern didactic pedagogical strategies such as scaffolding, chunking, and course design procedures to ensure that NT Greek not only has the right tools but also arranges those tools in the correct order.

Internal Validity

New Testament Greek is an educational field that needs more attention and participation while at the same time it suffers more and more from dwindling interest among ministry-focused students. This perceived lack of interest in NT Greek does not have a clear root cause,[5] but more and more schools are reducing their required amount of biblical languages to make their programs more appealing to the newer generation of students.[6]

---

5. There is no clear root because there has been no (known) research done on the subject. Although a few institutional surveys have been performed, many schools choose not to share the raw data with outside sources. Thus, researchers like this one are left to use the already-interpreted data and the pre-determined conclusions. A thorough survey of current students and recent graduates from dozens of prominent religious schools of higher education would yield much needed fruit on the subject and likely produce staggering findings to inform new and relevant pedagogical changes.

6. E.g., Daniel Streett, "Greek Immersion in the Seminary Curriculum–What's Needed to Make it Work? (Basics of Greek Pedagogy, pt. 7)," καὶ τὰ λοιπά, 21 September 2011, https://danielstreett.com/2011/09/21/greek-immersion-in-the-seminary-curriculumwhats-needed-to-make-it-work-basics-of-greek-pedagogy-pt-7/ (26 March 2018).

Many institutional reasons may lie behind a decision like this one (e.g., budgetary constraints, program size, faculty volume, limited professional resources, etc.), or there could be more didactic motivations (e.g., a desire for more "practical" courses, a lack of understanding of the modern–day need for such coursework, etc.).[7] The decision to reduce language requirements could also be a reaction to the collective voice (or wallet) of the students. Numerous students at Southeastern Baptist Theological Seminary alone switch each year from a Master of Divinity degree to a Master of Arts to avoid biblical language requirements, while others simply grit their teeth and push through the Master of Divinity's twelve credit hours as perfunctory hurdles.[8]

Regardless of the reasons behind the seemingly continuous change in biblical language requirements, emphasis needs to be placed on what can be changed immediately to improve the current educational condition. Four main components are involved in properly implementing NT Greek in higher education: the institution, the professor, the student, and the curriculum. Because institutional changes often require board meetings, panel discussions, trustee votes, and mountains of paperwork, the process of making needed changes is often long, tedious, and debate–filled. Therefore, it would be more efficient to work within the constraints of the current model available. The professor is considered the expert in the classroom and, assuming that he or she is highly trained and adaptable to the educational process, replacing them would be a misguided decision unless there are signs of negligence or ineptitude. The student is most often the recipient of the blame regarding waning classroom participation, poor retention numbers, and low post–graduation usage results on surveys. Although, this may be the case because many professors in higher education do not believe the blame can be placed on themselves or the institutions due to the reasons listed above. There is a possible fourth agent in the language learning process: curriculum. Although it is true that the professor and/or the institution bears the responsibility to select the books and resources used for each course, those books and resources can still be of poor quality/methodology/strategy. This does not leave the student to blame if the pedagogical methodology is designed around and presented through a flawed or

---

7. Wheeler and Ruger, "Sobering Figures Point to Overall Enrollment Decline: New Research From the Auburn Center for the Study of Theological Education," *In Trust* (Spring 2013): 5–11; and a more recent article, Seltzer, "Seminaries Squeezed," *Inside Higher Ed*, 27 May 2016, https://www.insidehighered.com/news/2016/05/27/traditional-theological-schools-explore-mergers-and-campus-sales-amid-financial (26 March 2018).

8. This researcher tutors several of these men every semester.

misguided instrument. On the contrary, if a worker is asked to dig a certain sized hole in the ground at a job site, but is given a snow shovel to complete the job, he will struggle mightily or fail because of the tool, not his lack of effort. Likewise, if a great professor asks a student of any educational level to complete a language task with a poor-quality tool, which element is to blame for a failure? Possibly the professor, merely for selecting and require the poor-quality tool, but certainly not the student. The constitutional question of this research is thus, is the current pedagogical tool (GTM), used in so many NT Greek classrooms, of good quality?

The highest care has been taken to ensure that internal validity is secured in this research. The survey steps were intentionally designed and carried out to be free from compulsion, and the participants were not pressured to agree with any particular research or methodology when questioned. Additionally, those surveyed were provided with a clear and unbiased definition of GTM before providing answers. This was done to establish a uniform understanding of the methodology being surveyed. Similarly, the survey stage was performed before the S.W.O.T. Analysis so to allow the experts to provide the strengths and weaknesses rather than the researcher. The intention was to make that stage less anecdotal and more expert-driven. In the end, the researcher's essential desire was to include prominent professionals in the research, use their experience-based opinions as the basis for the analysis, and then draw logical conclusions by comparing the results against proven language learning research. This process ought to assess the quality of GTM pedagogy for its use in the teaching of NT Greek.

External Validity

Although this research has been delimited to NT Greek pedagogy and the survey only included NT Greek professionals, it is this researcher's opinion that the results of the study can be transferred to other ancient research languages. In the case of the ministry-focused learner, NT Greek is often required alongside Old Testament Hebrew and the basic tenets for the first two semesters of these biblical languages ought to be easily transferable since both currently largely use GTM. Even though Latin and Aramaic are seldom required for ministry-focused students, this research may also apply to those languages.

Chapter Summary

This researcher has pored over publications, peer reviewed articles, dissertations, and master's theses to find any similar research on NT Greek pedagogy and found nothing more than a few passing comments or mentions of surveys done by an institution. While it is puzzling that this has not been done, it is not completely surprising. Many professors believe the best of their courses and their professional competency, as well they should. But, if the professor's professional acumen is not to blame for the systemic struggles in NT Greek, what is to blame? This question is precisely why a proper analysis and assessment of the pedagogical methodology is necessary.

Chapter 4

Research Findings

THIS RESEARCH PROCESS INCLUDED three components: an expert survey, a S.W.O.T. analysis, and a language teaching methodology comparison. This chapter is focused on the expert survey results and chapter five will explore the S.W.O.T. analysis and language comparison as conclusions of the data presented here. The objective is to find answers to the following research questions posited in chapter one:

1. What, if any, are the current benefits and detriments of the Grammar–Translation Method on New Testament Greek instruction in the twenty-first century?

2. To what extent, if any, can current, unique pedagogical methods help improve New Testament Greek instruction in the twenty-first century?

3. To what extent, if any, can the research and practices of Second Language Acquisition, Task–Based Language Teaching, and Targeted Learning help improve New Testament Greek instruction in the twenty-first century?

4. What would a modern, non–academically focused Greek pedagogy look like in today's theological educational setting?

These questions will help to assess the usefulness of current pedagogical practices and moving forward, determine the overall trajectory of biblical language learning in the twenty-first century.

Expert Survey

Responses to the survey questions from all of the NT Greek experts who participated are addressed below. Every participant was given the option to remain anonymous and some chose to do so. This option was given for a few reasons: (1) some people may not have participated if they had to go "on the record" publicly; (2) some people may be more open if their name was not attached to certain comments; and (3) some people may fear being taken out of context through the research and therefore want to participate and protect themselves at the same time. Overall, only a few participants chose to be anonymous and the results, either way, were honest, helpful, and sometimes quite blunt.[1]

GTM Strengths

The first question of the survey requested that the participants take part in the S.W.O.T. analysis by providing up to five strengths of the GTM from their own experience as an NT Greek professional. These are their exact answers, in no particular order:

- It enables the learner to have a framework for acquiring basic forms and vocabulary.

- It provides a systematic and categorized approach to learning the syntax of an ancient language.

- It develops a skill set when it comes to translating the Greek text, which is different from a conversational approach to a modern approach.

- Since Greek is a highly inflected language with many tense-forms and cases, it allows a learner to acquire a familiarity with every form within one year of study.

- It enhances the learner's awareness of English grammar to make them better students of their native language.

- Translation from the Greek text itself (as in Mounce's Workbook), rather than in made-up sentences (as in Machen/McCartney) helps to keep students encouraged. Students often comment about how exciting it is to actually be reading the Bible in Greek from the earliest weeks of the semester.

- The GTM conforms to many of the students' expectations for language-learning. They perceive immediate similarities between their Greek learning experience and the experiences they had of learning (or trying to learn) other languages (Spanish, French, German, sometimes Latin) in high school.

---

1. Each participant's name is attached to their response when quoted, unless the respondent chose to be anonymous; then they are referred to with a general title such as "professor," "expert," etc.

- A student can move quickly into interaction with biblical Greek, which is most of their motivation for learning Greek anyway, without having to learn what will seem superfluous terminology as in an immersion/speak–and–listen program (think of words like "ball," or "fun," or "email," which do not have a parallel in the Greek New Testament).
- The possibility of a solid understanding of the way Koine Greek works.
- Since Koine Greek is not a living language, GTM fulfills a narrower purpose of helping students to read (vs. produce) the language.
- Learning how Greek works can prevent students from using Greek in ministry (e.g., sermons) inappropriately (it can provide a solid linguistic foundation).
- GTM can be combined with more inductive approaches; i.e., getting students reading to learn the language (vs. learning the language to read) earlier in the process.
- Adult learners tend to think structurally, so a balance of deductive and inductive learning is helpful.
- It closes gaps such as rarer forms, etc.
- Reading biblical text as it appears (not just in example sentences) greatly aids the inductive learning process.
- It can be studied quickly.
- It is easy to review learned material.
- It helps students to learn their native language grammar better.
- It is a very systematic way to teach a language.
- It can be taught by people who do not control the language and who cannot speak even basic sentences in class.
- It uses the meta–language of many pieces of "help literature."
- Explicit systematic instruction is imperative for students to create an efficient and comprehensive framework for understanding Greek. It enables rapid assimilation of concepts leading to the comprehension and translation competency that is the primary goal of exegetical programs.
- Translation—Long–term feedback from alumni indicates that students with a broad vocabulary base and broad exposure to translation are the most likely to continue using Greek after college or seminary. By doing so they develop a facility in reading that allows them to use Greek without becoming labor intensive.

- Composition from English into Greek—While helpful on a basic level for learning noun and verb formation, overuse detracts from reading ability and an awareness of Greek syntax and idiom derived from broad reading.
- GTM requires a more deductive approach which results in time–saving.
- Another strength would be the potential for covering a larger amount of complex rules/grammar.
- Success can be measured very concretely.
- There are many, many resources to help with this method of teaching.
- Basic understanding of a language.
- Basic understanding of grammar; enhancement of understanding.
- Basic improvement in observation skills of language.
- Basic improvement of original language correcting bad theology.
- Basic improvement of understanding translations.
- Allows students to focus on the ultimate objectives: reading, translation, and exegesis.
- Remains text–based.
- Does not require students to become fluent in speaking the language.
- Honestly, I see little benefit. To me all it does is ready people for second year (if they perform well), but that needs review after a summer anyway. Unless a student is going to do advanced work (doctoral) they aren't going to keep reviewing forms and vocab once in ministry. They don't have to because of available tools, and won't have the time. And they have translations already. That's just the reality, and instead of inventing another reality we need to recognize this.
- Students are enriched as they see nuances of the text "come alive" through their study of the text in its original modes of expression.
- Students have a better grasp of the interpretive options of the NT texts they are analyzing as opposed to accepting those accepted by a given version of the NT.
- Students have an increased ability to interact with commentaries and other study tools that discuss aspects of the Greek text.
- Students gain a better grasp of English as they compare it with the grammatical modes of expression of NT Greek. This increased facility

- in English benefits them in all disciplines and particularly in learning to communicate for ministry.
- Students learn to think more logically and systematically as they grasp how thoughts are expressed through language.
- Students develop a stronger sense of competency and authority as they handle the biblical text, no longer being at the mercy of the decisions of the translators.
- It provides complete units of thought that are not too intimidating for the learner.
- It is easy to modify sentences to give practice for inflection of endings.
- It's easy to modify sentences to introduce and give practice for new vocabulary.
- It's easy to build upon the foundation of sentence structure.
- The use of both inductive and deductive learning is very helpful.
- Students translating in class show me who is falling behind.
- It is logical with a starting place.
- It helps the students understand their own language.
- Students end the year with some ability to read Greek.
- It reinforces grammatical concepts in one's primary language.
- It provides an explicit framework for better understanding one's primary language by forcing students to verbalize grammatical concepts/rules in both the target and native languages.
- Logical or systematic approach that works for many people.
- Many tools have been developed for using this system.
- It is the most popular system so there is continuity from one professor to another.
- It has stood the test of time. Other methods have been tried but don't seem to last.
- It worked for the professor, so it can also work for his/her students.
- Knowledge of syntax.
- Ability to parse forms.
- Textbooks designed this way.
- Fits with most students' educational backgrounds.

- Good for realistic amount of time students spend learning language.
- I'm comfortable with the method, mostly.
- Immediate access to original language.
- Progress toward goal of exegetical use.
- Concentration upon the most important factors for use.
- Results in a relatively short amount of time.
- Language reinforcement.
- The grammatical analysis enables students to see striking differences between the Greek language and the English language and understand the nuances of constructions for which no direct English parallel exists.
- The grammatical analysis enables students to understand features of the NT text which are difficult or even impossible to express fully in English translation.
- Students who understand how the language works can tackle any Greek text. Those who merely memorize English translations for phrases will not be able to translate Greek constructions not yet committed to memory.
- Most students will not learn to think in Greek. This ability to translate the text into their native language is necessary.
- Learning vocabulary.
- Gaining knowledge regarding declensions and conjugations in sentence–based context.
- Empowering students actually to read portions of the Greek NT quickly and with comprehension.
- Early memorization helps to avoid looking up forms later on.
- It is systematic in nature, allowing focus on topic at a time.
- Relatively easy to formulate Greek translation sentences that highlight the topic.
- Students learn better English grammar from the instructor (not the textbooks).
- Students become aware of the difficulties or complexities of translation.
- Students become more aware of details.
- Can increase student confidence in language acquisition generally.

- Students become aware of the politics of translation and that options exist that are only apparent when one is familiar with the Greek.
- There is a good measure of objectivity in using the grammatical method.
- It allows for a systematic and mechanical analysis of the text.
- There are a wealth of tools available for the grammatical method developed over the years.
- Understanding of points of emphasis in the text.
- Genuine understanding of the grammar of both source language and the target translation language as critical to sound semantic values being assigned.
- Student sense of confidence that they truly are engaging the text in interpretation as it was meant to be understood by the author.
- Sense of the "cultural" backdrop to the language and how ideas are expressed.
- It does require students learn English, often for the first time in any serious way.
- Structure.
- Generally moves from simpler/easier concepts to more difficult.
- Emphasis upon memorization/recall.
- Allows for concepts to be introduced one by one.
- Frequent assessment helps reinforce learning.
- Students understand WHY things are said in a certain way.
- Prepares students for more detailed examinations of the language.
- It is basically what the procedure is for exegetical work with the NT text for Bible classes and sermons for seminary students.
- It causes one to pay attention to nuances, including small nuances, of the target language.
- It helps students become aware of the nature of their own, receptor language.
- Improved analytical skills.
- Increased ability to think through the Greek way of looking at language.
- Appreciation of falsifiable hypothesis in doing exegesis.

- Method learned for determining meaning of words, sentences, paragraphs.
- Ability to think critically about the Greek NT.
- It gives the students a feel for Greek that will keep them from some grammatical fallacies. Just like learning Algebra in High School trains the mind to think in a certain way (granting the fact that they might not ever use it in real life), learning Greek trains the mind even if they do not keep up on the vocabulary and forms.
- Students are able to understand exegetical commentaries and the best exegetical literature that is available.
- Forces the students to slow down.
- Helps the students to understand English grammar.
- Helps them appreciate the interpretive decisions that need to be made in translation.
- Students learn to appreciate the variety of grammatical functions of primary and secondary word types.
- Students make it through the material.
- Students have clear goals for learning.
- Students learn in with a manageable structure.
- Students learn a method for ancient language learning that can be applied elsewhere (e.g., Hebrew, Latin).

Clearly many of these professionals like much of the GTM process of teaching NT Greek. These answers cover a broad range of aspects of GTM, from strengths for the student to benefits for the professor. Some of the most frequently repeated responses include structural or framework advantages, native language benefits, improved translation capabilities, and the fact that it helps the student to understand the text better.

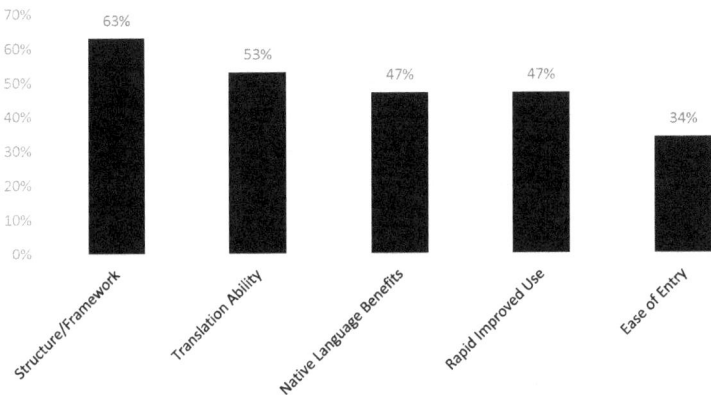

Structural/Framework

Sixty-three percent of participants indicate they believe the primary strength of GTM is that it is highly structured and laid out in a manner that helps the student learn and the teacher present the material more easily. GTM is highly structured and broken down into dozens of grammatical parts for better attainability. As mentioned in chapter two, the order and emphasis of these parts may change due to the author/professor's teaching objective, but in the end, structure is a primary element of this practice.

Translation

A surprisingly low 53 percent say this method improves translation skills. This may not initially appear surprising, but only sixteen professors out of thirty believe that the Grammar–Translation Method of teaching Greek improves translation skills. Logically, this number should be in the high 90s or even 100 percent. The fact that only just over half of the survey respondents identified translation as a strength of GTM may suggest that the very goal of the methodology is not being met in the classroom. Some prominent professors express concerns about whether two semesters of GTM can really provide the student with the necessary skills to engage the biblical text effectively.

Native Language

In what can be labeled a secondary benefit of GTM, 47 percent expressed that using this strategy for teaching NT Greek can, and often does, help the learner better understand their own native language. One major problem many Greek professors mention is that the student does not know enough about their own language's grammar to easily learn a new language's grammar. In other words, if a student does not know how to identify and properly use an adjective in English, then she will struggle to identify and properly use one in Koine Greek. This applies to every aspect of grammar and eliminates the benefit of Universal Grammar as mentioned in chapter two. But, it is concerning that half of these professionals say that one of the top five strengths of GTM is a benefit for another language rather than for Greek. Although this strength can serve double duty for both the native and target language, few professors would argue that the student has the capability to learn both English and Greek grammar at the same time. This is why Samuel Lamerson and others have published books aimed at preempting this issue by explaining English grammar before one attempts to add Greek grammar.

Improved Use of Greek

Less than half (47 percent) claim this process of learning NT Greek helps the student to use their Greek more often and with better accuracy. In this case, fourteen seasoned professors say that GTM can actually help the student use Greek. They did not specify whether they are referring to reading, speaking, exegeting, or some other use of Greek in their answer, but there may be further clarification on this point in the upcoming weaknesses section.

Ease of Entry

One–third of the answers suggest that the GTM format and structure make it easy for the student to begin learning the language. Although this is somewhat similar to the first benefit listed above, it is slightly different because the former speaks to the overall learning process and the latter addresses the ability for the average student to begin the learning process. To put it another way, 34 percent of these professors believe that almost any learner can step into a GTM classroom and begin learning NT Greek. Yes, they may struggle with Universal Grammar. And, yes, they may not be linguistically gifted, but, in theory, GTM is a system that is accessible to most learners.

CHAPTER 4

Other Strengths

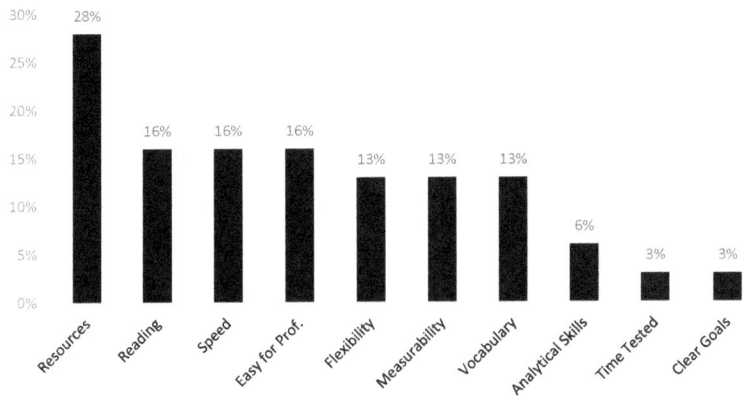

The participants provided several other categories, but none of them garnered more than 28 percent of agreement with other participants. For instance, 28 percent say that GTM has an abundance of related resources, which makes it easier to find "helps" and tools to assist the learning and retaining process. This is also true when looking for a textbook that fits a particular learning schema. There are dozens of NT Greek grammars to choose from and this can be a great blessing to both professors and students who may not follow Mounce's style as well as they do Porter's style of teaching. Additionally, 16 percent (five people) say that it helps the student read Greek better while flexibility of application, alacrity, assessability, and vocabulary all came in at 13 percent. Five professors claim that one of the top five strengths of GTM is that it is easy for the professor since they learned under GTM themselves when they began to study the language. Finally, with less than 11 percent, two people believe that it improves analytical skills and one person each attest that GTM stands on a time–tested methodology and provides clear goals for the student.

    It is very interesting that only one participant claims that GTM offers a clear learning objective and only two believe it has analytical benefits for the student. The survey did not ask if specific attributes of language learning were present or effective in GTM, rather each person was asked for up to five strengths and few of them gave more than three or four while some provided none at all. Therefore, since it was highly unlikely for one–hundred percent of the respondents to agree on any given answer, any answer that draws more than fifty percent agreement is noteworthy.

GTM Weaknesses

The second question asked the experts to provide up to five weaknesses of GTM from their experience.

Students struggle to retain much of the rules governing form and function of the various parts of speech.

- Students are not able to speak or read the language as a living language so they miss how to construct Greek sentences as well as proper pronunciation. In other words, a Greek speaker has an intuitive understanding of the language.
- The GTM method does not work well with every student in the way they learn and process language so some students don't learn it well enough to use Greek effectively.
- It heavily relies of memorization and repetition. While it is one of the best ways to learn, it is not necessarily the most engaging and exciting ways to acquire a new language.
- Depending on the textbook, it does not give students enough to translate both nouns and verbs quickly enough.
- The GTM approach is often overly-focused upon grammar. Really, language consists only of speaking, listening, reading, and writing. Grammar is simply a description of patterns that appear in the language to help with the learning process. But many students tend to think of grammar as being equivalent to the language itself.
- Since most of us using the GTM focus upon reading/translation alone (and do nothing with speaking and listening, and usually not much with writing/producing the language), the reinforcement that is usually gained from engaging in all four activities (speaking, listening, reading, and writing) does not get incorporated into this approach.
- Fluency also can be difficult to attain through this approach. If every sentence is simply translated from Greek into the receptor language (say, English), getting a feel for the language as it is in and of itself can be difficult to acquire.
- Related is the problem of reliance upon glosses for the meanings of particular words. Rather than possessing a fluency that allows one familiarity with the range of meanings of particular words, the student will often fall back on the one, two, or three meanings he/she memorized for particular words when he/she first encountered them in a beginning Greek textbook.

- Many students who take the language sequence do not retain enough from GTM to use much in subsequent settings (e.g., ministry).
- Learning the complexities of Greek grammar explicitly vs. implicitly (i.e., inductively through usage).
- The typically concentrated way Greek is taught and then (often) not followed up with more required usage.
- Speaking and reading aloud is usually downplayed.
- Rewards motivated students, but can be disheartening for less engaged students.
- Usually does not require generation of Greek sentences/language, but only one way translation.
- Can be boring if the instructor is boring.
- The emphasis on memorization can be overwhelming.
- Students usually fail to get a "feel" for the language.
- The categories we create to teach the language are many times imposed upon the language, not derived from an inductive study of the language.
- Most students do not continue using the language.
- Too much emphasis on unnecessary details; need BIG picture to see details.
- Too much emphasis on timed quizzes; give students time to complete.
- Too much emphasis on moving quickly over significant details.
- Not enough encouragement to see how language can make a difference in understanding theology.
- Not enough time dedicated to subject period.
- Requires large amounts of rote memorization.
- Requires adequate understanding of grammar.
- Can over-emphasize analysis of details at the expense of understanding the larger picture.
- It gives a false sense of "knowing" the language, especially in comparison to what literature majors have in other literatures/languages.
- The metalanguage tags (e.g. "present infinitive") take on a reality that may be against the language and that skew the language when the

student remembers pieces of it later on (e.g., there is no "present" time in the infinitive, despite the name present infinitive).

- Thinking in the language is derailed by interposing algorithms for many words (e.g. [α+ω, α+ειν] ἀγαπάω ἀγαπάειν instead of ἀγαπῶ ἀγαπᾶν).

- Practitioners with 20–30 years of work in the GTM system cannot think in the language, they cannot communicate with each other in the language the way literature profs can communicate in other languages.

- Insufficient translation exercises—Most grammars do not have an adequate amount of translation exercises and tend to utilize isolated sentences that make it more difficult for students to gain a sense of context or provide them with a consistent sense of Greek syntax and expression.

- Instruction often relies exclusively on rote memory and does not help students understand why things happen. Understanding why things happen in Greek (on some level) allows Greek to become familiar rather than an object to be deciphered. It is possible to introduce advanced concept at a beginning level to help understand why certain phenomena happen in Greek morphology, vocabulary building based n patterns of formation and basic stems, etc.

- Many programs teach translation based on decoding rather than comprehension of the Greek and conversion into the most appropriate English equivalent. As a result, many students continue to make mistakes that reflect a poor comprehension of Greek and a heavy reliance on tools.

- The tendency to rely on lists of grammatical categories rather than an understanding of what is happening frustrates students. In many programs students learn lists of acceptable categories for nominatives, genitives, etc. and in the process find themselves overwhelmed and unaware that they are merely describing how it is used, not trying to find the right answer. I have had faculty tell me that knowledge of these categories is essential to correct interpretation. Indeed it is, if you are teaching them how to decode without introducing them to a language they come to embrace as a living entity with a character of its own that they must embrace and learn. Instructors need to reinforce that these categories are a helpful stop-gap to show you the range of meaning you can otherwise only acquire by reading extensively. But they in my opinion students would be better served by the practice I was forced to employ in Classical Greek where our instructor reinforced labels in his own terminology, but forced us to come up with labels (any clear label) that indicated we understood the syntax. I learned more in his classes about the Greek language than in any of my other courses. Remove the intimidation of lists from our students and focus on understanding.

- Perhaps too teacher-centered.
- Passive students.
- Not inductive enough (though admittedly more difficult to accomplish in deductive learning).
- Requires memorization maintenance to be of any use.
- The above presumes a graduate/pastor will have the time to maintain translation level competency. That's contrary to reality and we all know it.
- Unless you get to a third year Greek course, you don't get sustained experience in exegesis (i.e., actually using your Greek). Second memorization of syntactical categories isn't exegetical proficiency. I took Greek syntax three times at three different schools—it was all the same. Memorize the categories. That isn't book study.
- When people don't have the time to retain translation proficiency after graduation and then do fine in ministry, this method teaches them they really didn't need those Greek classes.
- Many students struggle greatly with the languages due to a lack of native aptitude or poor language training in their previous educational experience. This can lead to frustration and a sense of failure in the student. (This is not so much a weakness of the method as it is a weakness in the student, nor is it an argument against requiring language study.).
- Since language acquisition requires a number of years of sustained effort, the introductory courses offered in seminaries can provide only the beginning of a process of lifelong learning that leads to competency.
- Because of the inherent complexity of language and the elementary nature of introductory Greek courses, students are tempted to oversimplify complex interpretive issues. Often this tendency toward oversimplification follows them into their ministries and can lead to the promulgation of exegetical fallacies.
- The compressed nature of seminary education often dictates that students attempt to master large amounts of detailed material in a short span of time. This is especially true with regard to intensive languages

courses, which in my view benefit only a small percentage of gifted students.

- The press and lack of integration of the seminary curriculum requires many students to lay aside their language training to focus on their other courses. This could be alleviated to some extent if the language courses were required to be taken in the first year and the other course reinforced the ongoing use of the original languages.
- Made-up sentences for pedagogical purposes soon become boring.
- But the NT is too familiar to most students to provide a true exercise of their Greek skills. I often used sentences from the LXX, with appropriately modified vocab.
- Sentence level translating implicitly trains students for an atomistic view of language that has to be undone when later teaching exegesis and the importance of context.
- Only the biblical languages are taught by focusing on one specific book (the Hebrew Old and Greek New Testaments). That is an artificial and somewhat myopic way to learn a language.
- If the work is not kept up, ability to translate is quickly lost.
- Students do not speak the language; thus, they don't really understand it.
- Because of the closed corpus of the NT, vocab is limited.
- Students cannot read very much of the more difficult books.
- Due to time constraints and ultimate goal, there is very little translation from English to Greek.
- It can become so rigid of a method that students sometimes fail to see the significance of the approach.
- It is not the best way to teach a purely inductive method of learning language.
- Too much memorization of paradigms.
- Learning of material that is not really necessary (relevant, common).
- Not enough focus on why learning Greek is helpful.
- Many students struggle with acquiring/memorizing a huge amount of information in a short period of time.
- Too much time translating and not enough time spent on how to use their knowledge of Greek.

CHAPTER 4

- GTM makes knowledge of Greek an adjunct to our knowledge of English.
- GTM makes Greek very forgettable
- With GTM one does not "read" Greek by any real definition of the verb "read," rather one decodes and translates.
- Not the way language is best learned.
- Perhaps "settles" for a lower level of proficiency among students.
- If not supplemented with some creative methods, it can fall a bit flat in inspiring students.
- Assumes knowledge of language not held by students.
- Intense learning and material to master.
- Incremental knowledge accumulation not typical of current learning techniques for other subjects.
- In my early years as an instructor, I used Summer's Essentials which required the memorization of a large number of paradigms. Students seemed to perform well on exercises and tests, but forgot much of their Greek soon after the course was completed because these paradigms were packed into their short-term memory. Using Mounce's Basics of Biblical Greek helped enormously since Mounce introduces students to elementary principles of Greek morphology and greatly reduces the amount of memorization necessary to learn and use Greek.
- In Elementary Greek students are given the impression that they can translate the Greek text based solely on familiarity with vocabulary and grammar. However, a good understanding of syntax is necessary for clear, precise, and exegetically helpful translation.
- More time needs to be allotted to beginning Greek classes (4 sem. hrs. each half-year term would be preferable).
- The goal of vocabulary learning should be 1000 keywords, as in Metzger's Lexical Aids book, which was based on a 17-week semester; present shorter semesters allow only about 800 words to be learned.
- Too many students attempt to take more hours per semester (e.g. 15+) than they should when taking a beginning language course (e.g. 12), mostly in an attempt to speed through an M.Div. program and to graduate.
- Mainly, I have to constantly urge them to review what they have learned

- Does not account for individual or unique competencies of students or lack thereof for studying languages.
- Needless focus on rote memorization and more on identifying patterns.
- False assumption that students who take one year of Greek will be able to use it with competency.
- Never sufficient practice exercises in textbooks to develop competency. Teacher must be prepared to augment in some way.
- Textbooks assume a certain level of student efficiency with grammar that is usually absent.
- Many students have very poor knowledge of English grammar and so find it difficult to grasp Greek grammar.
- Memorization of forms is very difficult for students.
- The payoff is delayed as students have to learn a great deal before they can use the tools effectively.
- Retention is difficult and many students do not continue to use Greek.
- Tendency to drive students crazy with all the variations on the "rules" in both morphology and in grammar/syntax . . . nature of languages, right, yet still tends to irritate students and make them impatient with learning when there are so many exceptions to the "rule."
- A loss of the sense of "flow" in reading the text . . . unless addressed.
- Overwhelming for students who struggle with memorization.
- Generally students do not begin to interact with Scripture for some time.
- When Scripture integration occurs, it is typically isolated verses.
- Tends to create focus upon isolated elements rather than flow of thought/larger structure of discourses.
- Focuses at times too much on micro–analysis to neglect of macro–analysis.
- Is not the way we learn language naturally.
- It can lead to students not seeing the forest for the trees, i.e., details can overwhelm if the teacher is not aware of this and teach so as to see the forest.
- Relatedly, the teacher must be aware of the danger of teaching a lot of "just in case" morphology, i.e., introducing rare forms "just in case" they come up but realistically do not.

CHAPTER 4   93

- Vocabulary skills.
- Intuitive sense of how Greek works.
- Reading.
- Speaking.
- Translating.
- Every year students seem to have a decreased ability to memorize even basic material. Students come with a poor background in English grammar (unless they are International students). This makes it very difficult to teach with GTM.
- It is an artificial approach to language learning.
- Very few students seem to continue on with review of the material or a robust use of it (But this could be said for many courses in a higher education curriculum—I was a chemistry major in college and used very little of that material in 10 years as a chemist.).
- It does not lend itself to learning pronunciation of Greek.
- The focus is translating Greek to English, but there is value in moving from English to Greek as well.
- The GTM usually enforces small segments and chunks of sentences rather than an immersive experience.
- Students who get behind or are slow learners tend to remain behind and do never catch up.
- It teaches language learning as "decoding".
- It makes Greek feel less like a language and more like a topic that needs to be mastered.
- Learning the GNT outside the realm of ancient Greek in general is efficient but lacks serious context beneficial for other aspects of exegesis (Word Study, Syntax analysis).
- Many approaches to GTM break up the language in many small pieces and don't put them back again. The first year grammars that I have used, tend not to be useful as reference grammars.

Of the weaknesses the participants provided, several overlapped with the strengths, while others uncovered unique insights. Where the strengths have two categories at or above 50 percent continuity, the weaknesses contain five areas in that range and the sixth close behind them. The experts pointed out weaknesses that range from GTM being poorly focused to being boring for the learner.

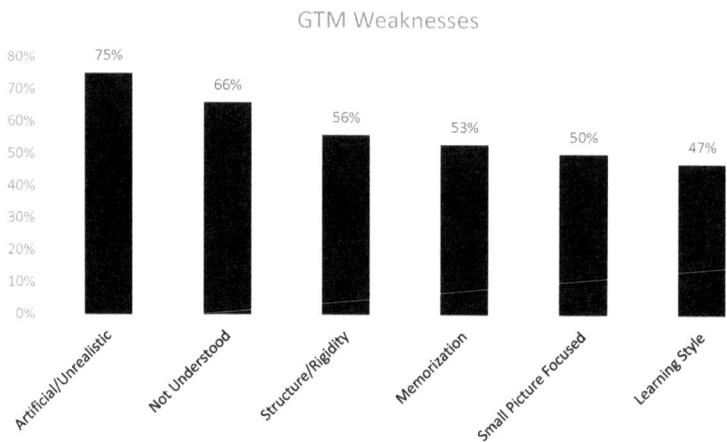

Artificial or Unrealistic

The largest and most agreed upon weakness of GTM is that it is an unrealistic approach to NT Greek. In fact, 75 percent of these participants posit that GTM is an out-of-touch methodology in some form or another. Contrast this number against the 53 percent of people who say it helps the student with their translation skills and it should become clear how staggering this number is. More people agree that GTM comes across more artificial than proficient at training students to translate NT Greek. GTM is certainly not a Natural Order approach as Krashen explains, nor is it a linguistic device that results in the student being able to speak the language. Some experts say that the method does not provide the student with enough ability to be useful and others suggest that it is simply outdated and antiquated for the modern learning environment. Either way, the view that GTM lacks a realistic and useful modus operandi should be a troubling reality.

Diminished Use

Two-thirds (66 percent) claim that GTM does not prepare the student to really understand NT Greek well enough to use it. To one degree or another, more than half of these experts say that GTM does not help the student to be able to apply their attained Greek skills in a useful manner. This is speaking of the typically required six credit hours of NT Greek often taken in theological higher education and does not include extensive coursework in syntax or NT book exegesis. But, it begs the question that if two semesters of Greek cannot properly prepare a student to use the language, then why is this still the norm for biblical languages in higher education?

Structure/Framework

With twenty people agreeing that the structure and framework of GTM is a strength and eighteen listing it as a weakness (63 percent and 56 percent respectively), it is a unique aspect of GTM, to say the least. While structure can help a student stay on track with the professor's aims in a Greek class, it can also be too rigid and daunting for the learner. For example, Mounce's text contains thirty-six categories broken up into four parts and a lengthy appendix. Black's textbook contains twenty-six categories followed by nine appendices. Gibson and Campbell's new book has a whopping eighty-three lessons before reaching the appendix. In just these three examples, it is clear that structure is a key component for GTM that can be changed drastically to fit any given professor's teaching goal. This is not a simple methodological differentiation; rather it can be a hurdle to understanding the language and the method to a student who is not familiar with why this type of variation exists. Koine Greek is already intimidating to many students, and this added facet of structural fluidity is just one more degree of difficulty to reconcile.

Memorization

Just over half (53 percent) of the survey participants claim that the amount of rote and systematic memorization is a detriment to the GTM process. For this very reason, many modern Greek textbooks have aimed to reduce the sheer number of paradigms and lists the student needs to memorize.[2] Although learning any new language requires the memorization of large amounts of vocabulary and usage rules, many living language pedagogies teach differing word forms and morphologies in a conversational manner instead of using paradigm charts.

---

2. This recent effort is not reflected in the 53 percent mentioned in this section since they are commenting on the GTM concept and not the current publishing trends in the field.

Focus

Half of the participants say that GTM is too small picture-focused and that it presents the language in a manner that forsakes the language as a whole. Many suggest that this is why a third semester (syntax) of a dead language is basically a requirement if the student intends to use their new skills. Similar to the view of structure being both a strength and a weakness, breaking down the elements of NT Greek into small "chunks" can assist the learner in attainment and possibly in retention, but can also place a high expectation on the student to put all of those small pieces together for themselves. The typical scope and sequence of a biblical language are as follows:

- Beginning Grammar 1—Teaches the very basic elements of the language such as the alphabet, pronunciation, punctuation, primary noun and verb function.

- Beginning Grammar 2—The student learns some of the more nuanced parts of the language like unique forms of nouns and verbs, participles, word order, etc.

- Syntax—The student learns how to combine the grammar elements into useful structures, differentiate between types of uses, and even to begin the early points of exegesis.

- Exegetical book studies—All of the elements are designed to come together; the student is expected to be functionally fluent with the grammar and apply the syntax so to draw out the meaning and purpose of a given pericope or book of the Bible.

Although this sequence is certainly well-intentioned, it is no longer as effective as it may have once been. Most seminaries only require a Master of Divinity student to take either the first two stages of both Greek and Hebrew (six credit hours of each; twelve total credit hours) or two stages of one and three stages of the other language (fifteen total credit hours). This means that the majority of ministry-focused students will only have the basic grammar elements of one language and a ground-floor level functioning ability in the other language.

Half of these experts argue that the student is being given a complex tool without knowing how to use it. Many professors strongly urge their Grammar 2 students to take a syntax course to learn how to utilize their base-level knowledge, but the majority of students do not heed this advice. In fact, it is because of the next listed weakness that many students limit their language exposure to their degree's requirements.

Learning Style

Almost half (47 percent) of these experts believe that GTM uses a learning style that is not conducive to general language learning. They argue that it does not help the student to really learn the language; rather, as one respondent said, it helps them learn to "decode" NT Greek. Additionally, several pointed out that this methodology is also not a familiar learning process for any other subject matter, therefore presenting the student with not only a new language but a new learning style that will have no relation to anything else they have learned. Putting that in perspective, a large portion of these experts say that using GTM for NT Greek results in an immensely steep learning curve due to its unrealistic goals (75 percent), the difficult form and structure (56 percent), its limited scope (34 percent), and its unique didactic methodology (47 percent). It is no wonder so many students express fear when considering courses in biblical languages in theological education.

Other Weaknesses

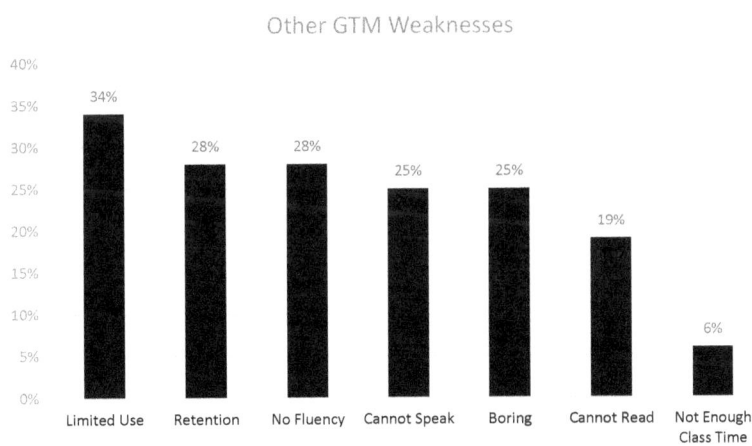

In the remaining seven categories of weaknesses, five categories stand above 25 percent in agreement. To begin with, 34 percent said that two semesters of GTM Greek cannot adequately prepare the student for daily or weekly use, especially coupled with the fact that 28 percent identified retention as a weakness. Several of these experts proposed that GTM is weak because it cannot provide the student with any kind of proficiency in the language, which is exemplified by the 28 percent who claim that it lacks student fluency since the student can neither speak (25 percent) nor read (19 percent) the text without regular assistance from "helps" or expert tools after they complete their studies. A few of these professional teachers and writers later make an argument for a Living Language approach to NT Greek, but these answers are based on the weaknesses of the GTM and not in contrast to another linguistic philosophy. Last, eight respondents (25 percent) agreed that GTM makes learning Greek boring or uninteresting while 6 percent made the case that there is not adequate class time to teach the language well. These last two groupings of answers may be related in the fact that students are known to learn better in an engaging and stimulating environment and to create such an environment takes time and skill for the professor to develop and deliver in each class meeting. Therefore, a deficiency of time can result in a lack of pedagogical creativity, intentionality, and differentiated instruction that is far more palpable in the student's experience than in the teacher's preparation.

Survey Questions

The survey questions were designed to serve several purposes in an effort to draw out honest opinions and provide rich insights from the thirty-two seasoned professors and authors. The first objective was to derive answers that were based on the participants' professional experience and not on philosophical ideals or platitudes. Second, the questions sought to identify the internal motivations of each teacher, a sampling of the expressed learning objectives for course material at multiple institutions, and the experts' opinions about the current and future state of teaching and learning NT Greek. Last, this survey was tailored to triangulate the responders' answers to create a clear understanding of their personal and professional views on GTM as a pedagogical methodology and the current state of NT Greek education.

Question #1—In your opinion, why should students in theological education take NT Greek courses?

When seeking someone's motivation for doing something, it is important to distinguish between their personal motivation and what they believe ought to be the proper motivation in general for that activity. In the case of this first question, the goal was to gain insight into why these professionals believed students should feel motivated to engage in learning a biblical language. The answers ranged widely from divine inspiration to practical utilization, but with few exceptions, these participants strongly believed that every serious Bible student needs to invest in biblical language training. Alan Bandy provides the following analogy:

> To study the Bible and or theology only in an English translation is like being a medical doctor or surgeon without ever having studied human anatomy. Such a doctor would be careless, sloppy, and entirely dependent on his colleagues who have studied anatomy. Knowledge of the original languages enables one to do exegesis and see things in the text not communicated in the translations.

Many of these experts echo this sentiment in various ways. David Croteau says that it "can help [students] avoid exegetical fallacies," while Delio DelRio adds that it also "aids in more accurate exegesis of the text." One professor says that it helps the student to read the Greek NT rather than simply "decode" it. Interacting with the text is a major theme in many of these answers; Samuel Lamerson believes that the study of biblical languages provides both answers and thoughtful questions from the text before he concluded that "sometimes being able to ask the questions are as important as the answers."

While literary and theological fidelity is crucial to the study of the text, many of these men and women placed a higher emphasis on the faithful and effective presentation of the gospel message. Although these two areas are not mutually exclusive, they do stand as unique motivators for the learner. Mark Strauss acknowledges that "for those who are in a teaching or preaching role, the ability to work with the Greek and Hebrew is important (if not always essential)." Croteau concurs when he writes that Greek provides "more confidence in their interpretation of the New Testament which will lead to more boldly proclaiming God's Word." And, it is difficult to put this idea more succinctly than Dan Wallace does when he says, "To know the mind of God so they can expound the scriptures faithfully. To connect to Jesus Christ and the apostles through the inspired material. To learn the importance of worshiping God with one's mind."

Whether the motivating factor is textual accuracy, divine familiarity, gospel proclamation, or something more personal, it is vital that the student knows why the study of biblical languages is important. Danny Zacharias commits the introduction of his elementary grammar to this idea and Robert Plummer and Ben Merkle dedicated an entire book to motivating Greek students to keep learning after they have finished in the classroom. One expert asks this poignant question, "What other class of leaders in the church will be accountable to the original languages of Scripture for the teaching of the church, if not pastors and teachers?"

Question #2—When speaking of biblical language courses, who do you believe holds the major responsibility for the course material ultimately being successful (professor, student, institutional methodology, etc.)? Why?

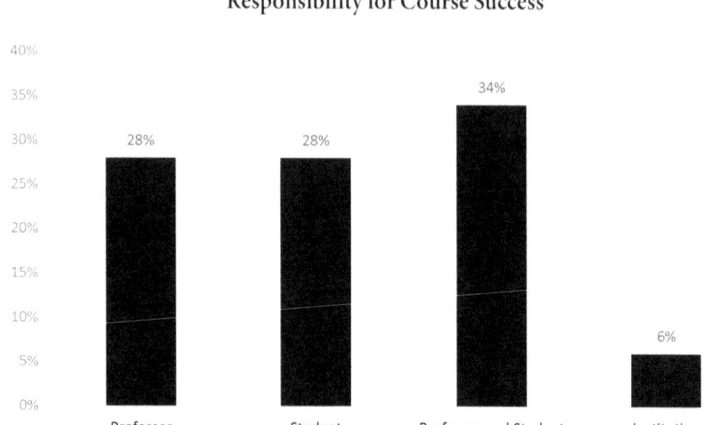

Responsibility for Course Success

Questions like this one are difficult to elicit an unbiased answer because the professor does not want to take the blame for poor results, but they often feel abashed if they blame the student or their institution. While only two professors assigned responsibility to the institution, 28 percent pointed to the professor (themselves) for sole responsibility for success, another 28 percent selected the student as the liable party, and 34 percent agree that there is shared culpability between the student the teacher for the success of language learning.[3] Although the institution is responsible for the hiring of the professor and, in some cases, the selection of curricula, the reality is that both the professor and the student must submit to this governing body, even if the institution does not favor one's particular department or degree program.

The Professor

This researcher assumes that theologically trained professors are chosen based on their merit and expertise in their content area, which presumes that they are highly knowledgeable and competent professional teachers. With that said, it is also highly likely that some of these professionals are brilliant scholars and, at the same time, below average teachers. This is likely the reason why

---

3. Two people chose not to answer this question due to a misunderstanding or disagreement with the semantics.

62 percent of these content experts assign at least part of the responsibility of successful education on themselves. One professor expressed her thoughts this way, "I do think the professor needs to work hard to make the material as accessible as possible, whatever method they use. The professor is also responsible for teaching linguistics well so that a simplistic or wooden view of language is avoided." Another professor believes, "The professor sets the tone of the course and has the responsibility to (1) explain to the students why Greek is important and (2) consistently demonstrate how that is the case." Similarly, William Varner argues that the professor is responsible for more than the dissemination of information when he says, "We must excite students about the language and not kill their spirit."

Danny Zacharias states that the professors need to "make the class their own" regardless of the publication being used and since Greek is such a difficult course the professor "shouldn't necessarily expect the student to be the driving force." Another professor synthesizes the thoughts of Varner and Zacharias when he writes, "It is the professor's task to explain to the student why an approach has merit, to build student trust, to encourage them to keep at it when they want to quit, and to motivate them by showing them the value of what they are learning." In the end, the professor is responsible for the pedagogy. Even if the school mandates the use of a particular text, the professor generally dictates the trajectory and tempo of how that curriculum is applied. Additionally, the professor is the content expert in the room and holds the ability to rule through encouragement or intimidation. The success of the student ought to be the professor's primary goal; that fact places a heavy weight on his or her shoulders.

The Student

Even though it is true that the professor holds a heavy burden in the learning process, the student must play an active role as well. Constantine Campbell says it well: "It remains true that unless the student puts in the effort even the best teacher will not cause them to succeed." Likewise, Charles Quarles agrees when he writes that "the student must invest hours studying, memorizing, and applying new principles. Without a significant time investment from the student, he or she will not learn Greek well." The memorization and regurgitation practice of GTM was a significant weakness listed previously (53 percent), but if the methodology requires it, the student must be willing and able to adapt. David Woodall echoes Campbell's point, "Ultimately success in the course is up to the student to put in the time and energy necessary to learn the material. Without this, you can have a great method and a great professor, but no success."

Delio DelRio brings up an excellent point when he identifies the student as the burden bearer in this process, but he places the blame for that burden on the institution. He says this:

> The current course structure of most institutions (at least as I've experienced them), as seen in, for example, sixteen-week or less semester length, proliferation of the online environment, and increasingly limited student and professor interaction in a workshop environment, results in an increasing need for self-directed learning.

In other words, the current education model is changing in a way that does not benefit the student's learning process, as much as it does their interest level.[4] DelRio pointed out that the shortening of the typical college semester, the abuse of the online learning format, and the lack of student–professor interaction has damaged the language learning process and afflicted the student. Although it is possible that the student could use a rude awakening regarding his level of educational engagement, thrusting it upon him may not be the wisest manner of drawing attention to the fact.

Both the Professor and the Student

Many of these experts argue that responsibility for educational success in this field ought to be equally divided between the student and the professor. A. Chadwick Thornhill puts it this way:

> I view education as a joint venture. Professors should do more than lecture. They should have an ear and eye turned toward the comprehension and retention of their students. Obviously, though, learning cannot take place if students are not engaged, applying themselves to the material, or completing (or at least attempting) assigned assessments.

Mitzi Smith resounds Thornhill's point and adds that these teachers need to "accommodate diverse learning styles" while they "encourage and motivate" the student who then must "put in practice time, be alert in the classroom

---

4. Several respondents commented on the fact that schools are making adjustments toward the goal of appealing to students who want less class time and shorter degree programs. This, of course, impinges on the teaching and learning process to the extent that institutions are laying off faculty and staff to fit this more stream-lined system.

CHAPTER 4

and ask questions." A boring and listless professor can easily dissuade an eager student just as a bored and unmotivated student can derail the efforts of an engaging teacher.

As any good student knows, time and effort are the two major keys to succeeding in the classroom at any level. But even these students, regardless of their personal time and effort, must take ownership of their education to excel. Mark House provides some personal insight here:

> All factors are, of course, important, and I'm not sure which is the most important. As a student of Greek I considered myself as ultimately responsible to master the material regardless of the competency of the instructor (who frankly put me to sleep). For most students, however, I am aware that the teacher and the methodology are extremely important. As a Greek instructor, I consider my role as immensely important, though I know that without some measure of self-motivation no student will thrive.

The student must understand their own needs and limitations to learn a biblical language. The learner must be fully invested in the process of learning. But Alan Bandy is quick to point out, "This is not to say that the professor is somehow absolved of the responsibility to communicate the material with clarity and making the best effort possible to make sure the students understand."

Question #3—What are the educational objectives for your first and second-semester Greek courses or personal textbook? (i.e., What do you want students to know, understand, and be able to accomplish by the end of their second semester)?

Educational objectives can be difficult to develop because the entire class and its outcomes are built upon them. For example, if a literature teacher wants her students to be able to identify the difference between various authors, genres, and writing styles, she needs to expose her students to Emily Dickinson, Mark Twain, Stephen King, and other authors while dissecting these literary styles and comparing them to each other. In the same way, if a NT Greek professor wants his students to understand morphology, then he must explain how the mood, tense, and person function within the Greek text. Additionally, these objectives must be assessed or tested in some form to know if the student has achieved the state goals of the professor. This may sound fairly simple, but if an objective is outside of the realm of the GTM course structure (i.e., reading, speaking, syntax, exegesis, etc.), then amendments must be made to the pedagogy, lesson plan, and assessment process to assure student competency.

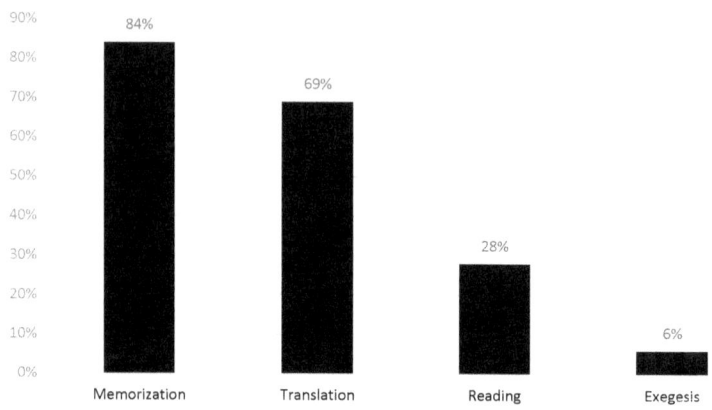

NT Greek Learning Objectives

While the answers to this question varied widely, the vast majority of the experts who participated in this survey (84 percent) say that they require a large amount of memorization.[5] This is no surprise; any new language learning process requires the memorization of vocabulary and some measure of morphology even if it is not a grammar–centered approach. And, as expected, the majority (69 percent) state that they require translation work from their students at some point during the learning process. Again, this is expected when the primary pedagogy is GTM.

What is more, 28 percent of these respondents express a requirement that the student be able to read portions of the Greek NT through the use of GTM. In contrast, only 16 percent chose GTM's ability to teach the student to read as a strength while 66 percent say that the methodology diminishes the student's use of their Greek at all. Assessing a student's ability to read their Greek NT requires more of the face–to–face time, which DelRio insists is in decline. Last, two professors require exegetical skills from their Greek students, which, as mentioned above, is outside the scope of GTM. In the case of reading and exegesis skills, both learning objectives require the professor to provide additional training above that which GTM offers. Although this is certainly possible, 35 percent of these experts complained about the limited time constraints placed on this language learning process.

In his unique approach to NT Greek, Danny Zacharias expresses his school's choice to limit the NT Greek requirement to one, three credit–hour course. Teaching a biblical language in such a compressed timeframe is quite a daunting task for any professor, but Zacharias took it as a challenge.

---

5. This number is likely much closer to 100 percent due to the nature of the language learning process, but only 84 percent expressed this objective specifically.

He expresses his creative objectives with a software-based grammar textbook this way:

> The objectives are to have a basic understanding of the entire Greek grammatical system; to seek and understand the exegetically significant points of the morphology (i.e. instead of teaching them to parse a word, I teach them what the significance is of its mood, tense, etc.); students should understand the basics of lexical semantics for proper word studies; Finally, the objective is for them to know how to access this information in Logos Bible Software.
>
> My textbook (and intro classes) is aimed at the single semester, but is also built to be used for a second semester by students such that they would end with the same outcomes as students using the normal Greek textbooks (like Mounce, Croy, etc.). In the second semester, they go through much of the textbook again, are introduced to some additional information and tables, and have more learning activities that focus on parsing and reading.

This professor's attempt to meet his school's effort to draw students required ingenuity and an unorthodox willingness to adjust the norm. This does beg the question about the abilities of his students compared to a traditional GTM-trained student, but, to his credit, it appears that he made the necessary adjustments to train his students with his personal objectives in mind.

Question #4—Do you have an instrument or process for measuring whether these educational objectives have been met? If so, how is this done?

Educational researchers like Robert Marzano and Walter Dick explain the first few steps to designing a course are:

- Identify instructional goals (i.e., what is the purpose of the course)
- Determine what skills and knowledge the students will need to reach those goals
- Analyze the educational level and context of a given course setting
- Write performance objectives
- Develop assessment instruments[6]

These five steps are crucial to the success of a class. These professional educators encourage every teacher to follow the ten steps listed in Dick and

---

6. Dick and Carey, *The Systematic Design of Instruction*, 8th ed. (New York: Harper Collins, 2014).

Carey's book to see the best possible results from student performance and the course effectiveness.

The experts were asked about their learning objectives and then their assessment strategy, because they reveal what they expect from their students each semester and how (or if) they measure their students' progress and success in an accurate manner. While thirty-one of the thirty-two respondents (97 percent) claim to use a variation of quizzes, tests, and exams, a few apply some more unique strategies for testing their students' progress. One professor prefers open-book exams to reduce anxiety and determine the students' ability to "identify syntactical categories and exegetical issues." Additionally, Con Campbell uses "reading groups" as part of his grading system, while William Varner and two other professors employ daily or weekly public, oral recitation as an assessment. Justin Langford employs "team competitions" and another professor requires one hour of tutoring (outside of class-time requirements) per week. Other unique additions to the normal assessment process are "guided word-study exercises," "personal interviews," and Robert Plummer's inclusion of his Daily Dose of Greek videos.

As mentioned earlier, due to the translation goal built into GTM's design and implementation, creating any other learning objective would require the addition of a specific assessment. Dick and others make clear that a learning objective must be measurable to be a true learning objective. In other words, if the professor desires the student to be able to "read" their Greek NT by the end of the first two semesters of language learning, they need to add a reading component to their methodology and a reading assessment to their grading.[7] Otherwise, the student may not be able to read and the professor would not be able to measure the student's competency in that area. For example, David Woodall and Delio DelRio both list a strong element of exegetical understanding in their previous answers (objectives), but neither expresses a specific assessment for that skill (this does not mean they do not exist though). On the other hand, Con Campbell requires his students to be able to read the first four chapters of Mark "with some assistance" and lists reading groups as one of his assessment aspects. Similarly, another professor requires reading skills and practices "personal interviews" in his courses to assure competence.

7. A few professors who contributed to this research outside of or in addition to the survey expressed their honest confusion regarding how a professor could define "reading." Some of the questions posited were: Is reading the act of orally presenting the NT Greek text (pronunciation)? Is reading defined as pronouncing a translation done on paper? Is reading defined as mentally translating the text in one's head out loud? And, so on. Not only does this cause confusion since each professor holds their own definition, but how can this objective be measured accurately? This topic could be a study of its own.

Question #5—Do you believe that two semesters of NT Greek (6 credit hours is the most common MDiv requirement) is sufficient to accomplish the objectives that you listed above? Why or why not?

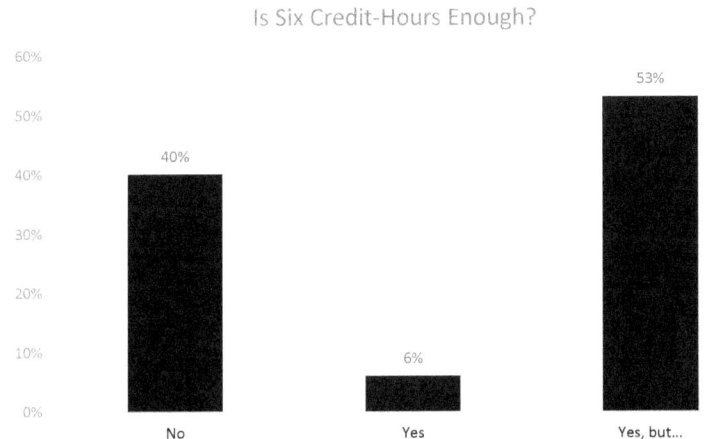

Throughout this survey, many of the experts mention that their school and others like theirs are slashing the mandatory amount of credit hours required for all degree programs, especially in the Master of Divinity tracks. This trend is aimed at attracting more students, but it leaves several areas wanting. By reducing the degree requirements, most departments must restructure and make respective cuts to meet the new institutional demands, and one of the harder hit areas has been languages. Markus Klausli explains his feelings, "The real issue relates to restraints in the curriculum. The current trend to reduce the number of hours in Master of Divinity programs makes it more difficult to prioritize the languages." Many schools, in recent years, require six credit-hours of one language and nine credit-hours of the other, but those numbers are going down. As exemplified above, Danny Zacharias teaches at a seminary that has reduced its number down to three credit-hours of each language for all Master of Divinity students.

When asked if these experts can achieve their learning objectives in a six credit-hour box, 44 percent said no. One professor conveys his worry regarding the trend "toward minimal credits" for Master of Divinity degrees in his answer. Michael Heiser is so convinced that the GTM system cannot be sustained in six credit-hours that he says, "You don't need to teach people to memorize. You need to teach people to think—how to ask questions about the text." William Varner writes, "Absolutely not. They are reeling by the end of the first year. They need additional time to process everything in first year Greek and then to build on that foundation." Randall Buth completely agrees with Varner: "It is woefully insufficient as a foundation for further work."

On the other hand, 31 percent of these experts say yes, they believe six credit-hours are enough to achieve their objectives. They also express that this is only possible because they have adjusted their objectives to meet the six credit-hour box. The professor mentioned earlier who began using open-book exams believes that practice solved her time problem. Robert Plummer says yes, but "barely." Charles Quarles agrees when he responds with, "Yes, but the approach is so fast-paced that weaker students are often left behind. I would much prefer to have 12 credit hours." Quarles continues, "Students who have had two years of Greek are much more comfortable working with the Greek New Testament and much more likely to continue using it in ministry because they have had greater opportunity to see the usefulness of the study." Of these ten experts who said yes, only two did not add a caveat regarding the quality of the success after six credit-hours. That is to say, the other eight ultimately answered: "yes, but . . . "

The final four participants specifically say "yes, but . . . " concerning whether they could meet their objectives in such a short time, and the remaining five say they are mixed on whether this would be possible or not. With these nine and the previous eight participants that seem to be on the fence, that would total 53 percent of the surveyed experts who say that it is possible to meet the objectives, but only to a certain extent. Furthermore, many of them provide commentary such as the following:

> "Yes, if it's rigorous enough. The great majority of first-year Greek instruction is not."—Dan Wallace

> "It's possible but proves difficult for most students in my experience. Most students struggle with the great amount of information that must be inductively learned (i.e., memorized) in such a short amount of time."—Delio DelRio

> "Yes, it is sufficient to accomplish these objectives. The bigger question is if these are the correct objectives. Students have considerable grammatical skills with this model but do not yet acquire significant interpretive or exegetical skills until their third or fourth semester."—A. Chadwick Thornhill

> "It is adequate to accomplish the objectives for the first-year Greek but not to equip students to use Greek in an informed way as part of exegesis and exposition."—Anonymous

CHAPTER 4

While institutions such as Dallas Seminary, Bethel University, Knox Seminary, Multnomah University, and others still require more than the standard six credit-hours of NT Greek, these schools are in the minority among those represented in this survey. One professor fears that this new trend will force schools to cut down their language programs or lose potential students to other schools that will require less language study.

Question #6—Do you believe the majority of students look forward to taking biblical language classes? Why or why not?

The intention of this question was to find out if these participants' students were anxious, nervous, or fearful before beginning their language studies. The aim was to discover if the anecdotal perception of students dreading biblical language courses was true or not from these experts' observations. Half of the participants (50 percent) explain that many students experience some level of fear when they see the language requirements on their degree plan. They used words like "afraid," "fearful," trepidation," "terrified," "intimidated," and even "dread." One professor writes, "They have heard that the classes are hard, boring, and have very little payoff." Another agrees, saying, "I would say about 25 percent are excited, another 25 percent are terrified, and other 50 percent are there because it is a requirement."

Some of the experts display a more optimistic tone about student perceptions. Robert Plummer says, "The majority of our students do [look forward to languages]. They are ravenous for the languages—for the most part. There are the occasional slackers." A. Chadwick Thornhill believes most students are excited: "They understand the importance of the languages typically, but also are terrified about the process." Based on the responses, it appears that just as many students look forward to language study as those who fear it, but there is reason for pause when weighing the students' perceptions. One prominent Bible professor tells her story this way:

> In my personal experience of seminary, I took Greek (and Hebrew) only because it was required. But while taking it I fell in love with the languages and discovered I was relatively good at them. Had the biblical languages not been required by the seminary, I would likely have opted out of them, and consequently my life would have taken another path.

It is exciting to know that somewhere around 50 percent of students look forward to learning a biblical language, and it is understandable that the other half are intimidated by the same process. Another professor sums these thoughts up well: "I think that most of my students in general are excited about the idea of knowing Greek, but most are afraid of passing through the process of learning Greek."

Question #7—In your opinion, what percentage of your students go on to study Greek beyond what their specific program requires (ex., Greek 3, exegetical courses, advanced degrees, etc.)?

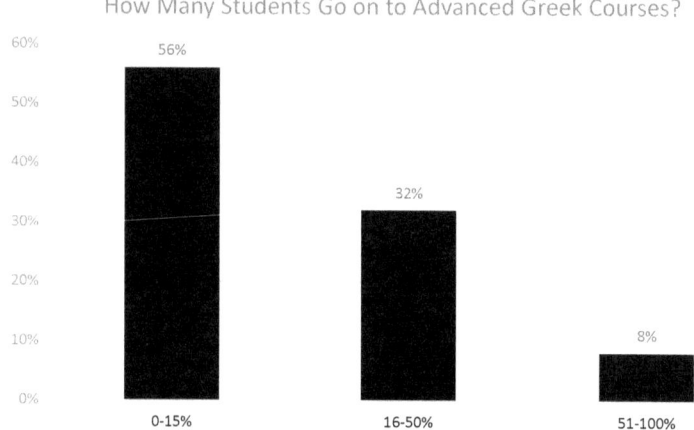

Determining how many students participate in intermediate or advanced Greek courses is a difficult task. A school's registrar would be a more accurate source of numbers for this question, but the goal was to find out what the professor thinks and contrast that (perceived) number with how these experts teach their courses. To put it plainly, if a professor assumes the majority of her students will not go on to further syntactical or exegetical work in NT Greek, what adjustments, if any, does she make in her first six credit-hours with those students? For example, if a professor thinks that his learning objectives cannot be adequately met in six credit-hours (as mentioned above) and that most of his students will not continue their language training past those six credit-hours, it would follow that he would change his objectives to fit the realistic educational constraints. The registrar can give accurate numbers, but they cannot provide a better understanding about a professor's realistic approach to teaching.

While there should be a slight curve in the numbers of this category due to the fact that three of the highest numbers represent schools that require advanced NT Greek courses, they will not be adjusted. Earlier, Figure 11 broke down what numeric percentage these experts say take syntax, exegesis, or other advanced NT Greek courses.[8] Examples of the other, non-numeric answers include seven of the eight respondents explaining their students are required to take advanced courses of one kind or another, and one, Markus Klausli, writes that "relatively few" of his students go on for more, non-required language work. This means that the students who studied under ten of the thirty-two experts (31 percent) do not have the choice to avoid these advanced courses. What this information exposes is that, of the 69 percent of the these experts' students who do have a choice regarding their advanced courses, 86 percent of the students represented by these participants do not elect to continue their formal language learning process.

Because 97 percent of the experts agree that six credit-hours of NT Greek is not enough for ministry proficiency and 88 percent say that less than half of their students elect to go on to receive more than the required credit-hours, then these numbers expose a substantial reason for an analysis and assessment of GTM. This means that the students who take their six credit-hours of NT Greek and do not continue on to advanced work (syntax, exegesis, and other advanced courses) are functionally incapable of using their linguistic skills with any confidence in their ministry.

Question #8—Do you believe the majority of students go on to use their NT Greek training after graduation in their regular ministry? Why or why not?

---

8. Eight participants did not provide a numerical answer; thus, their answers were not included in the final totals.

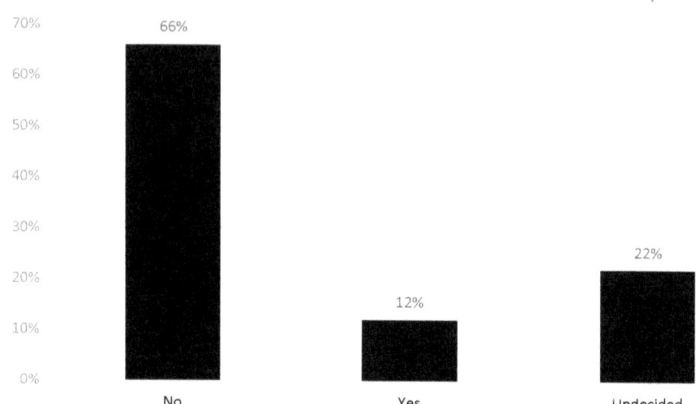

Do Students Go on to Use Their NT Greek in Ministry?

This question was designed to follow the previous ones to get an idea of whether these experts believe their students go on to use their language skills after two semesters of GTM after noting the learning objectives and lack of advanced training. Alan Bandy expresses his honest assessment this way:

> Only those who continue on for a second year of Greek have the skills to use their Greek on a regular basis in ministry. Those with only one year of Greek will typically forget about 85–95 percent of what they learned, but will attempt to sound like they know Greek in their sermons by mentioning the meaning of a Greek word or case/tense. [T]his sounds like I am being negative, but I have been in ministry for 25 years and I have known a lot of pastors who don't know Greek although they had a year of it in seminary.

This is a common theme among the answers on this survey. Randall Buth agrees when he says, "I think that most students do not use Greek because they have not reached a level of reliably extracting information in Greek." Along these same lines, David Croteau writes:

> No. Many reasons. 1) Some seminaries require a minimal knowledge (1 year of just grammar) of either Greek or Hebrew. By doing this, students never reach the level of comfortability to continue their study on their own. 2) They get into ministry and don't have the time to keep using it. 3) They were never taught how to actually use Greek in preparing sermons or teaching Bible studies. Greek professors typically teach Greek; homiletics

professors teach preaching. If there is no integration between the two, most students won't be able to do this on their own.

In fact, twenty-one of these experts (66 percent) agree that the majority do not use their Greek skills due to either a lack of adequate training (i.e., advanced courses) or time restrictions. Only four respondents say "yes" and the remainder are undecided. It is very likely that many of these answers are anecdotal, although a few experts refer to alumni surveys and other institutional data collection efforts.

Question #9—Do you believe theological institutions should require more or less biblical language courses at the bachelors or masters levels? Please explain your reasoning.

All but two of these experts agree that more language courses should be required; this is not a surprise though, because it is their profession. Two professors, Maurice Robinson and Mitzi Smith, both intimate that language requirements ought to be reserved for certain majors and educational tracks, but they also agree that more is better in this field. While some experts recommend a "tools"-based track for languages and others suggest an exegetical focus within the pedagogy, they all desire to see more room in the ministry degree programs for biblical languages. Although the respondents are in unison in this opinion, one reality-based concern came up often: other departments. Samuel Lamerson explains this well:

> I believe that in a perfect world most schools (including my own) need more Greek training. I also believe that almost every department feels this way. Historians feel that there is not enough history, Hebrew scholars that there is not enough Hebrew, etc. Thus, everyone must be willing to compromise somewhat. I think that the cut-off line for me would be at least 3 semesters of Greek. Any less than this is, I feel, not enough to enable the student to make real use of the language.

While several experts lean in the same sympathetic direction, they still look for ways to fit more Greek into the ministry-focused student's life. Another professor laments, "More, but good luck with that since [the] trend is toward [the] reduction of units in MDiv." Delio DelRio adds that it is "difficult to accomplish given the current educational state and student market climate."

Dan Wallace expresses his passionate thoughts on requiring more languages:

> Much more. This is the material foundation of our faith. We have been chipping away at the languages for a long time, in spite of what the Reformers stood for. The methodological battle cry of the Reformation—ad fontes!—and the formal battle cry—sola scriptura—are crucial for the evangelical faith. Second Timothy 4.2 comes to mind: "proclaim the word; be persistent whether it is convenient or inconvenient" (NAB).

It is obvious that these experts and many others are motivated to require as much language training as possible, but it is not always possible. Randall Buth says, "Obviously more is needed if we will treat the NT as God's Word, but qualitatively, this requires a new training paradigm, too." Languages need to find a place in every ministry-focused student's education, but this must come within the balance of the rest of the respective degree program. If six credit-hours are all that is currently allotted for a given biblical language, then the professor must find a way to adjust his pedagogy to fit that mold. As unfortunate as this reality might be, it is just that, reality. Michael Heiser and David Woodall push for a more technical approach while Mark House and Charles Quarles emphasize exegetical inclusion.

Question #10—If you could make ANY changes to the current pedagogical process of teaching Greek (ex., Grammar-Translation Method), what would they be and why?

The previous nine questions centered around the current NT Greek learning process; this question, on the other hand, sought desired changes as the process moves forward. Dan Wallace, Alan Bandy, Randall Buth, and a few others suggest moving toward a Living Language (immersion) approach while a prominent professor in the field disagrees when he writes, "I know that the immersion method is not the answer, as it requires a larger time commitment, an unreal environment, and does not produce the same tangible results for proportionate investment." David Croteau suggests starting with the infinitive mood as Spanish does, and others posit the addition of "more music," "solid linguistic principles," a more "community"-focused environment. Robert Plummer, Delio DelRio, and other professors request the addition of time to slow down and solidify the learning process, while another seasoned professor humorously suggests, "Medicate obsessive-compulsive teachers who love excruciating language details to the expense of good learning."

Chapter Summary

Many of the answers gleaned from these experts' survey responses have been helpful and a few have been quite revealing. The strengths and weaknesses of GTM painted a sharp picture of what professors have learned from their many years using GTM in theological education and their answers to the ten questions provided context and depth to that list of bullet points. The next step was to assess these responses and make logical conclusions about the GTM process and determine what, if any, changes need to be made to improve modern biblical language pedagogy and to prepare it for the emerging digital educational landscape to come.

Chapter 5

Summary and Conclusions

RESEARCH THAT IS CENTERED around analysis and assessment procedures is never easy and will always contain areas that can be strengthened and sharpened for stronger results. Although great effort has been expended to limit those weaknesses and research gaps, it is almost impossible to illuminate all such gaps. The goal of this research was to analyze a dominant pedagogical approach to a subject matter, assess its purpose, determine its practical usefulness, and, if necessary, propose a new path forward based on SLA and the twenty–first century student. The latter point is the focus of this chapter. What follows is a brief summary of the research and procedure, a description of the implications of the findings, an explanation of the limitations of such a process, and suggestions for further research in this area of study.[1]

Summary of Research and Procedure

This segment of the conclusion will include the S.W.O.T. analysis, the Language Teaching Methodology Comparison, and any final thoughts based on the survey results. The objective is to wrap up the research data into a concise assessment and move toward a pedagogical recommendation for NT Greek language teaching and learning.

---

1. In an effort for renewed clarification, when Grammar–Translation Method (GTM) is referenced in this manuscript, it is being referenced as a pedagogical methodology and not the simplistic effort of teaching grammar. In other words, the experts who participated in the survey and this researcher are not opposed to the act of teaching grammatical elements of NT Greek as a part of the language study. On the contrary, these opinions and remarks speak to the specific methodology that so many institutions use as a way of introducing students to the language in question.

S.W.O.T. Analysis

This portion of the research is designed to perform a final analysis and assessment of the survey findings and determine the overall usefulness of the Grammar–Translation Method of teaching NT Greek. Therefore, this section will not be long; it will simply act as a summary of the aforementioned data. The first two sections come directly from the survey numbers given in chapter four and the final two sections come from the following ten questions the experts answered. Therefore, this S.W.O.T. Analysis is directed and determined by the experts themselves and not the researcher or outside sources.

Strengths

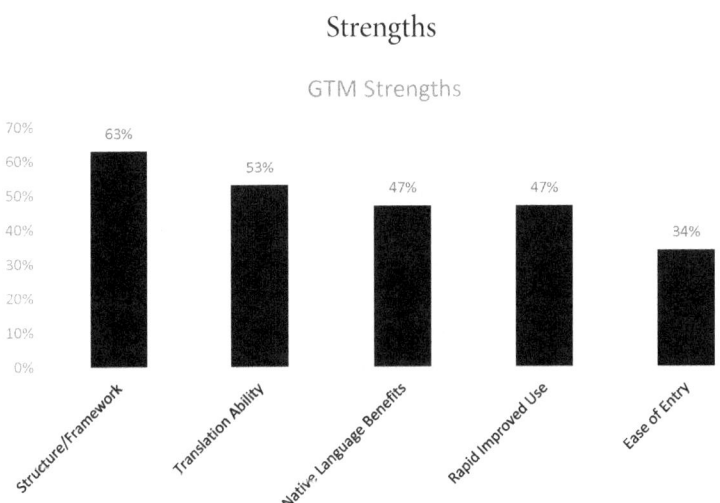

GTM Strengths

The strengths of GTM were fairly clear and easy to understand and have been listed in order of the most mentioned comments to the least mentioned. The thirty-two experts identified GTM as having a strong structure and overall framework for the student to learn from (63 percent) and a good method for teaching translation skills (53 percent). Other benefits were that it helps the student learn more linguistic properties of their own native language (47 percent) and improve the student's use of Greek in some measurable manner (47 percent). They also claimed that this pedagogy provides easy access for the new learner (34 percent), a multitude of resources (28 percent), and the ability to begin the Greek reading process (16 percent). A few of the more interesting aspects of the strengths list that did not garner a large amount of continuity deserve mention here. Ease of entry for the student (34 percent) and the number of related resources or "helps" (28 percent) provide very good support for the student on both ends of the learning process. These two noted strengths deserve mention due to their growing popularity and much-needed focus on the student.

Weaknesses

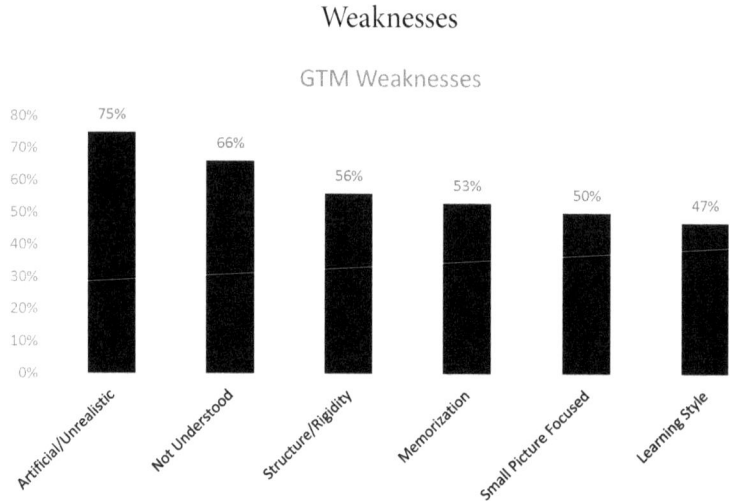

On the other side of the analysis, the experts listed the following areas of concern as weaknesses of GTM for NT Greek. Many saw this methodology as artificial and unrealistic (75 percent), and several others complained that it diminishes the student's use of Greek by only providing a limited ability to understand the language for use (66 percent). The wooden structure (56 percent) and the extreme focus on memorization (53 percent) made the top of the list as well, while GTM's narrow focus on grammar alone (50 percent) rounded out the top half of the group. Following close behind were the areas of GTM's poor learning style (47 percent), limited timeframe of 6 credit-hours (34 percent), and frustrating retention rates (28 percent). While Ohio State University's Language Files publication agrees with many of Larsen-Freeman and Anderson's principles explained in chapter two, it states that GTM's focus on translation is "misplaced" due to the learner's lack of natural inhibition to translate from one language to another.[2] Eight experts also listed GTM as "boring" for the majority of their students.

---

2. McManis, Stollenwerk, and Zhang, *Language Files*, 260.

CHAPTER 5

Opportunities

Because the S.W.O.T. analysis was originally designed for business ventures, the next two portions will require some explanation to understand their proper role in the didactic field. The content for the opportunities section comes directly from the breakdown of strengths and the experts' related answers. When analyzing opportunities, a few typical questions come to mind. How can the educational field benefit from the strengths listed above? What is the perception of the Grammar-Translation Methodology? Will the student grow in his or her use of languages with this methodology? Is GTM applicable within current educational trends? And finally, is the GTM practice suited for the future of biblical language pedagogy? These are important questions and they will be answered below, but most of the information for this section of the analysis and the next has already been presented; thus, these and other questions will be addressed briefly.

Only the top four listed strengths (structure, translation, native language benefits, and improved use) are mentioned here as they held the most continuity among the participants (63–47 percent respectively). According to this list of strengths, the primary benefit of GTM is structure, which aids the student in their entry and progression through NT Greek grammar. This is a very positive asset since so many of these experts brought up students' fear or intimidation of the language learning process before even walking into the classroom. Additionally, the chunking effect of this structure is a well-received educational practice that helps the student with learning, understanding, and retention throughout the process and afterward. Although structure will come up again in the next section, the complaint focused on the rigidity of the structure rather than the use of it. Therefore, as long as this strength remains somewhat pliable based on the course setting, timeframe, student-body makeup, and topic difficulty then it should remain a great opportunity for GTM and biblical language learning in general.

Translation is a unique strength because, as mentioned before, GTM ought to be outstanding at translation proficiency, but only 53 percent of respondents listed it as a strength. This fact should not detract from translation's place on this list though. If the instructor's objective is to teach the students how to translate the NT text, then this technique is designed for just that. On the other hand, if the professor desires for their students to read, speak, or exegete the NT text, then this methodology will not impress them. Translation is a useful skill when learning biblical languages, and many professors argue that every student needs to be able to attain this ability if he or she wants to move on to more serious language work. If the setting is a six credit-hour course load for NT Greek and the ultimate goal is for the student to translate, this is a reliable process.

The final two categories for this section are native language benefits and improved use; only 47 percent of the participants mentioned either category. In reality, the former strength is more of a strong byproduct than a strength of GTM. While it is wonderful that the student gains a more robust understanding of English as they progress through their Greek coursework, these students should ideally already have this native-language familiarity before attempting to learn a new language, especially a dead one. The latter strength posits that many students are able to interact with the biblical text fairly quickly in the language progression, which produces excitement and confidence. Understanding the grammar of NT Greek is a very positive asset and ought to be included in any pedagogy to some degree. To be fair, while 47 percent of these experts listed "improved use" as a strength, 44 percent said that GTM was not able to achieve their stated learning objectives and 53 percent said that it could but not without lowered expectations and additional training beyond the typical six credit-hours.

The respondents' perception of the GTM practice is mixed. Some of these experts believe it is valid and productive, while others argue that it is boring and unrealistic. It is possible that those thoughts are all true and Grammar-Translation can still be beneficial for the student and the learning process. Many experts identified GTM as seriously problematic when not supplemented with syntax and exegesis, and therefore the problem is not necessarily GTM, but the fact that GTM does not provide sufficient language training by itself. That statement does not mean that it is useless, simply that its place is not as the primary language pedagogy if six credit-hours (or less) remains the theological education standard requirement. At its foundation, what are the opportunities for GTM? Are these four areas beneficial to the student? Yes, with some additional instruction. Can these four areas function and remain viable in educational settings today and for future use? To some degree, yes. Although they require adjustments, these four areas, in particular, can remain beneficial if the student remains engaged with the process. And lastly, should GTM remain the primary pedagogy for teaching and learning biblical languages? No, but it offers some positives that should not be disregarded and even some assets that ought to be retained for future use.

CHAPTER 5

Threats

This final section of the S.W.O.T. Analysis examines the external factors that have or can threaten this linguistic practice. Threats to GTM can come in a variety of forms: the student's waning interest in the subject matter, the institutional jockeying to attract more potential students, the church's lackluster interest in exegetical discourse, and even the constantly shrinking availability of church and academic jobs in the employment market today. While all of these factors are threats to GTM and biblical language learning in general, they are not the dominant issue threatening GTM. Student non-participation in these GTM-focused courses will bring the demise of biblical language training if not properly addressed. Whereas the strengths list had four categories attested to by more than 47 percent of the experts, the weaknesses have six. More than half of these experts pointed to GTM being unrealistic, indiscernible, rigid, and too heavily dependent on rote memorization. These are massive weaknesses and 50 percent of the experts labeled GTM as too narrowly focused and poorly designed for the learner. If the professors see these weaknesses, then so does the student.

If the learner discerns that a particular skill or academic practice is outdated or impractical, they will either dismiss it or only devote minimal effort toward it. If they see no obvious benefit from it, they will avoid it altogether. This is just as true for biblical language training as it is for theological education altogether. So, how can these threats be resolved? The answer is unclear. The survey respondents wrote about their students being fearful and not having adequate training to understand or use their languages well in ministry. They also spoke about institutional trends that are strangling the necessary language preparation out of any influential position in a degree program and, in some cases, out of relevance, all to appeal to the disinterested student. It appears that some Christian schools and seminaries are aiming to please the lowest quality student rather than the highest quality student. Dallas Theological Seminary is a stalwart in this field; it is one of the few theological institutions that has not appeared to give in to the popular trend of moving away from stringent biblical language requirements. But not every school can begin requiring more and more languages without enormous sacrifices in their current curricula and future student body.

Dallas Seminary may well argue that its system works and others should follow their lead, but it may simply attract the language-heavy students that are leaving minimalist schools. There is not a clear consensus for a trend; instead, it may be that it is serving a niche that is just big enough to keep it afloat. In other words, if the rest of these theological schools desire to improve their biblical language process while not reorganizing their entire scope and sequencing, then they will have to do so within the six credit-hour system before that too is gone.

Language Teaching Methodology Comparison:

Grammar–Translation Method and Second Language Acquisition

Pedagogical language practices share key characteristics in some areas and vary widely in others. It is the intention of this final portion of this chapter to point out some of the similarities and differences that could offset the opportunities and threats of the GTM pedagogy. Because GTM's greatest strength is its structure/framework, this will not be examined. It is enough to mention that it is strikingly similar to the modern practice of "chunking" that is used in many educational fields to break up the content matter into easier to learn portions. As mentioned before, Black breaks up his Greek grammar into twenty-six units, Mounce dissects his textbook into thirty-six segments, and Gibson and Campbell, in the newest and most purposeful book of its nature, use eighty-three "chucks" for their grammar textbook.[3] On the other hand, translation is not a part of modern language learning and would be considered a personal choice based on whether or not the professor wanted to teach his or her students to translate by the end of the six credit-hours. Second Language Acquisition (SLA) teaches the learner the ability to speak, hear, and read a modern language; unless the professor subscribes to the Living Language approach for NT Greek, these skills are irrelevant.

In regards to the native language benefits, a student certainly needs to know how an adverb functions in their own language before understanding its use in Greek, but the Universal Grammar (UG) Hypothesis is highly debated and typically works the other way around. In UG, the student uses their already-acquired English grammar to assist in the learning of a second language; many biblical language students experience this process backward. Some of the experts in the survey mentioned that their students could begin translating and even reading some of the NT fairly quickly through the use of GTM (improved use). Again, this is beneficial only if translation and/or reading are the goals of the professor's pedagogy. Second Language Acquisition research aims for proficiency in speaking and understanding, thus the approach is different as well as the end results. In the case of the final two strengths—ease of entry and helps—they are not found in SLA strategies either. The ease of entry is based on basic grammar concepts that

---

3. Gibson and Campbell actually have ninety-five segments when one counts the "A" and "B" chapters separately.

SLA does not typically include early on, and the "helps" in the SLA process would be native speakers of the target language. While SLA offers videos, illustrated pages, and learning games, those "helps" are designed to be a part of the process, not a retention tool. GTM has two robust benefits for the student in these final two strengths even if the majority of the experts did not mention them.

When looking at the weaknesses and threats, it is clear that GTM needs serious adjustment to benefit the twenty-first-century theological student and to remain relevant in progressing educational technology. It is simply not acceptable for 75 percent of surveyed experts to claim that GTM is artificial and 66 percent say that it leads to underdeveloped language skills. GTM or some sort of grammar introduction can be very helpful and advantageous for the learner when working with a dead language like NT Greek. But when rote memorization, low retention, lack of strong focus, and learner boredom are listed as characteristics of a methodology for such an important subject matter as biblical language training, changes need to be made. SLA offers strong task-based language teaching techniques that cannot only chunk the information well, it can prioritize the information for the student. Additionally, the grammar may need to begin with the infinitive mood instead of the indicative mood as David Croteau suggested earlier in this research. It is a fairly common practice for modern language learning and this may be one step in the direction toward improving the learning process. Later, a pedagogical option will be presented that will utilize the strengths of GTM while mitigating its weaknesses and help the non-academic student be able to use his or her NT Greek in ministry in just six credit-hours of theological training.

Final Thoughts on the Survey

According to the survey data, there seems to be a clear disconnect between the comments the experts made and a search for a solution. In many cases, it is assumed that there are only two pedagogical options for teaching NT Greek: the Grammar-Translation Method or the Living Language approach (CTM). And of these two options, the former is described as artificial and severely limited and the latter is untested, unproven, and unfitting for a six-credit-hour institutional standard. Therefore, many professors simply default to the method they learned (GTM) and find a large number of their peers doing the same while finding very few detractors. It is unclear why there has been no serious analysis or assessment of the GTM practice if the numbers revealed in the previous data are accurate. Daniel Streett comments on this exact issue when he writes:

> I think the grammar-translation method has gotten a free pass when it comes to accountability. From the G-T classes I have taken (about 8 years' worth in 4–5 different institutions) the following hold true: a) Exams test rote memory of forms, vocab glosses, or entire paragraphs of "translations," b) Students are told almost exactly what will be on the exams so that the content is utterly predictable and requires no real understanding or comprehension of the language, merely a surface mastery of the metalanguage. c) If the student fails, it is his/her fault, not the professor's and surely not the method itself. d) Some professors have an almost infinite capacity for self-deception when it comes to how much their students are retaining. The assumption is often, "If I covered it in class, the students *got* it," or "If the student did well on the exam, he learned the material." But, at my institution we tested students 1–2 years after they had taken Greek, and their performance on even the most basic parsings and translations was abysmal. They retained virtually nothing.[4]

There is a growing number of professors who feel this way and they are becoming more vocal about their frustration. Michael Heiser includes this thought in his survey response:

> Honestly, I see little benefit [in GTM]. To me all it does is ready people for second year (if they perform well), but that needs review after a summer anyway. Unless a student is going to do advanced work (doctoral) they aren't going to keep reviewing forms and vocab once in ministry. They don't have to because of available tools, and won't have the time. And they have translations already. That's just the reality, and instead of inventing another reality we need to recognize this.

Like Streett, Heiser is passionate about this topic and it is evident in many of his survey answers. Experts wonder when this issue will be taken seriously and when changes will be made. Like a favorite son who seems to get away with anything with his parents, GTM is being treated like it is flawless and defended with little to no evidence of its effectiveness. This survey has exposed several areas of serious concern and brings to light not only its weaknesses, but more so its fatal flaws.

---

4. Aubrey, "Daniel Streett on Learning Greek," *Koine Greek*, 28 May 2009, https://koine-greek.com/2009/05/28/daniel-streett-on-learning-greek/ (27 March 2018).

The main concern with answers like those found in the survey responses is that they continue to build a case against the GTM as a primary pedagogy for biblical languages, not because GTM is an utter failure as an educational methodology, but because it does not provide enough proper training to for students to continue using their language skills once they enter the ministry in the current instructional setting. This begs the question: if theological institutions were to require more language instruction, would the student go on to use it more in their ministry? Dan Wallace says, "Absolutely." His certainty derives from the fact that Dallas Theological Seminary requires all of its Master of Theology students to take at least five semesters of each language to graduate. David Woodall expresses similar confidence from his seminary students at Moody Theological Seminary, but his understanding is based on his seminary's required use of software in the language learning process, which he argues "gives them greater tools to explore the use of Greek and Hebrew after graduation."

Knowing that 62 percent of these experts place at least half of the responsibility for success of the course on the professor,[5] that 97 percent of them agree that the noted objectives can only be partially met at best,[6] and that 50 percent believe the students approach the language learning process with trepidation, it would follow that these professors and content–expert authors would desire a thorough and detailed review of the prevailing methodology. But, sadly, this has not been the case. A pedagogical methodology that boasts such weaknesses as being artificial (75 percent), lacking understanding (66 percent), and being poorly structured (56 percent) needs to be assessed and most likely revised to attend to these serious issues. For instance, if a home building company constructed the walls of a house with the intention of securing those walls with ceiling joists and rafters, then the walls are not intended to stand by themselves. If the plans did not call for joists or rafters, then the walls would be designed and supported differently. When it comes to NT Greek, 97 percent of these experts say that GTM's learning objectives (the walls) cannot be met without further study (the rafters), but 86 percent of the students are not electing to sign up for the advanced courses. This exposes a serious issue that does not appear to be taken seriously. As a result, students are attracted to schools that are willing to reduce the number of language credits for their degree programs. The result of the current trajectory will either be multiple schools completely

5. Twenty–eight percent named the professor alone and 34 percent supported a joint responsibility between the professor and the student.

6. Forty-four percent said six credit–hours was not enough and 53 percent claimed that it might be enough, but that there would need to be multiple variables at play (yes, but . . .).

removing language requirements from all theological degree programs or an arduous and significant restructuring of their entire scope and sequence. Both options are costly in many ways.

If 97 percent of these experts agree that additional training is needed for the student to truly use their language skills, and 88 percent of these same experts believe that less than half will receive that extra training, then serious changes need to be made concerning how the first six credit-hours of NT Greek are taught. To return to the previous analogy, GTM is constructing walls that are obviously intended to be supported and stabilized by joists and rafters (syntax, exegesis, etc.), but the majority of these "walls" will never see those intended pieces of the design.

If schools and professors know that this is the case, then theological institutions are left with only a few options: (1) do not require any biblical language courses of their students; (2) require substantially more of these courses or; (3) significantly rethink the use of GTM-based language learning courses. The purpose of the theological school is to properly train students for their vocation, and if the current language methodology is not doing that, then it is the institution's responsibility to make the necessary changes through instructional design, professional development, specific hiring practices, or other means.

This may be a good time to reiterate that neither the professor nor the institution is being blamed for these failures and misdirected attempts at teaching biblical languages successfully. Many times, the professor simply uses the pedagogy that he or she is either most comfortable with or that the institution or department head requires that they use. Along these same lines, the institution seldom desires (nor should they) to take up the mantle of the content expert and require their faculty to change pedagogical approaches for any given department. One of the experts in this survey relayed a story about a fellow NT Greek professor who experimented with a more unique style of teaching Greek (CLT) only to be rebuffed by the school that employed him and required to return to GTM. It is not clear whether this new pedagogy was ineffective or just too different for the school's comfort level, but either way, it is possible that other theological schools are making similar decisions. It is also possible that professors continue to use GTM for two other reasons:

It is viewed as the lesser of two evils. As noted already, many professors say that they see two primary options for teaching NT Greek: GTM or Communicative Language Teaching (i.e., Living Language Approach). The view of teaching Greek as a living language is described as "unsustainable" or "unrealistic" by a few of the experts in this survey. That would make GTM a better option by default since it has a solid structural design for semester-based education and there are so few other sustainable or realistic options in this field.

They are not aware of the educational results. Many of these professors may simply use GTM because they assume that it works for their students as well as it worked for them when they learned NT Greek. Again, this researcher is not aware of another study that has attempted to analyze and assess the use and S.W.O.T. of GTM in theological institutions today. This leaves the professor at a loss for reliable data regarding the realities of GTM inside and outside of the classroom.

Therefore, it is not the purpose of this work to assign blame to anyone in particular because there is no clear culprit. The purpose of this work is to analyze and assess the reality of biblical language pedagogy today and, where necessary, expose the errors and, if applicable, suggest corrections. The numbers and conclusions from previous chapters (and those to come) are simply the results of the data collected and not a condemnation of the experts or their contemporaries in any way.

Implications of the Findings

After reviewing the data and analyzing the results of both the survey and the S.W.O.T. analysis, GTM clearly has several glaring weaknesses that need to be addressed through modern language acquisition techniques and didactic strategies. As mentioned already, the foundational bulk of GTM aims at teaching students how to translate, but few pastors, missionaries, and Bible study leaders have the time or see the profit in translating Scripture passages each week. This displays a weak practical methodology and a misguided educational objective. Therefore, it is highly unlikely, if not impossible, to teach biblical languages well using this strategy alone. But caution is necessary to avoid throwing the baby out with the bath-water. Professors like David Black, Stanley Porter, and, most recently, Richard Gibson and Constantine Campbell have all tried to address these issues by reformatting GTM to resemble a practical methodology and to direct it toward a useful objective, but these efforts have not addressed the primary weaknesses of the practice.

Throughout this research process, work has been done to define a set of "vital" requirements for a ministry-focused student to be able to use their biblical language training on a regular basis with reasonable confidence and accuracy.[7] Many of these requirements are covered in the basic grammar

---

7. In other words, this student will not acquire the educational level in a biblical language to translate large amounts of text without the help of tools. The goal is that

outlines of GTM, and therefore some of that systematic elements can and should be utilized in future approaches. Some of these areas where GTM can best prepare the student for future NT Greek study include the alphabet, pronunciation, punctuation, articles, and the basic concepts of philology. But the primary element of grammar that is needed is morphology; for example, the student needs to know the difference between a nominative and dative noun as well as an aorist and imperfect verb. The need for a student to memorize lengthy and difficult paradigms is highly debated, but the need to know the morphemes of any given word is not. The next few elements of NT Greek that are often prescribed are the ability to produce a detailed and accurate word study, an understanding of how verbal aspect works, the aptitude to diagram a Greek verse/phrase/sentence, a reasonable grasp of textual criticism, and an understanding of grammatical syntax and its related tools. All of these aspects of learning NT Greek should lead the student directly to the ability to perform proper exegesis of a biblical text.

There is no doubt that more pieces could be added to the previous list and several professors and authors argue their case for their preferences. But this list needs to be relatively short and able to be completed in two semesters to fit into the current institutional model. Also, it is not enough to simply make a list of necessary grammar/syntactical elements of a language and teach them to the student. If it were, GTM would thrive. On the contrary, a structured and objective–driven pedagogical system needs to be designed to deliver these linguistic elements properly and purposefully. The remainder of this section will explain how these required pieces of NT Greek could be applied to improve the teaching and learning process for NT Greek courses. Lastly, any pedagogical model that NT Greek professors might adopt needs to be adaptable for online education. It seems like an impossibility in this educational setting to design an onsite–only course anymore. Every school seems to be jumping on the distance education bandwagon, and for good reason. With online degree programs boasting all the financial benefits and none of the synchronous headaches of on–campus classes, the incentive for onsite courses to convert or perish is real.

A Proposal for a Pedagogical Solution: Exegetical Greek

The bulk of this chapter will be aimed at presenting a pedagogical proposal for teaching NT Greek that is focused on the student's success and the teacher's professional discretion. This proposed methodology is called Exegetical

---

the person be able to gain a deeper and richer understanding of the text that he or she desires to teach at a given time through the use of original languages.

Greek, based on its fundamental focal point on teaching the student how to exegete the biblical text from day one. Although the student will obviously not be able to exegete right away, each stage of the process is aimed at teaching specific skills and knowledge that will conclude with exegetical proficiency. The structure will be somewhat fluid with an à la carte design to allow the teacher to choose what they teach and when they teach it based on where they want the class to go. But the first thing any professor must do is select an ultimate objective for their students (translation, reading, speaking, exegesis, etc.) and then plan an intentional route to get their students to that objective. This step is referred to as instructional design and the layout process is known as scope and sequence. Next is a concise description of each step of the instructional design process with application derived specifically from this researcher's pedagogy for NT Greek.

Instructional Design for Exegetical Greek[8]

1. Identify Instructional Goals—Beginning with the end goal in mind helps the teacher develop the best possible process to follow since they have identified the beginning and the end. Someone cannot plan a trip without knowing where they are and where they plan to go. Many teachers design the class around the process instead of the goal and this often leaves the student confused about what they are supposed to learn.

   - The end result of this pedagogy is biblical exegesis; the student ought to be able to use their NT Greek knowledge to determine the meaning and, if possible, the intention of the author of the text. There should also be an element of application to help the student gain a practical use of this language and its exegesis.

2. Conduct Instructional Analysis—This step is designed to determine what skills the student needs in order to achieve the intended knowledge. If the student is not properly prepared for the class, then he or she may not meet the instructional goal(s).

   - Many professors believe grammar and syntax are the primary skills needed, but in this step of the process the instructor can dream a little. Several linguistic aptitudes are necessary for proper exegesis, including:
     - Grammar/morphology

8. E.g., Dick and Carey, *The Systematic Design of Instruction*, 8th ed. (New York: Harper Collins, 2014).

- Biblical software
- Word study
- Verbal aspect
- Text diagramming
- Textual criticism
- Syntax

These skills and others can help in preparing the student for a detailed and accurate exegesis of the biblical text.

3. Analyze learners and context—One must determine the audience and the setting before launching into strategy. In this case, the teacher needs to know who they are teaching, considering age, gender, education level, language, timeframe, etc. and then move forward accordingly.

- In the case of this study, the students would be freshmen in college or higher who desire to go into non-academic ministry fields after graduation. The setting would be an American theological institution with the restriction of six credit-hours of introductory NT Greek language training.

4. Write performance objectives—In this step, the professor determines what the "student will be able to . . .". What should they know at the end of the course/unit/day and what should they be able to do with that information? These performance objectives, as mentioned earlier, must meet three key parameters: (1) they must be obtainable within the course timeframe; (2) they must be measurable; and (3) they must be measured.

- The student will demonstrate their knowledge of the required Greek vocabulary.
- The student will gain a better understanding of NT Greek grammar and its core elements.
- The student will learn how to use a Bible software in conjunction with their NT Greek language training.
- The student will develop the skills necessary to utilize the following language tasks with their NT Greek knowledge: syntax, word studies, verbal aspect, diagramming, and textual criticism.[9]

---

9. *Language tasks* are units of study that help the student build towards a larger language goal or objective.

- The student will be required to employ the previously listed language tasks in their exegesis of the biblical text.

5. Develop assessment instruments—Now that the performance objectives have been identified, the teacher can design assessments to measure the success of the student and the course itself. If the student does poorly on the assessment, then it could be either a failure of their personal effort or a failure of the pedagogy (step 9).

    - Although some quizzes and tests are used throughout this process for vocabulary and grammar elements, they are not a major part of this pedagogical structure. This methodology is measured through the student's ability to demonstrate their proficiency rather than their ability to recall memorized material. Therefore, assessments in this method consist of the student displaying their ability to complete the language task and produce an assignment that illustrates their understanding of the task. For example, students are shown how to perform a detailed word study in class; they then use the tools and proper steps necessary for a word study to do one in class, and then they are required to complete several of these word studies for the following class that will function as their assessment. This process is then duplicated (with some adjustments) for each of the language tasks leading up to the exegetical assessment. This procedure is called the Present–Practice–Produce methodology that Gibson and Campbell employed in their new textbook. The final assessment includes a long and detailed exegetical paper (20–30 pages) that requires the inclusion of each language task to display the student's understanding of each aspect of the six credit-hour course and their ability to use each language task in their exegetical process. This type of assessment was selected for three primary reasons: (1) it allows the student to prove their Greek language skills through production rather than through regurgitation; (2) it helps the student assign practical use for each of these language tasks since they will ultimately be amalgamated into one final project; and (3) it reduces the ability (or temptation) for the student to cheat during their on-site or online courses. In the end, the student is graded by their abilities for complete the tasks required and not their retention capacity. This reduces the student's anxiety and provides the teacher with a clear picture of the student's level of understanding of the information and their ability to apply it.

6. Develop an instructional strategy—Once goals and objectives have been set and the assessments have been designed to properly test the student's performance, then the strategy must be planned out to guide the student from assessment to assessment successfully. What information will they need? How long should they go between assessments? The teacher designs the plan and provides a logical and strategic path to follow.

- This is where GTM both succeeds and fails: its structure is easy to follow and fairly intuitive, but it also changes from professor to professor and has little actual stability. The current proposal offers a direct and intentional framework that walks the student from an introductory grammar all the way through exegesis, and it is flexible enough to serve beginning students who have never taken a Greek course before, up to students looking for a refresher course. At its core, this pedagogy begins with grammar and then moves on to any number of language tasks that build upon the grammar foundation and teach the student to apply these tasks to the final exegetical project.

7. Develop and select instructional materials—Selecting the correct books, articles, videos, etc. for a course is vital to making sure the student can follow the strategy. These materials need to point directly to the previously set goals, prepare the students for the assessments, and possibly even dictate/mirror the pace of the strategy used. Many professors rely on the textbook they learned. That can certainly work, but only if the objectives and strategy are similar.

- This stage of the instructional design is the most difficult since no available textbook offers similar objectives or anything that mirrors this strategy. What follows is a tentative list of books that can fit each language task, but this is not conclusive:

- Grammar—While Dan Wallace uses William Mounce's text for his two-semester "lightning Greek" course, it is not for the faint of heart. Similarly, Black and Gibson/Campbells' works are excellent for introductory grammar but would need serious reduction to be used well. The only readily available textbook that fits this one-semester mold is Danny Zacharias's NT Greek Stripped Down, which combines the shorter timeframe and integrates the use of a Bible software into the process.

- Zacharias, Daniel. NT Greek Stripped Down: Mastering Greek Essentials in Conjunction with Bible Software. Web-Based: Scholar's Publisher, 2012.

- Software—A brief analysis of each of the major software programs that were tested during this research process appear later in this chapter.

- Syntax—The literary choice for this task is almost an automatic selection, but there is reason to pause. While Dan Wallace's text has been and still is a staple for learning syntax, the recent addition from Köstenberger, Merkle, and Plummer is impressive. Each book uses different approaches and both provide an excellent tool for the student; therefore, either one is an excellent choice.

  - Wallace, Daniel. Greek Grammar Beyond the Basics: An Exegetical Syntax of the New Testament with Scripture, Subject, and Greek Word Indexes. Grand Rapids: Zondervan, 1997.

  - Köstenberger, Andreas, Benjamin Merkle, and Robert Plummer. Going Deeper with New Testament Greek: An Intermediate Study of the Grammar and Syntax of the New Testament. Nashville: B&H, 2016.

- Word Studies—This task does not require a textbook, although a well-constructed explanation of the process and a detailed list of strong tools and resources would be an excellent place to start. It should cover areas such as etymology, semantic range, broader semantic-domain, and theme-study. This is one of the most-used language study tools by twenty first-century pastors, and often the most abused as well. Extreme care must be taken to help ministry-focused students to avoid common word study mistakes and errors and to bring them to an appropriate and controlled use of this task.

- Verbal Aspect—Although there are several books on the market for this task and several differing philosophies on the subject, Campbell published a concise and well-rounded text that would help the student as a reasonable introduction to the topic.

  - Campbell, Constantine. Basics of Verbal Aspect in Biblical Greek. Grand Rapids: Zondervan, 2008.

- Diagramming—This is a key aspect of learning an exegetical language like Greek or Hebrew that many students never learn how to do. Whereas Doug Huffman's book is a quick and well-written text that would work as an excellent introduction to the topic, Kantenwein's book includes both Greek and Hebrew diagramming.

- Huffman, Douglas S. The Handy Guide to New Testament Greek: Grammar, Syntax, and Diagramming. Grand Rapids: Kregel Academic, 2012.

- Kantenwein, Lee H. Diagrammatical Analysis. Winona Lake, IN: BMH Books, 1991.

- Textual Criticism—Understanding textual variants is not incredibly difficult, but it can be daunting if care is not taken when explaining it. While Aland does an excellent job doing just that, Black's text is considerably shorter and does very well for what this type of course would be looking for from a text.

- Aland, Kurt, and Barbara Aland. The Text of the New Testament: An Introduction to the Critical Editions and to the Theory and Practice of Modern Textual Criticism. 2nd ed., rev. and enl. Grand Rapids: Eerdmans, 1995.

- Black, David A. New Testament Textual Criticism: A Concise Guide. Grand Rapids: Baker, 1994.

- Exegesis—This is the most important task to understand for students in this methodology. Even if the previous tasks are taught well, exegesis is the final, capstone step and cannot be misunderstood. All of the books below are rich and exceptionally helpful. Fee is longer and slightly more technical, while Black and Carson's books are timeless and provide immediate application. Plummer's text is a series of forty questions and answers that can be used more as a reference resource than a textbook.

- Fee, Gordon D. New Testament Exegesis: A Handbook for Students and Pastors. 3rd ed. Louisville, KY: John Knox Press, 2002.

- Black, David A. Using New Testament Greek in Ministry: A Practical Guide for Students and Pastors. Grand Rapids: Baker, 1993.

- Carson, D. A. Exegetical Fallacies. 2nd ed. Carlisle, UK; Grand Rapids: Paternoster, 1996.

- Plummer, Robert L. 40 Questions About Interpreting the Bible. Grand Rapids: Kregel, 2010.

8. Design and conduct a formative evaluation of instruction—This is an opportunity to determine the effectiveness of the course as one goes through it. Did an assignment fail to produce the desired results? Did a group activity go particularly well? Were the grades on a difficult assignment lower than expected? The first iteration of a course is not always successful, but this is where the teacher can make notes about successful and unsuccessful aspects of the course as they are implemented.

    - This process has not been exercised yet, but it is vital to the evolution of a course if the teacher desires a healthy and well–polished product to offer to their students year after year.

9. Revise instruction—Many believe this step can be done as the ninth or tenth step, but either way, it should be an integral part of the evaluation results. A teacher needs to evaluate the course and make necessary changes to be in a constant cycle of improvement. This consideration should always be in the top drawer of a teacher's desk, as the teacher constantly desires to make changes and improvements where deficiencies are found. One can never assume that the same process or methodology works for very long. Some educational experts suggest a complete evaluation and, if needed, revision of all course materials and methodology every two to three years.

    - The pedagogy being proposed here is not a concrete solution; it is just a proposal. It will need to be assessed as it is introduced, revised along the way, and evaluated after each semester to determine its benefits and effectiveness for the students and the institution alike.

10. Design and Conduct Summative Evaluation—The formative step is done during the course, whereas the summative step is performed after the course is completed. Here, the teacher can determine the effectiveness of the assessments, strategy, materials, etc. and make the determination of their continued use. Also, the teacher should evaluate the pace of the material, the style of pedagogy, and the need for more or less differentiation in the planning of the course. Notes from the formative evaluation are instrumental here. In the end, was the course done well and is it worth doing again?

    - This methodology is unique, but not a radical departure from what many professors are used to; it is simply formatted differently and strategically aligned along didactic lines. It might be a risk to attempt to implement it, but some risks need to be taken to right the direction that many schools are currently heading. And ultimately, this pedagogy will need revision and alteration over time; every course will need this step of the process at some point.

Structural Elements of Exegetical Greek

With the instructional design aspect planned, it is time to select and employ specific structural elements of this pedagogy. These structural components function as the supportive skeleton upon which the methodology's information is presented. Each piece of this skeleton has a unique function, but all of them are equally important to the viability of the pedagogy.

Software

Bible software is often considered a crutch or a hindrance in the learning process for the student, but this mentality must change. Twenty-first-century education does not require handwritten assignments, candlelit classrooms, or even chalkboards anymore. Technological advancements have changed everything about modern education—everything but NT Greek pedagogy. While many professors encourage the use of Robert Plummer's Daily Dose of Greek, his work on that site would not be possible without Koine Greek fonts, digital recording, and advanced software. Professors know these software are an asset, which is why they use them in their own studies and research. Gone are the days of counting lemmas and searching for hapax legomenon; these results are at the software user's fingertips in just seconds. Does a chalkboard still get the job done in front of a class? Yes, but it is messy and noisy. Dry erase boards are cleaner and easier to see and digital screens are even better still. Avoiding the use of a powerful and intelligent software may very well be the reason that NT Greek pedagogy has not advanced with its counterparts. The "helps" and tools that have been designed to surround GTM have been an enormous advancement, but the teaching methodology itself has changed very little over the years.

Liberty University offers a software-based online program, while Moody Theological Seminary decided to construct all of their language courses on software and have seen strong benefits from this decision. In a world where smartphones allow the learner to review vocabulary while they wait in a Starbucks line and perform a detailed word study with a few screen taps, it is only logical to incorporate these tools into the NT Greek language learning process. What follows is a breakdown of the usability of several major Bible software programs that have been tested and analyzed throughout this research process. These descriptions are not meant to act as full-fledged product reviews; rather, they are intended to give the reader an understanding of how these tools can help their students when learning a biblical language.[10]

Logos Bible Software (version 7.13)

Logos boasts a large library of books and resources with a one-stop shopping mentality. For the purposes of this research, Logos offers dynamic language tools and commentaries all at the learner's fingertips. The student can hover over a word to see its origins and click on it for further study, but the main issue is that the user must purchase resources to unlock the best assets of the software. While this is true everywhere in language study, the base language package does not include BDAG or other major linguistic tools, and the Collector's Edition of the software costs $10,000. As for functionality, Logos is impressive with the right resources and provides its user with more tools and gadgets than they may ever use. For pastors, it offers sermon outlines, PowerPoints, handouts, and other helpful tools. For academics, it offers word studies, text comparisons, and diagramming tools. One of this company's greatest benefits is its mobile application that allows the user to take much of their Logos software with them anywhere they go. The company also offers excellent online courses for its software training and language learning classes at a reasonable price. As a whole, Logos is an excellent package for anyone desiring to learn a language, and even though it can be a steep financial commitment at first, it can pay off well over the long run.

Accordance Bible Software (version 12.1.5)

Accordance made it clear that it does not normally provide "reviewer copies" of their software, but it was very interested in this dissertation and elected to participate. The layout is significantly different than most Bible software, but once the user spends enough time on the program this is not a serious issue at all. Much of Accordance's functionality is similar to Logos, but it is geared more toward Apple users. It too offers a free version and a library of resources to make the user's experience much fuller. Their format and commands have become more universal and less Apple-specific, but it is still slightly difficult for a PC user to navigate. This is also the case for

---

10. The researcher contacted each of the major Bible software companies to request a "review copy" of their software with a languages package for this purpose. Although some do not normally allow this and some declined to participate, most were happy to lend their product to such a venture.

their recently-launched mobile application, but over time, this too ought to become more universally user-friendly. Apple users get the most bang for their buck with Accordance because this was the program's original audience, but it is a strong program either way. For this research, Accordance tested well and would be a good prospect, but in the end, its Apple-focused approach makes the software difficult for many users to grasp and it is a few steps behind Logos for mobile availability.

BibleWorks 10

While BibleWorks is a major competitor in the language study department for Bible software, its representative chose not to participate in this research. Although this researcher has some access to the product, it is not the most recent version and therefore it would not provide an accurate representation for the reader.

WORDSearch 11 (version 11.0.3)

This software is currently owned by LifeWay Christian Resources and offers several packages to its users. The software starts at $40 and runs as high as $2,000 for the top-tier package. The major difference between the previous products and WORDSearch is that this software is aimed at pastors and not academics. It does offer a few language tools, but the goal is to help the pastor in his weekly sermon preparations instead of his detailed exegesis of original languages.

Other Bible Software

There are dozens of Bible software programs on the market. Unfortunately, not many of them devote a large amount of their time and resources to biblical language tools. They all make searching the biblical text easier and more productive, but for these purposes, it appears there are few from which to choose.

Task-Based Language Teaching and Chunking

The Task-Based Language Teaching (TBLT) methodology would aid the GTM process by providing smaller, more achievable goals for the student. Similar to chunking, TBLT follows the thinking that small and specific

CHAPTER 5

chunks of information are easier to remember and apply; thus, breaking a course or a unit up into these tasks can benefit the student greatly. In chapter two Mike Long identifies two different forms of tasks: target tasks and pedagogical tasks. The former is a task that is done in the language, but outside of the class, while the latter focuses on teaching tasks to be done inside the classroom. Target tasks are specifically designed for modern, living languages, and pedagogical tasks are more flexible and can be adapted to a dead language. This researcher suggests the use of pedagogical tasks as a way of breaking up the elements of NT Greek. Figure 14 depicts the recommended tasks for Exegetical Greek:

Example of Tasks (Chunking)

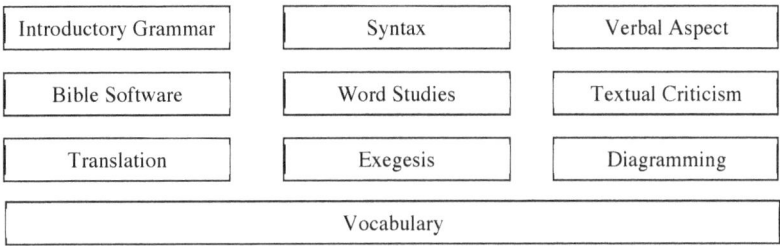

It is always good to establish these tasks early on, but it is equally important to arrange them in a meaningful and intentional manner or they are nothing more than good ideas.

Scaffolding

Scaffolding is the crucial part of instructional design. If done properly, the course will be easy to follow, easy to assess, and easy to repeat. If this step is not done with care, it could spell disaster for the students and the professor. Figure 15 presents a simplified example of how many professors use GTM scaffolding:

Example of GTM Scaffolding

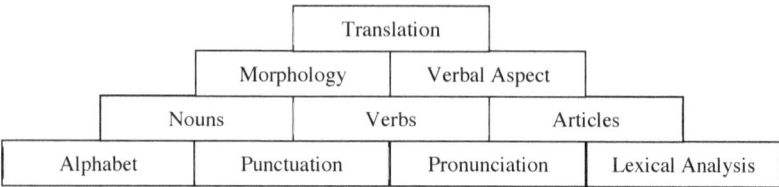

Again, this is a simplistic example, but the main idea is that the basic elements are arranged at the bottom (introduced early in the class) and the process works upward toward the more advanced skills until the main learning objective has been met (final exam). Exegetical Greek functions the same way, introducing simple elements early (e.g., grammar) and working toward the goal of exegesis.

Learning Targets

Learning Targets is built upon the same philosophy as scaffolding, but it combines chunking (or tasks) with the idea and turns it on its side:

Learning Target Illustration

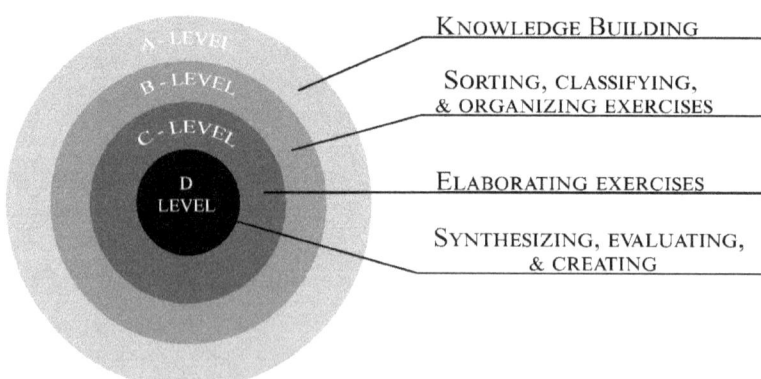

What a learning strategy like Learning Targets does is direct the student from the outside of the target toward the middle. Again, this is not that different from scaffolding. The PPP method fits very well into this system with present on the outside, practice in the middle layers, and produce on the very inside of the target. This can get considerably more technical regarding self–regulation, thinking metacognitively, goal setting, and differentiated instruction, but the objective is to introduce how the concept works and why it was chosen.

The Resulting Product: Exegetical Greek

Designing a NT Greek pedagogy requires more than restructuring the Grammar–Translation Method; it entails a new direction and an intentional approach that students can follow and use in their future ministry position. Many scholars and professors agree with Michael Heiser's thoughts from a few years ago:

> What discipline in the world embraces a 90 percent failure rate and calls it a success and the right course to follow? Swimming instruction? (90 percent drown, but at least somebody's using that skill). Explosives training? Emergency medicine? Construction engineers? Good guesses, but the answer is: seminary language training. . . . We're trying to improve what happens in the pulpit; to fix the failure in some small way. We don't think the strategy of trying to turn people into translators can provide evidence that it's actually working for the mass of seminary graduates. . . . Our concern is with the great majority of *seminary graduates* who just don't use what they were taught in their language classes. We think perhaps a tool-based approach that front-loads the payoff will work better. At the very least we could try it instead of doing the same thing over and over again and expecting different results.[11]

Why would theological institutions continue to use this broken system when it does little for the student and less for the church? Constantine Campbell says just that in his concluding thoughts from Advances in the Study of Greek:

> As fewer and fewer students elect to study Greek, as more institutions lessen their emphasis on languages, and as nearly all students struggle to retain what they've learned, Greek pedagogy has probably never been more important. It is essential that Greek instructors and professors everywhere consider how to teach Greek in the most effective manner possible. This may

---

11. Heiser, "Why Don't Scholars Understand Logos' Learn to Use Greek and Hebrew?" (sic), *NakedBible*, 11 December 2012, http://drmsh.com/scholars-understand-logos-learn-greek-hebrew/ (27 March 2018).

mean tweaking long-held practices. It may mean completely rethinking one's pedagogical approach. While we tend to cling to methods we know—which may be comfortable and safe—good teachers ought to be willing to adapt and change for the sake of their students. Ultimately, what is good for Greek students will be good for Greek, and good for the exegesis, teaching, and preaching of the Greek New Testament.[12]

The GTM process is failing the student and failing the church, and it is the responsibility of those who teach NT Greek to make the necessary changes. This proposal is not perfect, but it addresses several of the weaknesses the experts identified and it aims to connect what happens in the classroom with what the student will do in his or her ministry field.

Exegetical Greek helps the teacher to know exactly where he or she is going in each unit, in each semester, and with each student. The tasks are somewhat flexible and interchangeable depending on the student's readiness to move forward to the next task. Figure 17 provides an example of how the course would be laid out over two, three credit-hour semesters beginning at the bottom of the structure and working toward the top:[13]

Exegetical Greek Scaffolding

Exegesis	
Textual Criticism	Diagramming
Word Studies	Verbal Aspect
Syntax	
Bible Software	
Introductory Grammar	

VOCABULARY →

The basics of grammar are explained first through the use of the Bible software. This helps the student know where to find specific features and resources in the software in order to repeat this process when preparing for a Bible study on Wednesday night. The next step is to introduce syntax and explain how to use the reference resource the professor selects. The next four tasks students learn would help shape their sermon preparation and deepen

---

12. Campbell, *Advances in the Study of Greek*, 222.

13. Vocabulary is a language task, but in this illustration and the next, it will be placed outside of the structural example and applied throughout both semesters of the course. This was done to show that it will be an over-arching task through all the other tasks.

their understanding of the text every time they open their Bible. Having the professor walk through word studies, verbal aspect, textual criticism, and diagramming using the PPP method provides students with hands–on experience with these highly useful aspects of language study. Vocabulary is a key aspect of any biblical language training and is for this proposed methodology as well. The memorization of vocabulary words allows the students to identify and properly work through a chosen passage with greater ease because they would not need to constantly look words up. Although software provides the student with the ability to hover over a word to find its translation, the memorization of words used more than twenty to thirty times would greatly speed up the learning process for each of the tasks that make up this strategy. Therefore, vocabulary is displayed on these illustrations as an ongoing task that is both an active and passive process throughout the coursework as the professor sees fit.

The student learns the basic concepts from their professor and practice these exercises in class under the expert eye of the professor or in a small group. Then they produce an assignment that demonstrates their proficiency. For example, the professor explains how to conduct a proper word study and explains common errors many pastors and public speakers make in the process. He then hands out sheets of paper with a passage on it and asks the class to get into groups of three and discuss what words appear to be important in the passage and deem necessary for a detailed word study. Each group uses either their Bible software or a physical resource to produce a short word study to present to the rest of the class. The professor can then make suggestions and correct errors during these presentations before letting the students go home and produce two or three lengthy and more detailed word studies due at the next class meeting. This assignment stands as the student's assessment for this task. Each task looks different and requires its own style and resources for the student to learn practical, hands–on skills that they will use regularly. The goal is to set students up to succeed during the course and afterward in their vocational setting.

Exegetical Greek Learning Target

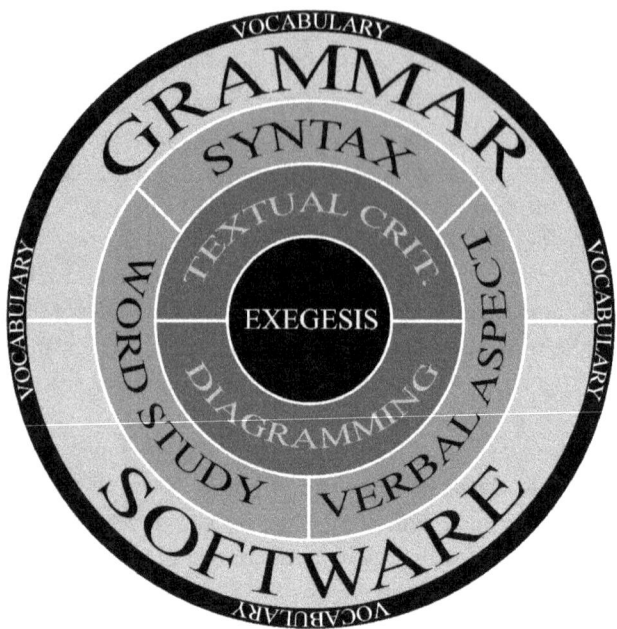

Figure 18 shows what a course looks like with the same elements and philosophies as task-based and scaffolding strategies, but with a learning target layout. There is little difference between these two structures other than shape and visual orientation; otherwise, they function the same. This design is arranged to help the student understand where the course is going and why they are learning each task in this particular order. This concept can also be applied to each language task individually as well to assist students in their understanding of each separate task and the course as a whole. Figure 19 displays how the course would break down with individual learning targets from the overall structure, to the individual tasks per semester, and then an expanded breakdown of an individual task.

CHAPTER 5

Exegetical Greek Structure

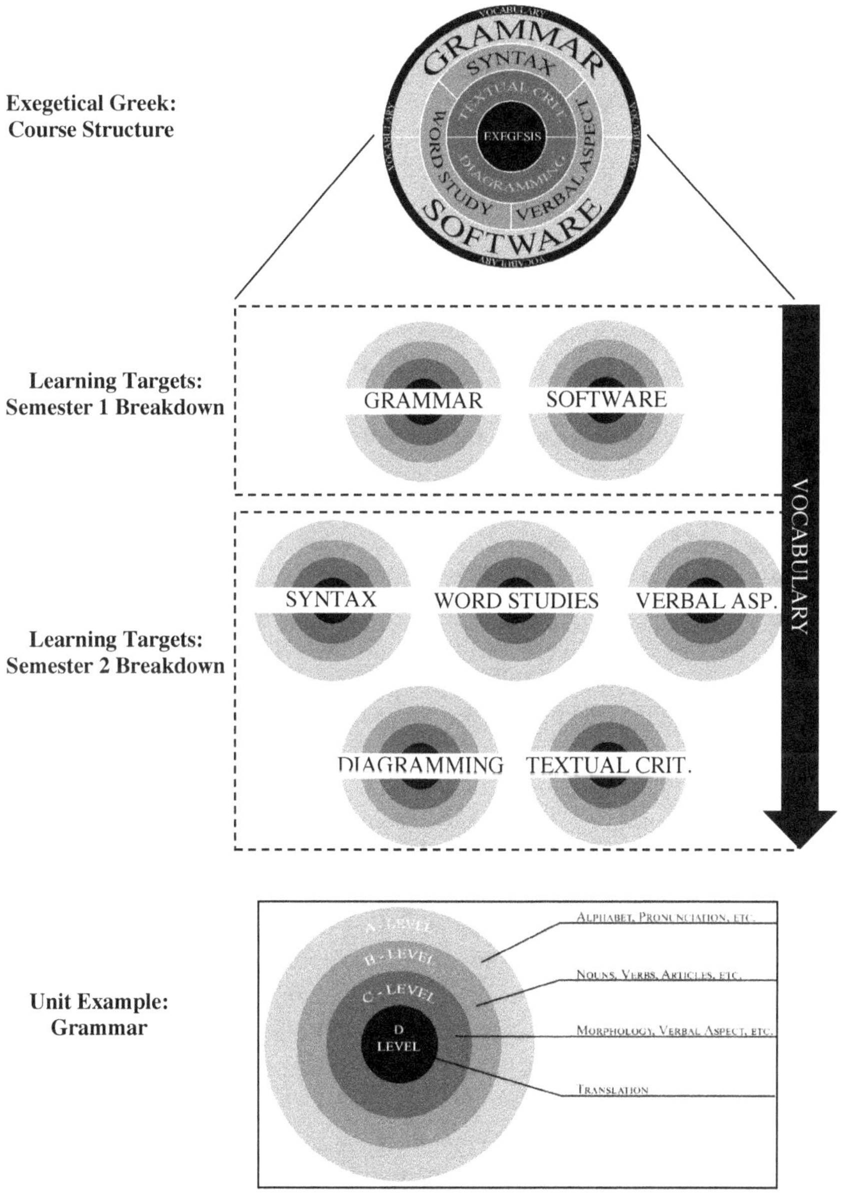

**Exegetical Greek:
Course Structure**

**Learning Targets:
Semester 1 Breakdown**

**Learning Targets:
Semester 2 Breakdown**

**Unit Example:
Grammar**

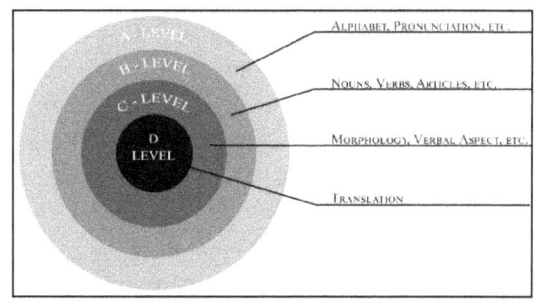

Ontological Benefits

In a format like Figure 19 displays, every element is vital and no time can be wasted. Because grammar is cut down to one semester instead of two, only the essential elements can be taught, which requires more forethought and planning. Likewise, the instructor would find it impossible to complete the process if he or she spends too much time on unnecessary details for any given task. These tasks are selected to provide the student with hands-on experience with tools and resources that will be useful immediately after completing the NT Greek training.

Application of Exegetical Greek

The Exegetical Greek pedagogical methodology is designed and arranged with two people in mind: the student and the professor. The student is served by the format, the process (PPP), and the course objective of exegesis. The professor is served in the same areas but in different ways. First of all, the format may be unique, but the content is not. There is nothing radically different in this methodology from what most NT Greek professors are already used to. Yes, these language tasks are not normally found in the first year of learning NT Greek, but many of their core principles can be found in how most Greek courses are taught. Lexical analysis is typically included in grammatical morphology and therefore word studies would not be a reach for a first-year student. Similarly, elementary explanations of verbal aspect and textual criticism are both introduced in many early Greek classrooms and can simply be expanded for the student. This is the case for each of the language tasks listed above. In the end, this pedagogy allows the professor to teach the students what he or she deems necessary.

What might be the most unique aspect of this teaching methodology is that it is designed to let the professor be the professional. For instance, the teacher chooses what he or she covers in the grammar task and how they explain it when tying it into the exegesis task. Also, the teacher gets to choose and arrange the second-semester tasks however he or she sees fit. Although syntax is a logical next step after grammar, the professor may elect to begin with verbal aspect to introduce an exegetical element early into the second semester to provide the student with much-needed motivation. In some ways this pedagogy can be an à la carte methodology that encourages the professor to be creative while exploring which format fits his or her personal interests. Additionally, some schools require more credit-hours per semester for biblical languages than they do for other courses. For example,

Moody Bible Institute only offers four-credit-hour NT Greek courses for its undergraduate students (eight total credit-hours for the first year), and Bethel University requires seven and a half credit-hours for its first two semesters of NT Greek. Institutions that still only require two semesters, but offer more time per semester, can either expand their tasks to fill the extra time or add tasks they believe the student needs on top of the ones suggested earlier. The professor would no longer be limited by the six credit-hours that many listed as a weakness. Instead they would have the room to develop a scope and sequence for non-academic students in their own class and eliminate the rigid structure that GTM imposes.

This final point of application may be the most important one for the student and the professor alike. Stephen Krashen expresses three key aspects of language success from the student's perspective. He calls them "affect filters":

> (1) Motivation. Performers with high motivation generally do better in second language acquisition (usually, but not always, "integrative").
>
> (2) Self-Confidence. Performers with self-confidence and a good self-image tend to do better in second language acquisition.
>
> (3) Anxiety. Low anxiety appears to be conducive to second language acquisition, whether measured as personal or classroom anxiety.[14]

While instructors cannot control their students' personal lives or mental states, they can control what happens in their classroom. Each of these three "filters" will be addressed separately next, but it is worth remembering that 62 percent of the surveyed experts agree that the professor holds at least half of the responsibility for the success of the course.

Motivation

Multiple experts agree that they see themselves as the cheerleader or encourager for the student as they learn Greek. Many professors take it upon themselves to remind the students often that although the work is difficult, it will pay off in the end. If a primary factor for student success is that the student receives proper motivation throughout the learning process, then the professor needs to prioritize time in each class to give them a fresh

---

14. Krashen, *Principles and Practice*, 31.

reminder of why NT Greek is important now and in their future ministry. Often the student does not see the innate benefits of learning biblical languages and therefore views the required credits as perfunctory and possibly even a waste of their time and money. The Exegetical Greek pedagogy is designed to show the student the purpose, direction, and ultimate goal of the course from the beginning. GTM only shows the student a large number of minor steps leading to translation proficiency that the student, and apparently the experts as well, would describe as "unrealistic" in their regular ministry use. It is crucial that the student knows the end–goal of the course, what the educational plan is to get there, and how it can apply to their vocation. Translation is not a learning objective; it is a task. It is a piece to a larger language skill that comes through syntax and exegesis, but many students do not elect to take those advanced courses and thus learn only the task of translation with no operational NT Greek language proficiency. Professors must properly motivate their students if they want to see success and practical application of Greek in the church.

Self–Confidence

The term self-confidence alone suggests the professor has nothing to do with this "filter," but that is not completely accurate. Many people gain self–confidence from others' words and actions; spouses and parents provide great examples of this. Professional athletes and academics alike often point to their parents or dedicate their books to a parent or spouse who instilled confidence in them to keep pushing or pursuing their dreams. A professor can do the same in many ways. Encouragement is always a great trait in a teacher; it helps the student feel better about their efforts, even if they are not ultimately successful. Volunteering a wrong answer in class can be met with shame or a balanced response of correction and reassurance. Correspondingly, volunteering a correct answer can be met with a simple acknowledgment or verbal praise. Poorly done assignments often have nothing more than a grade written on them, but what that student may need is feedback and encouragement to either keep trying or an offer to help the student with their shortcomings. If a student believes someone else has confidence in them, they may develop stronger self–confidence from that belief. Academics are just like sports in that the participant needs to be self–confident to succeed. Therefore, coaches and professors alike need to be able to provide the appropriate balance of positive feedback and corrective encouragement. Often, if students are properly motivated, they will have fewer struggles with self-confidence in that area of their lives, and they will experience less anxiety as well.

Anxiety

Anxiety often comes with the unknown. Suspenseful movies are built on keeping information from the viewer until the filmmaker believes the audience's anxiety level is at its apex. Surgery and gambling both build anxiety because the outcome is uncertain. For a student, anxiety comes from not knowing what will be on a quiz or test or from hoping they did well on an assignment. One way a professor can limit this anxiety is by revealing all of the questions that will be on a given quiz or test, but educators discourage this practice. The student will know exactly what to study, but they will also know what not to study, and may consider the leftover information worthless. Instead, the professor can eliminate much of the needless anxiety by offering performance-based assessments rather than quizzes, tests, and exams. Stony Brook University provides a well-thought-out explanation of the differences between tests and assessments, and the school boils the difference down to a lesser focus on grades and a greater focus on understood knowledge.[15] Exegetical Greek uses assignments at the end of each task instead of tests or exams because it allows the student to display their understanding of the information in a practical, direct manner. This can reduce or eliminate rote memorization in the majority of learning NT Greek, aside from vocabulary. The exegetical paper at the end of the six credit-hours of NT Greek functions as a capstone project that incorporates every language task the professor selected and taught in his course in place of a cumulative exam. This capstone assessment shows the professor where the student's strengths and weaknesses are in each task and throughout the entire language learning process. It also allows the student to apply each language task toward an exegetical assignment that will be repeatable, in a more abridged fashion, during sermon and Bible study preparation. This reduces anxiety during the writing of the capstone assignment, which greatly improves their ability to think clearly and perform better.

It is worth noting that although nothing in this pedagogy is radically different for the professor, it would be for the student. Through personal conversations with dozens of professors and New Testament doctoral students over the last two years of conducting this research, one thing has been

---

15. Stony Brook University, "Understanding the Difference Between Assessment and Testing," *The Faculty Center*, https://facultycenter.stonybrook.edu/articles/understanding-difference-between-assessment-and-testing (27 March 2018).

made very clear: academics do not like change. The most often repeated sentiment has been some form of, "The current model worked for me, it should work for everyone, they just need to study as hard as I did." The problem with that type of thinking is that it dispels the idea that people learn differently and that some people have a natural propensity for languages while others do not have that ability. If every student had the same learning style, teaching would be easy and schools would be equally successful at all levels. This is certainly not the case. Also, if everyone had an equal ability to learn a second language, this research would not be necessary because there would be no pedagogical issues to analyze in the first place. Is the argument that Michael Jordan is the greatest basketball player ever based on the premise that no one has ever practiced as hard as he did before games? Was Billy Graham the most revered evangelist simply because no one has ever read the Bible more than he did? Of course not. These men embodied an innate, God-given quality that other men did not have. So, why do some assume that this is not the case with academics or language learning? The Grammar-Translation Methodology is responsible for teaching many men and women biblical languages for many years. Many of these men and women have gone on to become successful professors and some even served as the experts in this dissertation's research. But, as mentioned earlier, the seminary was designed to serve the church, not itself. GTM may be successful at training academically gifted professors and authors for the seminary, but what about the church? If those believers who are gifted for a vocational ministry behind a pulpit, leading a weekly Bible study, or sharing their faith on the mission field are required to learn biblical languages from a pedagogy that is not suited for those ministry fields, then they will be ill-prepared and cheated of their money and time.

The survey results are clear: GTM, as a broad-spectrum pedagogy, does not work for non-academic students in theological education in the twenty-first century. They fear the idea of the work and doubt its usefulness in their vocation. This needs to change. The Exegetical Greek approach may not be the solution to the larger problem; it is designed to address specific issues found in the current model and to provide the learner with a focused approach. But it is an attempt to right the ship. More attempts need to be made and more research needs to be done if this generation of theological educators desire to see biblical languages used in the church for the glory of God.

Limitations

This research was delimited in several areas to ensure that the topic could be covered well without spreading out the data too thin or squeezing in too much. Unfortunately, that meant leaving out certain areas of research and some angles could not be explored due to the desired focus. It would have been helpful to survey more experts. While fifty experts were contacted, several either did not respond or declined to participate. A 64 percent response rate for a survey is generally very good, and for the candidate pool being considered, it is very good. However, having 100 or more completed surveys would have produced a stronger data pool from which to draw results. Additionally, surveying an equal number of alumni who have taken NT Greek at these experts' schools would have added a helpful dimension. But since every school offers multiple Greek professors, pedagogical strategies, textbooks, and formats to their students, it would have been incredibly difficult to determine a fair representation of equal students to survey. Lastly, the original preference was to include some of the more popular textbook authors in the field. Because David Black is the advising professor for the research, he was not available, but William Mounce, S. M. Baugh, and N. Clayton Croy were specifically sought out for participation. Croy's contact information was not available, Baugh politely declined due to previous commitments, and Mounce did not feel that he was a good fit for the dissertation topic. Therefore, although the experts who did participate were all excellent choices, the four top-selling textbook authors in the field were not part of the survey participants.

Suggestions for Further Research

Several areas of research would significantly help improve the findings and narrow the possible cause behind the lackluster use of biblical languages in everyday ministry. Possible additional research processes could include:

- Perform an analysis and assessment of the use of GTM in OT Hebrew.
- Perform a large-format, longitudinal survey of students who have taken NT Greek courses to find out if they currently use their Greek language skills.
- Engage the institutional leadership of several theological schools about their choice of the scope and sequence of their degree programming, where biblical language study fits, and why.

- Design a survey that compares the student retention rates of on–site NT Greek courses and online courses.

- Research the possible structure, pedagogy, application, and use of a Living Language approach in NT Greek in theological education.

- Research whether biblical language courses would be better taught on their own unique semester schedule rather than forced to fit into the same format as all other courses.

- Explore the possibilities of mixing biblical language courses with hermeneutics and/or homiletics to increase retention and usability in ministry vocations.

- Discover if the highly practical PPP method of teaching can be implemented in online courses to improve their success rates.

Chapter Summary

In an effort to avoid belaboring the point, this summary will be brief and direct. Biblical languages are a key component to faithfully understanding the Word of God, therefore they need to be taught and taught well. Until now, there have been little to no efforts to determine if the pedagogical methodology being instituted for this subject matter is producing desirable results. Anecdotal evidence pointed to a lack of continuity and poor retention for ministry use. This expert survey has revealed that those anecdotal suspicions were correct. GTM, as a methodology, is failing the student and desperately requires bolstering through modern SLA research and cutting–edge educational practices. NT Greek needs more than a fresh approach, it needs a well–designed and intentional approach that places the success of the student and a vocational focus at the forefront of its pedagogical design.

Appendix 1

List of Experts

The list of voluntary, expert participants along with the names of their employers at the time of the survey are listed alphabetically (by last name) below:[1]

Name:	School/Corporation:
Alan Bandy	Oklahoma Baptist University
Ken Berding	Talbot School of Theology
Jeannine Brown	Bethel University
Randall Buth	University of the Holy Land
Con Campbell	Trinity Evangelical Divinity School
David A. Croteau	Columbia International University
Delio DelRio	New Orleans Baptist Theological Seminary
F. David Farnell	The Master's Seminary
John Harvey	Columbia International University
Michael S. Heiser	FaithLife Corporation (Logos)
Mark House	Reformed Theological Seminary
Karen Jobes	Wheaton College
Markus Klausli	Columbia International University
Karl Kutz	Multnomah University
Samuel Lamerson	Knox Theological Seminary
Justin Langford	Louisiana College
Ben Merkle	Southeastern Baptist Theological Seminary
Gerald Peterman	Moody Bible Institute
Robert Plummer	Southern Baptist Theological Seminary
Stanley Porter	McMaster Divinity College
Charles Quarles	Southeastern Baptist Theological Seminary

---

1. Some of the participants opted to list their answers as "Anonymous" in the results, but they were notified that they would be listed here for accountability.

Name:	School/Corporation:
Maurice Robinson	Southeastern Baptist Theological Seminary
Gary Shogren	Seminario ESEPA (Escuela de Estudios Pastorales)
Mitzi Smith	Ashland Theological Seminary
Mark Strauss	Bethel University
John Terveen	Multnomah University
A. Chadwick Thornhill	Liberty University
William C. Varner	The Master's Seminary
James W. Voelz	Concordia Seminary
Dan Wallace	Dallas Theological Seminary
David Woodall	Moody Theological Seminary
Danny Zacharias	Acadia Divinity College

Appendix 2

GTM Expert Survey Transcript

Survey Inquiry Email

The initial email that was sent to each of the potential experts was worded as follows:

Good morning [participant's name and title],

I pray that your semester is going well. My name is David R Miller, and I am a doctoral student at Southeastern Baptist Theological Seminary in North Carolina studying under Dr. David Alan Black. I am currently working on a dissertation which will analyze NT Greek pedagogy in theological institutions, and I would like your assistance in my research. I am researching some of the current methodologies being used and determining if an improved direction should be pursued in light of current educational trends and ministry application. There has been very little research done in their field which is why I am seeking your help. I have decided to go directly to the source of this issue by contacting several experienced professors, influential authors, and content experts. You are one of the professionals who I believe can provide outstanding feedback for this study.

What I am asking of you is to consent to participate in my short survey which will be used as an instrument to inform much of where biblical language pedagogy currently is and where any possible deficiencies may be that need to be addressed. The format of the survey will be as follows:

PART 1: A short biographical portion (You can choose to be anonymous in the results, but I would still need the information for my own professional and academic accountability).

PART 2: Your thoughts on the popular Grammar-Translation Method of teaching NT Greek.

PART 3: Your experienced feedback about teaching NT Greek in a theological setting (I value your time and do not wish to take more than a few minutes).

(Optional) PART 4: A supplementary opinion section (This would only be used if you would like to provide me with any further thoughts or resources on this subject).

(Optional) PART 5: Recommending any additional experts in this field who you believe may be beneficial to this work.

I understand that you are a very busy person and that your time is valuable. Thus, my aim is to request as little of your time as possible. But, the truth is, your professional opinion is quite valuable to my research, and I would greatly appreciate any time you could spare for this work.

If you would please, reply to this email whether you would like to participate in this survey or not (so that I will be aware of your position and will not bother those who choose not to participate). As a side note, this is NOT a blanket email that has been sent to hundreds of professors. I have selected a small number of professionals to participate in this study, and you are one of those few that I am requesting assistance from, please consider your participation prayerfully.

Thank you very much for your time and consideration,

David R Miller

Actual Survey

The actual survey that was sent to each of the participants worded as follows:

PART 1: Demographics:
Name—
Contact email—
Current employer—
Number of years Teaching/Publishing/Advising NT Greek materials—
Primary textbook(s) used—
Do you wish to remain anonymous in the paper? (Note: I will still need your info for my personal/academic references, but your information will not be shared publicly in any way.)—

APPENDIX 2

PART 2: In my research, I am performing a S.W.O.T. (Strengths, Weaknesses, Opportunities, Threats) analysis of the GTM as it is used in modern-day NT Greek pedagogy through an educational framework. I would greatly appreciate your opinions on the following questions related to this process.

Definition: Grammar-Translation Method (GTM) is "a traditional technique for foreign-language teaching based on explicit instruction in the grammatical analysis of the target language and translation of sentences from the native language into the target language and vice versa."

http://www.dictionary.com/browse/grammar-translation-method

—Please list up to five (5) STRENGTHS that you have experienced with any form of the GTM through your education in and/or teaching of NT Greek.

—Please list up to five (5) WEAKNESSES that you have experienced with any form of the GTM through your education in and/or teaching of NT Greek.

PART 3: In addition, I will also be researching modern Second Language Acquisition methods to assess whether they could benefit the biblical language learning process in our modern theological education system. Please give your personal views regarding the questions below.

—In your opinion, why should students in theological education take NT Greek courses?

—When speaking of biblical language courses, whom do you believe holds the major responsibility for the course material ultimately being successful (professor, student, institutional methodology, etc.)? Why?

—What are the educational objectives for your first and second-semester Greek courses or personal textbook? (i.e., What do you want students to know, understand, and be able to accomplish by the end of their second semester)

—Do you have an instrument or process for measuring whether these educational objectives have been met? If so, how is this done?

—Do you believe that two semesters of NT Greek (6 credit hours is the most common Master of Divinity requirement) is sufficient to accomplish the objectives that you listed above? Why or why not?

—Do you believe the majority of students look forward to taking biblical language classes? Why or why not?

—In your opinion, what percentage of your students go on to study Greek beyond what their specific program requires (ex., Greek 3, exegetical courses, advanced degrees, etc.)?

—Do you believe the majority of students go on to use their NT Greek training after graduation in their regular ministry? Why or why not?

—Do you believe theological institutions should require more or less biblical language courses at the bachelors or masters levels? Please explain your reasoning.

—If you could make ANY changes to the current pedagogical process of teaching Greek (ex., Grammar-Translation Method), what would they be and why?

(Optional) PART 4: If you have any further comments or suggestions for my research that you believe would be helpful or clarifying, please do not hesitate to add them here. This would include your further opinion, personal experience, resource titles, recommended contacts, related materials, etc.

(Optional) PART 5: If you know of any other NT Greek professional who might be willing to provide useful information for this research, please send me their contact information, and I will seek their participation. Thank you very much for your valuable time!

Appendix 3

GTM Expert Survey Response Transcripts

The exact answers from all of the participants on the GTM expert survey are provided below. The formatting and instructional matter has been removed to save space and the only editing that has been done was to fix spelling errors. Those eleven participants who chose to have their answers kept anonymous have been listed as such and all the participants' answers have also been placed in random order to protect those anonymous people.

GTM Strengths

Michael Heiser

> Honestly, I see little benefit. To me all it does is ready people for second year (if they perform well), but that needs review after a summer anyway. Unless a student is going to do advanced work (doctoral) they aren't going to keep reviewing forms and vocab once in ministry. They don't have to because of available tools, and won't have the time. And they have translations already. That's just the reality, and instead of inventing another reality we need to recognize this.

Anonymous 9

> The possibility of a solid understanding of the way Koine Greek works
>
> Since Koine Greek is not a living language, GTM fulfills a narrower purpose of helping students to read (vs. produce) the language
>
> Learning how Greek works can prevent students from using Greek in ministry (e.g., sermons) inappropriately (it can provide a solid linguistic foundation)

> GTM can be combined with more inductive approaches; i.e., getting students reading to learn the language (vs. learning the language to read) earlier in the process

Charles Quarles

> The grammatical analysis enables students to see striking differences between the Greek language and the English language and understand the nuances of constructions for which no direct English parallel exists.
>
> The grammatical analysis enables students to understand features of the NT text which are difficult or even impossible to express fully in English translation
>
> Students who understand how the language works can tackle any Greek text. Those who merely memorize English translations for phrases will not be able to translate Greek constructions not yet committed to memory.
>
> Most students will not learn to think in Greek. Thus ability to translate the text into their native language is necessary.

Anonymous 6

> Basic understanding of a language
>
> Basic understand of grammar; enhancement of understanding
>
> Basic improvement in observation skills of language
>
> Basic improvement of original language correcting bad theology
>
> Basic improvement of understanding translations

Con Campbell

> Adult learners tend to think structurally, so a balance of deductive and inductive learning is helpful
>
> It closes gaps such as rarer forms, etc.
>
> Reading biblical text as it appears (not just in example sentences) greatly aids the inductive learning process
>
> It can be studied quickly
>
> It is easy to review learned material

Anonymous 7

> Translation from the Greek text itself (as in Mounce's Workbook), rather than in made-up sentences (as in Machen/McCartney) helps to keep students encouraged. Students often comment about how exciting it is to actually be reading the Bible in Greek from the earliest weeks of the semester.
>
> The GTM conforms to many of the students' expectations for language-learning. They perceive immediate similarities between their Greek-learning experience and the experiences they had of learning (or trying to learn) other languages (Spanish, French, German, sometimes Latin) in high school.
>
> A student can move quickly into interaction with biblical Greek, which is most of their motivation for learning Greek anyway, without having to learn what will seem superfluous terminology as in an immersion/speak-and-listen program (think of words like "ball," or "fun," or "email," which do not have a parallel in the Greek New Testament).

Mark House

> Students are enriched as they see nuances of the text "come alive" through their study of the text in its original modes of expression.
>
> Students have a better grasp of the interpretive options of the NT texts they are analyzing as opposed to accepting those accepted by a given version of the NT.
>
> Students have an increased ability to interact with commentaries and other study tools that discuss aspects of the Greek text.
>
> Students gains a better grasp of English as they compare it with the grammatical modes of expression of NT Greek. This increased facility in English benefits them in all disciplines and particularly in learning to communicate for ministry.
>
> Students learn to think more logically and systematically as they grasp how thoughts are expressed through language.
>
> Students develop a stronger sense of competency and authority as they handle the biblical text, no longer being at the mercy of the decisions of the translators.

Anonymous 1

> It provides complete units of thought that are not too intimidating for the learner.
>
> It is easy to modify sentences to give practice for inflection of endings.
>
> It's easy to modify sentences to introduce and give practice for new vocabulary.
>
> It's easy to build upon the foundation of sentence structure.

Samuel Lamerson

> The use of both inductive and deductive learning is very helpful.
>
> Students translating in class shows me who is falling behind.
>
> It is logical with a starting place.
>
> It helps the students understand their own language.
>
> Students end the year with some ability to read Greek.

Mitzi Smith

> Students learn better English grammar from the instructor (not the textbooks).
>
> Students become aware of the difficulties or complexities of translation.
>
> Students become more aware of details.
>
> Can increase student confidence in language acquisition generally.
>
> Students become aware of the politics of translation and that options exist that are only apparent when one is familiar with the Greek.

Alan Bandy

> It enables the learner to have a framework for acquiring basic forms and vocabulary.
>
> It provides a systematic and categorized approach to learning the syntax of an ancient language.
>
> It develops a skill set when it comes to translating the Greek text, which is different from a conversational approach to a modern approach.
>
> Since Greek is a highly inflected language with many tense-forms and cases, it allows a learner to acquire a familiarity with every form within one year of study.

It enhances the learner's awareness of English grammar to make them better students of their native language.

Justin Langford

It reinforces grammatical concepts in one's primary language.

It provides an explicit framework for better understanding one's primary language by forcing students to verbalize grammatical concepts/rules in both the target and native languages.

Anonymous 2

Logical or systematic approach that works for many people.

Many tools have been developed for using this system.

It is the most popular system so there is continuity from one professor to another.

It has stood the test of time. Other methods have been tried but don't seem to last.

It worked for the professor, so it can also work for his/her students.

Dan Wallace

Improved analytical skills

Increased ability to think through the Greek way of looking at language

Appreciation of falsifiable hypothesis in doing exegesis

Method learned for determining meaning of words, sentences, paragraphs

Ability to think critically about the Greek NT

Anonymous 5

Knowledge of syntax

Ability to parse forms

Robert Plummer

Textbooks designed this way

Fits with most students' educational backgrounds

Good for realistic amount of time students spend learning language

I'm comfortable with the method, mostly

Anonymous 8

> Immediate access to original language
>
> Progress toward goal of exegetical use
>
> Concentration upon the most important factors for use
>
> Results in a relatively short amount of time
>
> Language reinforcement

Maurice Robinson

> Learning vocabulary
>
> Gaining knowledge regarding declensions and conjugations in sentence-based context
>
> Empowering students actually to read portions of the Greek NT quickly and with comprehension.

Anonymous 10

> Early memorization helps to avoid looking up forms later on
>
> It is systematic in nature, allowing focus on topic at a time
>
> Relatively easy to formulate Greek translation sentences that highlight the topic

Danny Zacharias

> Forces the students to slow down
>
> Helps the students to understand English grammar
>
> Helps them appreciate the interpretive decisions that need to be made in translation
>
> Students learn to appreciate the variety of grammatical functions of primary and secondary word types

Anonymous 3

> Allows students to focus on the ultimate objectives: reading, translation, and exegesis
>
> Remains text-based
>
> Does not require students to become fluent in speaking the language

APPENDIX 3

Mark Strauss

> There is a good measure of objectivity in using the grammatical method
>
> It allows for a systematic and mechanical analysis of the text
>
> There are a wealth of tools available for the grammatical method developed over the years

Anonymous 11

> Understanding of points of emphasis in the text
>
> Genuine understanding of the grammar of both source language and the target translation language as critical to sound semantic values being assigned
>
> Student sense of confidence that they truly are engaging the text in interpretation as it was meant to be understood by the author
>
> Sense of the 'cultural' backdrop to the language and how ideas are expressed
>
> It does require students learn English, often for the first time in any serious way

A. Chadwick Thornhill

> Structure
>
> Generally moves from simpler/easier concepts to more difficult
>
> Emphasis upon memorization/recall
>
> Allows for concepts to be introduced one by one
>
> Frequent assessment helps reinforce learning

David Croteau

> It helps students to learn their native language grammar better
>
> It is a very systematic way to teach a language
>
> Success can be measured very concretely
>
> There are many, many resources to help with this method of teaching

William Varner

> Students understand WHY things are said in a certain way
>
> Prepares students for more detailed examinations of the language

James Voelz

It is basically what the procedure is for exegetical work with the NT text for Bible classes and sermons for seminary students.

It causes one to pay attention to nuances, including small nuances, of the target language

It helps students become aware of the nature of their own, receptor language.

David Woodall

It gives the students a feel for Greek that will keep them from some grammatical fallacies. Just like learning Algebra in High School trains the mind to think in a certain way (granting the fact that they might not every use it in real life), learning Greek trains the mind even if they do not keep up on the vocabulary and forms.

Students are able to understand exegetical commentaries and the best exegetical literature that is available.

Markus Klausli

Students make it through the material

Students have clear goals for learning

Students learn in with a manageable structure

Students learn a method for ancient language learning that can be applied elsewhere (e.g., Hebrew, Latin)

Randall Buth

It can be taught by people who do not control the language and who cannot speak even basic sentences in class.

It uses the meta-language of many pieces of 'help literature'.

Anonymous 4

Explicit systematic instruction is imperative for students to create an efficient and comprehensive framework for understanding Greek. It enables rapid assimilation of concepts leading to the comprehension and translation competency that is the primary goal of exegetical programs.

Translation—Long-term feedback from alumni indicates that students with a broad vocabulary base and broad exposure to translation are the most likely to continue using Greek after college or seminary. By doing so they develop a facility in reading that allows them to use Greek without becoming labor intensive.

Composition from English into Greek—While helpful on a basic level for learning noun and verb formation, overuse detracts from reading ability and an awareness of Greek syntax and idiom derived from broad reading.

Delio DelRio

GTM requires a more deductive approach which results in time-saving

Another strength would be the potential for covering a larger amount of complex rules/grammar

GTM Weaknesses

Anonymous 2

Too much memorization of paradigms.

Learning of material that is not really necessary (relevant, common).

Not enough focus on why learning Greek is helpful.

Many students struggle with acquiring/memorizing a huge amount of information in a short period of time.

Too much time translating and not enough time spent on how to use their knowledge of Greek.

Alan Bandy

Students struggle to retain much of the rules governing form and function of the various parts of speech.

Students are not able to speak or read the language as a living language so they miss how to construct Greek sentences as well as proper pronunciation. In other words, a Greek speaker has an intuitive understanding of the language.

The GTM method does not work well with every student in the way they learn and process language so some students don't learn it well enough to use Greek effectively.

It heavily relies of memorization and repetition. While it is one of the best ways to learn, it is not necessarily the most engaging and exciting ways to acquire a new language.

Depending on the textbook, it does not give students enough to translate both nouns and verbs quickly enough.

David Woodall

Every year students seem to have a decreased ability to memorize even basic material. Students come with a poor background in English grammar (unless they are International students). This makes it very difficult to teach with GTM.

It is an artificial approach to language learning.

Very few students see to continue on with review of the material or a robust use of it (But this could be said for may courses in a higher education curriculum—I was a Chemistry major in college and used very little of that material in 10 years as a chemist.)

Anonymous 9

Many students who take the language sequence do not retain enough from GTM to use much in subsequent settings (e.g., ministry)

Learning the complexities of Greek grammar explicitly vs. implicitly (i.e., inductively through usage)

The typically concentrated way Greek is taught and then (often) not followed up with more required usage

Anonymous 6

Too much emphasis on unnecessary details; need BIG picture to see details

Too much emphasis on timed quizzes; give students time to complete

Too much emphasis on moving quickly over significant details

Not enough encouragement to see how language can make a difference in understanding theology

Not enough time dedicated to subject period

APPENDIX 3

Con Campbell

> Speaking and reading aloud is usually downplayed
>
> Rewards motivated students, but can be disheartening for less engaged students
>
> Usually does not require generation of Greek sentences/language, but only one way translation
>
> Can be boring if the instructor is boring

Maurice Robinson

> More time needs to be allotted to beginning Greek classes (4 sem. hrs. each half-year term would be preferable).
>
> The goal of vocabulary learning should be 1000 key words, as in Metzger's Lexical Aids book, which was based on a 17-week semester; present shorter semesters allow only about 800 words to be learned.
>
> Too many students attempt to take more hours per semester (e.g. 15+) than they should when taking a beginning language course (e.g. 12), mostly in an attempt to speed through a M.Div. program and to graduate.

Anonymous 3

> Requires large amounts of rote memorization
>
> Requires adequate understanding of grammar
>
> Can over-emphasize analysis of details at the expense of understanding the larger picture

Michael Heiser

> Requires memorization maintenance to be of any use.
>
> The above presumes a graduate / pastor will have the time to maintain translation level competency. That's contrary to reality and we all know it.
>
> Unless you get to a third year Greek course, you don't get sustained experience in exegesis (i.e., actually using your Greek). Second memorization of syntactical categories isn't exegetical proficiency. I took Greek syntax three times at three different schools—it was all the same. Memorize the categories. That isn't book study.

When people don't have the time to retain translation proficiency after graduation and then do fine in ministry, this method teaches them they really didn't need those Greek classes.

Anonymous 1

Made-up sentences for pedagogical purposes soon become boring.

But the NT is too familiar to most students to provide a true exercise of their Greek skills. I often used sentences from the LXX, with appropriately modified vocab.

Sentence level translating implicitly trains students for an atomistic view of language that has to be undone when later teaching exegesis and the importance of context.

Only the biblical languages are taught by focusing on one specific book (the Hebrew Old and Greek New Testaments). That is an artificial and somewhat myopic way to learn a language.

Robert Plummer

Not the way language is best learned

Perhaps "settles" for a lower level of proficiency among students

If not supplemented with some creative methods, it can fall a bit flat in inspiring students.

Samuel Lamerson

If the work is not kept up, ability to translate is quickly lost.

Students do not speak the language; thus, they don't really understand it.

Because of the closed corpus of the NT, vocab is limited.

Students cannot read very much of the more difficult books.

Due to time constraints and ultimate goal, there is very little translation from English to Greek.

Justin Langford

It can become so rigid of a method that students sometimes fail to see the significance of the approach.

APPENDIX 3

It is not the best way to teach a purely inductive method of learning language.

Markus Klausli

Students who get behind or are slow learners tend to remain behind and do never catch up

It teaches language learning as "decoding"

It makes Greek feel less like a language and more like a topic that needs to be mastered

Learning the GNT outside the realm of ancient Gk in general is efficient but lacks serious context beneficial for other aspects of exegesis (Word Study, Syntax analysis)

Many approaches to GTM break up the language in many small pieces and don't put them back again. The first year grammars that I have used, tend not to be useful as reference grammars.

Anonymous 5

GTM makes knowledge of Greek and adjunct to our knowledge of English

GTM makes Greek very forgettable

With GTM one does not 'read' Greek by any real definition of the verb 'read,' rather one decodes and translates.

David Crotcau

The emphasis on memorization can be overwhelming

Students usually fail to get a "feel" for the language

The categories we create to teach the language are many times imposed upon the language, not derived from an inductive study of the language

Most students do not continue using the language

Delio DelRio

Perhaps too teacher-centered

Passive students

Not inductive enough (though admittedly more difficult to accomplish in deductive learning.

Anonymous 8

>Assumes knowledge of language not held by students
>
>Intense learning and material to master
>
>Incremental knowledge accumulation not typical of current learning techniques for other subjects

Charles Quarles

>In my early years as an instructor, I used Summer's Essentials which required the memorization of a large number of paradigms. Students seemed to perform well on exercises and tests, but forgot much of their Greek soon after the course was completed because these paradigms were packed into their short-term memory. Using Mounce's Basics of Biblical Greek helped enormously since Mounce introduces students to elementary principles of Greek morphology and greatly reduces the amount of memorization necessary to learn and use Greek.
>
>In Elementary Greek students are given the impression that they can translate the Greek text based solely on familiarity with vocabulary and grammar. However, a good understanding of syntax is necessary for clear, precise, and exegetically helpful translation.

Dan Wallace

>Vocabulary skills
>
>Intuitive sense of how Greek works
>
>Reading
>
>Speaking
>
>Translating

Anonymous 10

>Mainly, I have to constantly urge them to review what they have learned

Mitzi Smith

>Does not account for individual or unique competencies of students or lack thereof for studying languages.

APPENDIX 3   173

Need less focus on rote memorization and more on identifying patterns.

False assumption that students who take one year of Greek will be able to use it with competency.

Never sufficient practice exercises in textbooks to develop competency. Teacher must be prepared to augment in some way.

Textbooks assume a certain level of student efficiency with grammar that is usually absent.

Anonymous 11

Tendency to drive students crazy with all the variations on the 'rules' in both morphology and in grammar/syntax . . . nature of languages, right, yet still tends to irritate students and make them impatient with learning when there are so many exceptions to the 'rule'

A loss of the sense of 'flow' in reading the text . . . unless addressed

Mark Strauss

Many students have very poor knowledge of English grammar and so find it difficult to grasp Greek grammar

Memorization of forms is very difficult for students

The payoff is delayed as students have to learn a great deal before they can use the tools effectively

Retention is difficult and many students do not continue to use Greek.

Randall Buth

It gives a false sense of "knowing" the language, especially in comparison to what literature majors have in other literatures/languages.

The metalanguage tags (e.g. "present infinitive") take on a reality that may be against the language and that skew the language when the student remembers pieces of it later on (e.g., there is no "present" time in the infinitive, despite the name present infinitive).

Thinking in the language is derailed by interposing algorithms for many words (e.g. [α+ω, α+ειν] ἀγαπάω ἀγαπάειν instead of ἀγαπῶ ἀγαπᾶν)

Practitioners with 20-30 years of work in the GTM system cannot think in the language, they cannot communicate with each other in the language the way literature profs can communicate in other languages.

William Varner

Focuses at times too much on micro-analysis to neglect of macro-analysis

Is not the way we learn language naturally

James Voelz

It can lead to students not seeing the forest for the trees, i.e., details can overwhelm if the teacher is not aware of this and teach so as to see the forest.

Relatedly, the teacher must be aware of the danger of teaching a lot of "just in case" morphology, i.e., introducing rare forms "just in case" they come up but realistically do not.

Anonymous 7

The GTM approach is often overly-focused upon grammar. Really, language consists only of speaking, listening, reading, and writing. Grammar is simply a description of patterns that appear in the language to help with the learning process. But many students tend to think of grammar as being equivalent to the language itself.

Since most of us using the GTM focus upon reading/translation alone (and do nothing with speaking and listening, and usually not much with writing/producing the language), the reinforcement that is usually gained from engaging in all four activities (speaking, listening, reading, and writing) does not get incorporated into this approach.

Fluency also can be difficult to attain through this approach. If every sentence is simply translated from Greek into the receptor language (say, English), getting a feel for the language as it is in-and-of-itself can be difficult to acquire.

Related is the problem of reliance upon glosses for the meanings of particular words. Rather than possessing a fluency that allows one familiarity with the range of meanings of particular words, the student will often fall back on the one, two, or three meanings he/she memorized for particular words when he/she first encountered them in a beginning Greek textbook.

Danny Zacharias

It does not lend itself to learning pronunciation of Greek

The focus is translating Greek to English, but there is value in moving from English to Greek as well

The GTM usually enforces small segments and chunks of sentences rather than an immersive experience

A. Chadwick Thornhill

Overwhelming for students who struggle with memorization

Generally students do not begin to interact with Scripture for some time

When Scripture integration occurs, it is typically isolated verses

Tends to create focus upon isolated elements rather than flow of thought/larger structure of discourses

Anonymous 4

Insufficient translation exercises - Most grammars do not have an adequate amount of translation exercises and tend to utilize isolated sentences that make it more difficult for students to gain a sense of context or provide them with a consistent sense of Greek syntax and expression.

Instruction often relies exclusively on rote memory and does not help students understand why things happen. Understanding why things happen in Greek (on some level) allows Greek to become familiar rather than an object to be deciphered. It is possible to introduce advanced concept at a beginning level to help understand why certain phenomena happen in Greek morphology, vocabulary building based on patterns of formation and basic stems, etc.

Many programs teach translation based on decoding rather than comprehension of the Greek and conversion into the most appropriate English equivalent. As a result, many students continue to make mistakes that reflect a poor comprehension of Greek and a heavy reliance on tools.

The tendency to rely on lists of grammatical categories rather than an understanding of what is happening frustrates students. In many programs students learn lists of acceptable categories for nominatives, genitives, etc. and in the process find themselves overwhelmed and unaware that they are merely describing how it is used, not trying to find the right answer. I have had faculty tell me that knowledge of these categories is essential to correct interpretation. Indeed it is, if you are teaching them how to decode without introducing them to a language they come to embrace as a living entity with a character of its own that they must embrace and learn. Instructors need to reinforce that these categories are a helpful stop-gap to show you the range of meaning you can otherwise only acquire by reading extensively. But they in my opinion students would be better served by the practice I was forced to employ in Classical Greek where our instructor reinforce labels in his own terminology, but force us to come up with labels (any clear label) that indicated we understood the syntax. I learned more in his classes about the Greek language than in any of my other courses. Remove the intimidation of lists from our students and focus on understanding.

Mark House

Many students struggle greatly with the languages due to a lack of native aptitude or poor language training in their previous educational experience. This can lead to frustration and a sense of failure in the student. (This is not so much a weakness of the method as it is a weakness in the student, nor is it an argument against requiring language study.)

Since language acquisition requires a number of years of sustained effort, the introductory courses offered in seminaries can provide only the beginning of a process of lifelong learning that leads to competency.

Because of the inherent complexity of language and the elementary nature of introductory Greek courses, students are tempted to oversimplify complex interpretive issues. Often this tendency toward oversimplification follows them into their ministries and can lead to the promulgation of exegetical fallacies.

The compressed nature of seminary education often dictates that students attempt to master large amounts of detailed material in a short span of time. This is especially true with regard to intensive languages courses, which in my view benefit only a small percentage of gifted students.

The press and lack of integration of the seminary curriculum requires many students to lay aside their language training to focus on their other courses. The could be alleviated to some extent if the language courses were required to be taken in the first year and the other course reinforced the ongoing use of the original languages.

Survey Questions

1—In your opinion, why should students in theological education take NT Greek courses?

Danny Zacharias

> Please refer to my introduction to my intro Greek textbook, as this is the precise question I try to start with—since it is the question students are asking! (I hope this is an okay answer)

Markus Klausli

> One of the main goals of theological education should be to prepare students to handle the Biblical text accurately. While knowledge of content is certainly important, in order for students to engage fully the biblical text, they need to be able to interact with text in its original form as well as with other resources that are biblical languages based.

Anonymous 7

> In my opinion, students should take NT Greek courses because: 1) studying Greek will enable them to see the syntactical/exegetical options for interpretation more clearly than they can using English translations alone, 2) reading in the Greek NT will slow students down and help them think more deeply about what they are reading, 3) looking at the NT in Greek will cause students to ask questions of the text that they would not otherwise know to ask.

Anonymous 9

> At least those students in theological education who are going to be primary teachers and preachers in the church should, I believe, take NT Greek. What other class of leaders in the church (in addition to experts in Greek and the NT—a small group comparatively) will be accountable to the original languages of Scripture for the teaching of the church, if not pastors and teachers?

Randall Buth

> Because the GNT is part of God's revelation to mankind. We need to take that seriously, at least as seriously as Jews take Hebrew and Muslims take Arabic.

Michael Heiser

> They shouldn't take GTM or 2nd language acquisition methods (by which I presume some sort of speaking proficiency is in view?). How will they keep up such a skill? How many Greek speakers will they have the time for, or access to, in a given week in ministry? That approach suffers from the same denial of ministry realities. The only way to get graduates to consistently use Greek or Hebrew in their sermon / teaching prep is to have them develop tools-based skills (unless they go on for PhDs, but that's a different story—and less than 5% of our students—so why not serve the 95%, too?). It's time Greek and Hebrew profs stop looking for their next doctoral student and serve the vast majority of pastoral students. The doctoral people will emerge anyway. We should be teaching tools-based competency to EVERYONE in EVERY program in seminary, then offering a traditional set of courses for those who want more—that's where the doctoral students will emerge.

Robert Plummer

> To be more faithful readers and teachers of the Bible

Anonymous 8

> Students in theological education usually (or at least should) draw upon the New Testament (as well as the rest of the Bible) as the basis of their lives, teaching, ministry, etc., and if the student does not have facility in Greek the student can never claim full access and expertise in knowledge of the New Testament.

Mark House

> Please refer to my listing of the strengths in the first question. In addition, even students who struggle with languages will receive the kinds of benefits students universally receive from studying a second language. They will simply become more competent users of language and consequently will be better critical thinkers.

Anonymous 10

> They should either take enough instruction (2 years) to really be able to use it, or not study it at all. For those who take it seriously, there are benefits—another dimension to Bible study, the "braking" effect that reading in the original has of slowing down the reader to notice the details.

Mitzi Smith

> N/A

Anonymous 1

> I believe the Old and New Testaments to be the Word of God, and theology to be the study of God, so theology is necessarily bound to the Bible as it was originally given.

Justin Langford

> In short, theology comes from the text, so students in theological education must be familiar with the text in its original language. "Familiarity" may vary with each student, but exposure to and study of the languages is imperative to navigating not only textual or theological issues but also practical or cultural issues that arise from the text (textual criticism questions, NT use of the OT, socio-cultural expressions/formulations that must be "translated" into a different culture, etc.).

Anonymous 2

> Greek Is the Language of the New Testament
>
> Greek Increases Our Ability to Rightly Interpret the Bible
>
> Greek Saves Time in Ministry
>
> Greek Demonstrates the Importance of God's Word

Con Campbell

> It is essential for a serious handling of the NT longer answer: Language "tools" are precisely that: tools. They provide information but not interpretation. If an individual hopes to interpret and communicate the message of the NT accurately, he or she needs to be able to make informed decisions about the grammar, syntax, and discourse structure

of the text. Commentaries provide selective interpretations, but leave the individual dependent on the decisions of others.

Anonymous 5

In order to read the Greek NT. By 'read' I do not mean decode and translate.

Charles Quarles

The basis for sound theology is the God-breathed Scriptures given in Hebrew, Aramaic, and Greek. A knowledge of Greek is necessary for clear and precise interpretation, since English translations often communicate either less or more than the Greek text expresses. This knowledge enables students to use the best commentaries and often helps them weigh competing interpretations of the text. A mastery of Greek prevents students from becoming slavishly dependent on the views of their favorite expert.

Anonymous 4

Student who are doing theology need to understand the issues and are not able to do so if they only deal with it in English translation.

Delio DelRio

Knowing the biblical languages aids in more accurate exegesis of the text.

Maurice Robinson

Probably the answer is obvious: to be able to read, interpret, translate, exegete, and apply material from the NT directly through their own study and research without having to be dependent upon varying opinions of others.

Alan Bandy

Any student of the Scriptures, which is the foundation for theological education, must be able to read them in their original languages.

To student the bible and or theology only in an English translation is like being a medical doctor or surgeon without ever having studied human anatomy. Such a doctor would be careless, sloppy, and entirely dependent on his colleagues who have studied anatomy. Knowledge of the original languages enables one to do exegesis and see things in the text no communicated in the translations.

I have personally heard a lot of very bad interpretations or messages that miss the main point of the text by well-intentioned pastors who simply lack the exegetical skills that only knowing Greek enables.

To not learn the original languages is lazy and unacceptable for someone who wants to do theology or teach the bible.

David Woodall

It gives them the tools to understand the Bible better.

Mark Strauss

There is a measure of authority one gains when able to read the Scriptures in their original languages. If the Jehovah's Witnesses who knock on your door know more Greek than you do, it is difficult to speak with authority on exegetical questions. For those who are in a teaching or preaching role, the ability to work with the Greek and Hebrew is important (if not always essential). A knowledge of Greek also allows access to the best commentaries and other tools.

David Croteau

It them to have more confidence in their interpretation of the New Testament which will lead to more boldly proclaiming God's Word. It can refine their understanding of the text. It can help them avoid exegetical fallacies. They won't have to be slaves to technical commentaries, but will be able to discern good grammatical arguments from poor arguments.

Anonymous 6

Helps them understand translations and finer points of belief// theology

Anonymous 3

Short answer: In order to be able to interpret and communicate the message of the NT accurately.

Anonymous 11

> Not all necessarily should, though those whose key area of ministry will be as teachers of scripture (those who preach or teach regularly) surely should since it will . . . give intelligent access to the best interpretive works/commentaries . . . require the preacher/teacher to interact more thoroughly with the text on its own terms . . . help the preacher/teacher to see more clearly the various 'structures' within the text that point to the author's intentions . . . increase the likelihood that the point/s of the text (the author's intentions) will be the point/s of the pastor teacher still today (he will 'preach biblically' and feel confidence in doing so)

Samuel Lamerson

> The student who is to teach or preach the word of God should care enough about it to want to read it in the original. There are things that simply cannot be understood by the use of a translation. In fact, there not only are there answers but there are questions that the student cannot ask without having studied the original. Sometimes being able to ask the questions are as important as the answers.

A. Chadwick Thornhill

> Biblical languages and social/cultural context are absolutely essential for understanding the meaning of the text. Translations are helpful tools but cannot fully communicate the meaning of the text like the original, cannot preserve emphasis and various rhetorical devices which can be seen in the languages. Even comparing translations, which is a valuable practice, cannot substitute for knowing the languages. In my opinion, for those who will be teaching/preaching the text, there is no substitute for the languages.

William Varner

> Because the primary text is in Greek

Dan Wallace

> To know the mind of God so they can expound the scriptures faithfully. To connect to Jesus Christ and the apostles through the inspired material remains. To learn the importance of worshiping God with one's mind.

James Voelz

> Because the NT is written in Greek and interpreting from the original is not only valuable but easily valuable. I tell students early on that there are three things that make all the difference in the world knowing the original Greek, three things that translation routinely ignore or suppress, three things that pay huge dividends without overwhelming investment in learning: a) verbal aspect b) word order c) middle voice. Translations often are not sure what to do with these factors specific to Greek and so ignore them. I know this from my work on the ESV (Acts/1 Peter). I was told specifically that they were going to under-translate differences between, say, present and aorist infinitives, because there was no agreement on how to handle the differences. What a testamonium paupertatis! Again, it's actually not that hard to notice and to convey to one's people real differences in the target language. In my book, Fundamental Greek Grammar, you are introduced to all three factors by chapter 9.

2—When speaking of biblical language courses, whom do you believe holds the major responsibility for the course material ultimately being successful (professor, student, institutional methodology, etc.)? Why?

Randall Buth

> Ultimately, it is the institution. The institution hires the professors and sets the parameters for the training. The poor control of Greek within Christian academy (e.g. the professors cannot communicate with each other in the language) is a reflection of priorities set by the institutions and the Church as a whole.

Con Campbell

> Hard to say; all are essential. But it remains true that unless the student puts in the effort even the best teacher will not cause them to succeed.

Anonymous 7

> I believe that the primary responsibility for learning a language (Greek or otherwise) is always with the learner. Honestly, I don't believe that languages are taught; I believe that they are learned. A language teacher, then, is more like a language-helper, coach, and guide than one who

explains. There are a few exceptions to this, as in the moments when a particularly tricky grammatical issue needs explanation and examples, but in general I think that the onus is on the student to learn. Having written this, I think that Greek teachers ought to labor hard in their craft to encourage, push, incentivize, tutor, and even cajole their students to learn as much as the students possibly can.

Markus Klausli

In post-secondary and especially post-graduate contexts the responsibility for a successful course is shared by both professor and student. The professor is responsible for organizing materials in a way that can be grasped by the student, providing a framework for learning, and most importantly, giving feedback on student work. Students are responsible for engaging the material, learning it, submitting assignments according to the instructions, and integrating feedback into future work.

Anonymous 6

Professor and teaching technique employed

Anonymous 3

The student. Because learning the biblical languages is a skill that requires regular review regular practice. Only the student controls those aspects of skill development.

Michael Heiser

This question isn't answerable, as you haven't defined "success".

David Croteau

The student. As a teacher, I need to provide a path, a step-by-step process, for them to learn the language. I hold them accountable for memorization with exams and quizzes. I need to help them understand the grammatical concepts. This last part, understanding the concepts, is really the key component for the teacher: students will rarely grasp the predicate nominative the first time it's explained. However, if they don't memorize the paradigms, don't memorize the vocabulary, don't do the homework diligently, or avoid asking questions for clarification, there is nothing I can do to make them successful. Greek teachers are cheerleaders, to a certain extent. Some Greek teachers try to accomplish this through intimidation; others through love or mercy. But we try to motivate our students (one way or another) to put the effort in. But they are ultimately responsible.

The institution can handcuff the students and faculty by forcing them to squeeze what should be a year-long study of the grammar into one semester. Several schools are doing this now to minimize the hours for the degree programs. It's not impossible to learn Greek that way, but it makes it harder. But the institution is not ultimately responsible.

Mark House

All factors are, of course, important, and I'm not sure which is the most important. As a student of Greek I considered myself as ultimately responsible to master the material regardless of the competency of the instructor (who frankly put me to sleep). For most students, however, I am aware that the teacher and the methodology are extremely important. As a Greek instructor, I consider my role as immensely important, though I know that without some measure of self-motivation no student will thrive.

Anonymous 1

The student. Ideally the professor and methodology don't put obstacles in the students' way, but I fully believe that the student of any topic must take ownership of the success of their own education.

Samuel Lamerson

The professor must make the class less intimidating than the student imagined, and perhaps even a little fun. The student must study vocabulary and memorize the things the professor tells them. Thus, both are responsible, and the class cannot be considered successful unless both work hard.

Anonymous 9

I would say it's a mix of all of these factors. I do think the professor needs to work hard to make the material as accessible as possible, whatever method they use. The professor is also responsible for teaching linguistics well, so that a simplistic or wooden view of language is avoided.

Justin Langford

> The professor holds the primary responsibility because he/she should know the students and institutional approach and he/she can make adjustments along the way to best meet the students' needs for learning the language.

Anonymous 2

> The Professor. The professor sets the tone of the course and has the responsibility to (1) explain to the students why Greek is important and (2) consistently demonstrate how that is the case.

Robert Plummer

> A lot of the weight falls on the professor, but after a quality teaching job has been accomplished, it's up to the students.

Anonymous 8

> Student, then professor, and last institutional methodology. The learner is always responsible for learning. Teachers only provide opportunities and encouragement, but students must become self-teachers for educational success. Teachers can make things more difficult or more accessible, but the major responsibility rests in the student's hands. Gilbert Ryle, I believe, used the analogy of learning to read. No one taught us to read. We only learned to read when we taught ourselves to read, even if encouraged and provided access by others. All of learning is in fact like this.

Charles Quarles

> The student holds primary responsibility. Even the best professor using the best curriculum cannot effectively teach Greek in the small number of hours allotted in the typical seminary program now. The student must invest hours studying, memorizing, and applying new principles. Without a significant time investment from the student, he or she will not learn Greek well.

Anonymous 5

> Hard to say. Method, student, professor.

Maurice Robinson

> Certainly the student is responsible for his or her own mastery of the materials. The professor, however, also must be responsible for the proper and accurate communication of such material. So I see this as a joint symbiotic effort.

Anonymous 10

> Professor. Because the professor has learned the language him/herself and also has enough experience to know the pitfalls and the legitimate shortcuts.

Mark Strauss

> I would say the responsibilities are pretty equal. The professor needs to use a pedagogy that is effective and enables most students to be successful. But, ultimately, the student must invest the time necessary to learn this difficult language.

Anonymous 11

> Combination of all the above, eh? Professor must bring a 'passion' and 'devotion' to the work that draws from the student a sense of its value . . . and therefore commitment to excellence. Pedagogical methods are ways that we as teachers can make the difficult understandable and the weak strong . . . .

A. Chadwick Thornhill

> I view education as a joint venture. Professors should do more than lecture. They should have an ear and eye turned toward the comprehension and retention of their students. Obviously, though, learning cannot take place if students are not engaged, applying themselves to the material, or completing (or at least attempting) assigned assessments.

William Varner

> Professor. We must excite students about the language and not kill their spirit

Dan Wallace

> Professor and student share this responsibility.

Delio DelRio

> Student. The current course structure of most institutions (at least as I've experienced them), as seen in for example sixteen-week or less semester length, proliferation of the online environment, and increasingly limited student and professor interaction in a workshop environment, results in an increasing need for self-directed learning.

David Woodall

> This is a hard one because a case could be made for several options. Ultimately success in the course is up to the student to put in the time and energy necessary to learn the material. Without this you can have a great method and a great professor, but no success.

Mitzi Smith

> Both the professor and student. Professor chooses the methodology(ies) and must find ways to accommodate diverse learning styles and levels of prior knowledge of grammar and the language. I have also found it necessary to encourage and motivate students along the way because of the amount of material one attempts to cover in a year or less. Students must put in the practice time, be alert in the classroom and ask questions.

James Voelz

> Professor. He's got to make is understandable, desirable to learn, and exciting. After taking the course, every student should be able to see the value of what is being offered, and, if a student does not pursue it or maintain proficiency, he should feel bad at having something slip that is of inestimable help.

Danny Zacharias

> The professor. Most professors need to make the courses their own, even if their is some sort of institutional methodology. Greek is usually among the hardest courses so professors shouldn't necessarily expect the student to be the driving force.

Anonymous 4

> The professor. It is the professor's task to explain to the student why an approach has merit, to build student trust, to encourage them to keep at it when they want to quit, and to motivate them by showing them the value of what they are learning.

Alan Bandy

> I think the responsibility ultimately falls on the student. At the end of the day, a professor can explain the syntax or grammatical rule very well and the book can provide all the data they need, but if a student does not spend the time everyday studying the material they will not attain language proficiency. I have had very smart students do very poorly in Greek, not because they did not understand the material, but because they did not fully apply themselves when it came to memorizing forms and vocabulary. Yet, I have also seen poor students do extremely well because they were highly motivated to learn the language. This is not to say that the professor is somehow absolved of the responsibility to communicate the material with clarity and making the best effort possible to make sure the students understand. My own success in Greek was because I believed it was essential for me to learn the language so I poured myself into it. While I had some good professors, I could not have learned Greek just from my class lectures and reading the textbook—I had to work at it and memorize forms/vocab every day.

3—What are the educational objectives for your first and second-semester Greek courses or personal textbook? (i.e., What do you want students to know, understand, and be able to accomplish by the end of their second semester)

Anonymous 7

> By the end of the second semester of Greek, I expect my students to be able to sight-translate any passage out of the New Testament that they encounter in a reader's Greek NT (that is, in one of the two resources that define words that occur fewer than 30 times in the New Testament). Thus, I expect them to be able to recognize every word on the page that isn't defined in the notes below, parse out of their heads any (except the strangest) of the words that they know definitions for, and be encouraged enough that they want to continue reading throughout

the summer that spans the end of beginning Greek and the start of intermediate Greek. Note that during the final six weeks of the second semester, students are required to sight-translate (for a grade) through 1 John, which gives them confidence that they will be able to continue reading during their summer months.

Alan Bandy

By the end of the second semester I want the students to know the forms well enough to be able to parse every now and verb they encounter and that they have enough of a vocabulary (all words occurring 50 times or more in the NT) that they can read 1 John directly from the Greek without much or any outside aids.

Con Campbell

All the basic grammar and vocabulary down to 50x. Be able to read first four chapters of Mark's Gospel (with some assistance)

Anonymous 9

By the end of the second semester, I expect students to be able to identify words occurring over 50 times in the NT and all basic grammatical forms, as well as be able to identify possible syntactical categories in particular NT uses (e.g., genitives, infinitives). They should also be able to identity in particular situations whether an exegetical issue is text-critical, lexical, grammatical or syntactical and the appropriate tools to use for adjudicating the issue.

David Croteau

Greek 1:

A. General: To develop a knowledge of basic paradigms, syntax, and vocabulary as a foundation for translation and exegesis of the Greek New Testament.

B. Specific: Upon completion of this course, you should be able to

1. Explain the elements involved in word formation of NT Greek, especially verbs.
2. Reproduce from memory the declension and conjugation paradigms of NT Greek.
3. Recall basic vocabulary used in NT Greek.

4. Explain the basic syntactical elements of NT Greek and their significance.

5. Translate selected NT passages from Greek to English.

Greek 2:

A. General: To develop a knowledge of basic paradigms, syntax, and vocabulary as a foundation for translation and exegesis of the Greek New Testament.

B. Specific: Upon completion of this course, you should be able to

1. Explain the elements involved in word formation of NT Greek, especially verbs.

2. Reproduce from memory the declension and conjugation paradigms of NT Greek.

3. Recall basic vocabulary used in NT Greek.

4. Explain the basic syntactical elements of NT Greek and their significance.

5. Translate selected NT passages from Greek to English.

Anonymous 6

Basic parsing/translation on level of 1 John; awareness of basic exegetical issues.

Randall Buth

I want a foundation of being able to understand basic texts both through reading and listening.

Anonymous 3

General: To develop a knowledge of basic paradigms, syntax, and vocabulary as a foundation for translation and exegesis of the Greek New Testament.

Specific: Upon completion of both courses, you should be able to

1. Explain the elements involved in word formation of NT Greek, especially verbs.

2. Reproduce from memory the declension and conjugation paradigms of NT Greek.

3. Recall basic vocabulary used in the Greek NT.

4. Explain the basic syntactical elements of NT Greek and their significance.

5. Translate selected NT passages from Greek to English.

Mark House

They need to have a functional beginning vocabulary and a good grasp of the word forms and rules of Greek grammar.

They need to have a basic ability to translate NT Greek sentences.

They need to be prepared to go on to the second-year exegetical courses.

In our curriculum, students are also to have a basic grasp of textual criticism (which I think would be better left for the advanced courses).

Michael Heiser

The first-year textbooks are designed to produce translating skills. I do this online now for people who want it, not for an institution. But I encourage everyone to learn tools-based methods anyway.

Samuel Lamerson

By the end of the second semester I expect the students to be able to read many passages of the NT with the aid of a lexicon. In my class, we read selections from 1 John, Mark, and John. We either use a reader's lexicon or BDAG as an aid. I constantly remind them during the semesters that our aim is to read the text and know more about God, not just to learn the language.

Justin Langford

Our first two Greek courses here at my institution bring students through Mounce's Basics of Biblical Greek. By the end of the second semester, students should:

–Comprehend the basic principles of Greek grammar and translation

–Have a working knowledge of Greek vocabulary of the words that occur 50 times or more in the NT

–Value the importance of the original languages for sound exegesis

–Be prepared to translate from selected portions of the Greek NT using appropriate translation aids

SURVEY QUESTIONS

Anonymous 1

> An appreciation of what is involved in learning to read the Bible in original languages.
>
> An awareness that the Bible, though perhaps a very familiar text in translation, is truly an ancient artifact produced in cultures unlike our own.
>
> A mastery of the most frequently occurring Greek words in the NT.
>
> An understanding of what an inflected language is, mastery of the case system of nouns and principle parts of verbs, a basic knowledge of participles and how tense should be understood in Greek.
>
> An increasing understanding of how language works, with an ability to parse nouns and verbs for translation accuracy and relate parts of a sentence to the whole (e.g., adverbs, prepositional phrases, etc.). I find sentence diagramming to be an excellent way to accomplish this, and to identify grammatical ambiguities. Students seem to either love diagramming or hate it.
>
> A growing ability to read the text of the Greek NT, at least the texts of straightforward syntax.

Anonymous 2

> Understand the basic grammar of NT Greek.
>
> Memorize a sufficient number of words so that reading is not slowed down by lack of vocabulary (currently they memorize words that occur 17 times or more in the NT).
>
> Grasp the basic syntax of NT Greek.
>
> Gain confidence by reading through an entire NT book (1 John).
>
> Know how to use some of the basic tools to do research (BDAG, Louw & Nida, etc.).

Mitzi Smith

> I want students to know basic grammar (verb conjugations various tenses and moods; noun declensions by case, gender, number; different uses of adjectives and infinitives; verbal nouns etc), develop a basic vocabulary, know how to use a lexicon, and be able to translate simple sentences from Greek to English and more complex sentences. Students should be able to provide literal word-for-word translations

as well as smooth English translation. Students should develop facility with Greek pronunciation.

Anonymous 8

The goals for the end of two semesters of Greek learning are all of the major morphosyntactic categories, vocabulary down to about 12 times or more, ability to manipulate morphology and basic syntax in exercises, and ability to translate, with help on vocabulary and more difficult constructions, of representative passages from the major portions of the New Testament.

Charles Quarles

Students will be able to recognize a working vocabulary of the most frequently occurring words in the Greek New Testament.

Students will be able to demonstrate a basic working knowledge of the grammar and syntax covered in the first semester, ultimately enabling them to begin translating and interpreting passages from the Greek New Testament.

Students will be able to identify the various exegetical and reference tools to further their ability to interpret the Greek New Testament and use it in ministry.

Students will be able to identify and synthesize the benefits of Koinē Greek for life in the ministry.

Anonymous 10

All declensions, all tenses, verbals, moods, pronouns, basic conditional sentences, subordinate clauses, translation from Johannine literature, 368 vocabulary words, basic semantics.

Anonymous 5

Read simple portions of the GNT (e.g., 1John, Gospel of John) with comprehension and answer simple questions. The questions are posed in Greek and answered in Greek.

Robert Plummer

> I want them to love Greek, to believe it makes a difference in studying the Bible, and to know well the defined course content (e.g., vocab words, paradigms, syntactical categories, translation ability, etc.)

Mark Strauss

> I want students to know enough basic morphology and syntax that they can translate the Greek New Testament and identify the functional relationships of phrases and clauses.
>
> I want to enable them to use the best Greek tools available, such as high-level commentaries, grammars and lexicons.
>
> Learn enough about linguistics that they avoid common words study errors as well as common grammatical errors (errors like the claim that the aorist means once-for-all time action or that words have a "literal" meaning)

Maurice Robinson

> My objectives tended to be very simple: to have a mastery of a working Greek NT vocabulary and various declension, parsing, and basic syntactical forms so as to be able to read with a general understanding most portions of the Greek NT without needing a word-by-word recourse to lexicons and grammatical tools, thus reserving look-up needs for those forms or constructions that are more problematic.

William Varner

> I teach second and third year Greek. They should be able to identify all grammatical constructions they will encounter in the GNT.

Anonymous 11

> We expect students to know by memory the vocabulary of the Greek NT to words that occur 25 or more times in the GNT . . . know by memory the basic working paradigms for morphology (as given in the text, in this case D. A. Black's text) . . . know by memory basic grammar and syntactical matters (as given in the first year text) . . . and be able to translate 1 John and 1 Thessalonians from Greek into English without undue 'helps'

A. Chadwick Thornhill

> We follow Mounce's BBG structure in a two semester approach. Students thus learn the most common vocabulary words in the NT (about 80% of word usages) as well as learn the declensions and conjugations in order to recall/recognize forms when reading the text. The skills emphasized are parsing, translation, declining and conjugating, and vocabulary recall.

James Voelz

> See the answer to question 1. They should have the basic morphology and syntax under control, but most important, they should understand how verbal aspect, word order, and middle voice open up the world of the language and its nuances. They should know what to look for and where to look (e.g., at stems for verbal aspect, at endings for voice, etc.).

Dan Wallace

> Read the Greek NT and the Apostolic Fathers (selections of both); ability to analyze the forms and constructions (morphology and syntax); translate the Greek NT and Apostolic Fathers (selections of both); know what alternatives the Greek author has for expressing the ideas; appreciate the value of NT Greek for exposition of the Word; fall more deeply in love with Jesus Christ through the study of the Greek NT.

Delio DelRio

> Understand the vocabulary and grammatical principles needed to translate and interpret the Greek New Testament. Demonstrate the application of the grammatical concepts to the translation and exegesis of the Greek New Testament. Be able to communicate clearly the meaning of selected New Testament passages based on a grammatical exegesis of the Greek text

Danny Zacharias

> I will likely have a different answer than most here, and I need to give a two-tier answer. The reason I wrote my grammar was because of a curriculum change at Acadia Divinity College. With the revamp to the M.Div., we decided that the new requirement would be one semester of Greek and one semester of Hebrew.

The learning outcomes for a single semester was to give the students an overview of the entire grammatical system, and help them to access and interact intelligently with the Greek New Testament utilizing the tools available in Bible Software (Logos in particular). I evaluated every intro NT Greek textbook, and none of them would work for a single semester, nor are any accommodating to Bible Software.

With that pre-amble aside, my primary focus is on the outcomes of a single semester. The objectives are to have a basic understanding of the entire Greek grammatical system; to seek and understand the exegetically significant points of the morphology (i.e. instead of teaching them to parse a word, I teach them what the significance is of its mood, tense, etc.); students should understand the basics of lexical semantics for proper word studies; Finally, the objective is for them to know how to access this information in Logos Bible Software.

My textbook (and intro classes) is aimed at the single semester, but is also built to be used for a second semester by students such that they would end with the same outcomes as students using the normal Greek textbooks (like Mounce, Croy, etc.). In the second semester, they go through much of the textbook again, are introduced to some additional information and tables, and have more learning activities that focus on parsing and reading.

Markus Klausli

By the end of the first two semesters, students should be able to parse any verb and do a rough translation of any part of the Greek New Testament with access to a Greek Lexicon and grammar.

David Woodall

Pronounce the Greek text accurately (Performance and Action)

Memorize a list of frequent New Testament Greek words (Engagement and Motivation)

Translate portions of the Greek New Testament (Knowledge and Understanding)

Investigate the basic tools included in Bible research software (Reflection and Critique)

Summarize the basics of Greek exegesis and the use of Greek in ministry (Judgment and Design).

Anonymous 4

A knowledge of approximately 600 Greek words. These are preferably learned a week before they are utilized so that students are not restricted in their comprehension of new material by encountering words they do not know.

2) Extensive translation work. Completion of at least five-hours of translation per week. Extensive translation assignments allow students for whom language comes naturally to read long passages. On the other hand, students with more difficulty in language acquisition are given time limits to keep their homework within acceptable limits.

3) Self-graded translation work in which students are required to not only identify what they got wrong, but why they got it wrong. This reinforces concepts more than just being told the answers. Moreover, because they have already worked on finding solutions, the in-class time can devote attention to issues they could not resolve and more focus on helping them focus on oral comprehension (see below), translation theory, sight-reading skills that move beyond prepared work, etc.

4) Students practice oral reading during every class devoted to translating with the goal of training mental pathways so they can move beyond pronunciation to actually comprehending Greek before translating rather than simply decoding.

5) Students are able to replicate the paradigms for noun and verbs.

6) An understanding of concepts and ideas even if they do cannot produce the conventional labels. Are we teaching them to read and understand Greek or read and understand commentaries? There is a subtle difference.

4—Do you have an instrument or process for measuring whether these educational objectives have been met? If so, how is this done?

Con Campbell

Quizzes, exams, and reading groups

David Croteau

Many quizzes and several exams.

Anonymous 3

>Unit exams (three per semester)

Alan Bandy

>Because the language is learned in a piecemeal fashion, so it the assessment and measurement of the students' progress. This is primarily accomplished through three or four instruments:

>Vocabulary and syntax quizzes on a daily/weekly basis. These quizzes determine how the students are learning the material as they learn it. Quizzes also motivate students to memorize the material.

>Translation of Greek sentences in class where individuals are put on the spot to translate in front of all their peers. This allows me to not only assess the student, but also give further instruction where they may need it.

>Exams. I normally give two exams each semester that are comprehensive and test three areas: (1) vocabulary acquisition; (2) grammar and syntax (rules and forms); (3) the ability to put into practice by translating large portions of the Greek text of Scripture (usually drawn from their workbook so they have already see the verses before).

Randall Buth

>The written side is the easiest to test at present, although some pieces of oral testing can be done and have been done.

Anonymous 7

>Yes. At the end of the second semester, they are expected to sight-translate one biblical passage and one non-biblical passage (usually from the Apostolic Fathers) and to parse anything I ask them to parse. That evaluative tool is a written exam. In addition, as already mentioned above, I expect my students to come to class ready to orally translate and parse a chunk of 1 John that I have assigned ahead of time. They are graded on the spot (in small groups) on their ability to do this.

Anonymous 9

>I use an open-book exam (Greek NT, English translations, lexicon, Mounce, Wallace; but no commentaries) to determine whether they

are able to identify syntactical categories and exegetical issues (as in last sentence in #3).

Anonymous 6

Tests; quizzes; comprehensive finals

Michael Heiser

It's the eyeball test. I've been a believer for 30+ years and have met perhaps 1-2 pastors who can translate now like they did when they left seminary. It's a failed approach.

Samuel Lamerson

Second semester Greek has a final exam which consists of several short passages which the student is to translate, parse certain verbs, and decline chosen nouns. The student is allowed to use a lexicon, but the test is timed. This is an attempt to measure the student's ability to work with the language at a basic level.

Anonymous 1

I've spent countless hours in faculty meetings discussing this. Until "assessment" became such a hot topic in education, I always thought quizzes and exams fulfilled this purpose. And perhaps a report/review of a book on Greco-Roman times and culture.

Mark House

This is done primarily through the final exam, which includes a and b above. Students also complete course evaluation surveys, and the results of these are fed back to instructors. Ordaining bodies also have basic Greek competency tests students must pass for ordination, although I rarely get feedback on how my students perform on these.

Justin Langford

I use the following to measure student objectives: vocabulary quizzes and exams, sectional exams that include translation and grammar, in-class participation at the board and team competitions, discussions and assessments on the cultural background of texts and their interpretation, and workbook completion.

Anonymous 5

Exams and personal interview.

Anonymous 2

Yes. Quizzes, exams, and guided word-study exercises.

Charles Quarles

Exams and exegetical worksheets

Maurice Robinson

I used regular (weekly) quizzes on cumulative vocabulary learned as well as practical translation exercises based on sentences that were constructed to read like biblical passages, although not precisely such.

Anonymous 10

Weekly quizzes, weekly group participation, exams.

Mitzi Smith

Homework, classroom participation and oral and written quizzes and exams.

Robert Plummer

Regular quizzes and tests

Anonymous 8

Examinations, quizzes, student completed exercises, and in-class modeling and response.

Mark Strauss

Scores on quizzes and exams, as well as working with individual students through workbook exercises.

Anonymous 11

Mostly it is quizzes/exams . . . vocabulary quizzing is done via 'mastery quizzing' online (take weekly vocabulary quiz repeatedly that week till you get the score you want) . . . similarly with grammar matters . . .

translation assignments are worked through each week . . . a separate hour for tutoring is required each week, taught by a different professor but over the same material

A. Chadwick Thornhill

Yes. We use a combined assessment of daily quizzes, homework/workbook exercises, and exams.

James Voelz

At CSL we have an Entry Level Competency Examination (ELCE).

Dan Wallace

Exams, quizzes, class interaction, workbook assignments, composition workbook assignments, syntactical analysis sheets.

Delio DelRio

If so, how is this done?--translation exercises, vocabulary quizzes, and grammar exams

David Woodall

We use a comprehensive final exam as the major criteria for success. It gives a good indicator of where the students are in their understanding. It is fairly rigorous, and I need to curve the exam. Sometimes students fail the exam but still pass the course because of their work on other assignments.

William Varner

Daily recitation in class. Every class is an oral exam.

Markus Klausli

These are measured by course assignments and exams in Gk 1 and 2.

Danny Zacharias

Not in the textbook (though this is a good idea!), but in the class the final assignments and exams perform this function.

Anonymous 4

1) Vocabulary—Weekly quizzes and a final vocab exam given at the end of each semester one week before the translation final. That way students are given a chance of focus on review and solidify their vocab.

2) Translation work - Students turn in assignments with self-graded annotations and comments and an indication of their total time spent.

3) Oral reading - Apart from in-class reading, students have a prepared reading each semester that ranges from 5-6 verses first semester and approx 15 verses during second semester. The readings are read at the start of each class period during the semester and students present an oral reading in the 11-12th week of class. Students are graded on a pass / fail basis, but are required to read it with correct pronunciation, clear diction, and evidence of comprehension while reading.

4) Paradigms - tested on quizzes and exams

5—Do you believe that two semesters of NT Greek (6 credit hours is the most common MDiv requirement) is sufficient to accomplish the objectives that you listed above? Why or why not?

Mark House

Given the limited objectives I have listed, I do believe our "beginning" Greek courses are sufficient to meet them. However, I make clear to my students that the courses are to be considered introductory and that learning Greek well requires years of sustained work. Our curriculum offers advanced, "second-year" courses that provide additional training necessary to equip students toward mastery.

Markus Klausli

Learning a language well—especially and ancient one, is not really possible in 2 semesters. The real issue relates to restraints in the curriculum. The current trend to reduce the number of hours in MDiv programs makes it more difficult to prioritize the languages. Because of this reality, highly efficient approaches to learning Greek are needed, and thankfully, they exist in multiple formats. Given the materials, in spite of the restraints there is really no reason why the above goal cannot be achieved.

Anonymous 4

No. If the goal is for students to use Greek in exegesis, they must first understand the language. Moreover, anyone intending to go into ministry with a teaching focus should have language background. If not, then they should enroll in a chaplaincy program. The problem with many programs is the assumption that Greek competency can be achieved through a basic understanding of grammar and a decoding approach to Greek. Such approaches are constantly evident in sermon and a source of continuous frustration to anyone who knows Greek.

Con Campbell

It is sufficient for basic beginning Greek, yes. But ideally students will have a second year for intermediate study and exegesis.

Anonymous 7

I believe that six credit hours is indeed sufficient to accomplish the objectives I listed above, which were only objectives for elementary Greek. But I do not believe that six credit hours is sufficient to make Greek useful to students over the long haul. For that they need at least twelve credit hours. Actually, students who have only taken elementary Greek make regular exegetical mistakes, largest because they haven't interacted with the necessary syntactical categories (think of Wallace's intermediate grammar), haven't had Greek exegetical method modeled for them, and still usually haven't attained a strong enough fluency to continue using their Greek.

David Croteau

Yes. Because our objectives for the first year are reasonable. If you expect your student after 2 semesters to read the Greek New Testament with ease or to memorize an insane amount of vocabulary, then you are asking too much.

Anonymous 6

No, but the trend is toward minimal credits; not maximal credits in an area for MDiv//reduction of requirements

Anonymous 3

> It is adequate to accomplish the objectives for the first-year Greek but not to equip students to use Greek in an informed way as part of exegesis and exposition. (See the answer to 3.1 above.)

Michael Heiser

> See above—I favor only a tools-based approach for all students in every program. That can be followed by a traditional course for anyone who wants more. But the end result is that everyone can use software tools and (hopefully—here's where the professor comes in) understand the value of languages for interpretation. That will depend on examples. Students should be taught how to mine data and then think carefully about the data. That means understand terms and concepts, and then seeing actual examples where those terms and concepts matter for interpretation. You don't need to teach people to memorize. You need to teach them to think—how to ask questions about the text. They can get English glosses and parsings in seconds, so let them. What they can't get is why it all matters—that's why they need courses and professors.

Anonymous 10

> Yes, they are adequate, although an additional semester or two are needed to reinforce and practice learning.

Mitzi Smith

> No. Students learn at different paces and most of my students have either never studied a language or studied it a long time go. Sometimes as the instructor I have to slow down and spend more time with a difficult subject like participles. If my goal is to just expose them to, for example participles, that's one thing. But I want to give them the opportunity to learn grammar so that they can use it. I took Greek twice before doing doctoral studies—in an undergraduate BA in theology and years later in an MDiv program. I don't feel my wonderful instructor in my BA program taught with the intent that we would use the Greek in meaningful or practical ways in preaching and ministry beyond the classroom. It was a requirement. It definitely gave me a foundation when I studied Greek ten years later in my MDiv program. So I teach with the goal of providing a solid foundation and with the intent of preparing students to use it in ministry. But still time is not

always on our side. This has to change. Students benefit but not in terms of continued and/or practical use beyond the classroom.

Anonymous 1

Not really. Two semesters is enough to embolden students to think they know Greek, but not enough to master the objectives to the extent that will serve them if they'll be using Greek professionally or in grad school. I found four semesters, with the fourth focusing on reading large amounts of Greek text and introducing NT exegesis to be the threshold.

Samuel Lamerson

Absolutely not! Even three semesters are really not enough. When I first started teaching at Knox, the administration required five semesters of Greek. We now require three semesters and I believe that most students can at least make some exegetical decisions and syntactical choices by the end of the third semester. I could campaign for more required Greek classes, but it would be at the expense of other fields.

Anonymous 9

Yes; I begin open-book work about midway through the second semester and we practice the skill of determining the nature of exegetical issues using the various Greek tools through that last half of the semester as well as into the summer ½ term. (We have 7.5 credits of Greek.)

Randall Buth

It is woefully insufficient as a foundation for further work.

Justin Langford

Yes, though not every student will get to that point, in my experience. However, I teach at the undergrad level, so I don't want to speak for the MDiv level.

Anonymous 2

No, but that's all most students take so I do my best. Without a knowledge of Greek syntax, one cannot interpret NT Greek.

David Woodall

> Yes, six hours are fine for seminary education. This gives students that basic grammar covered in Mounce and other basic grammars. This is not enough time, however, to develop the syntax categories discussed in Wallace. We do not cover the Exegesis section in Mounce (third edition) since it is covered in Greek Syntax and Exegetical Method. Our undergraduate faculty, however, have argued strongly for 8 hours for first year Greek.

Anonymous 8

> It used to be, but with the current generation of students it is increasingly difficult, as they bring less academic preparation in language and study habits.

Charles Quarles

> Yes, but the approach is so fast-paced that weaker students are often left behind. I would much prefer to have 12 credit hours. Students who have had two years of Greek are much more comfortable working with the Greek New Testament and much more likely to continue using it in ministry because they have had greater opportunity to see the usefulness of the study.

Anonymous 5

> This is an odd question. The answer is Yes. But 6 hours is not sufficient for reading all the NT with comprehension.

Robert Plummer

> Barely. And we teach an entire intro grammar in one semester—at lightning speed.

Maurice Robinson

> Yes, but . . . as noted above, more time is needed for such study (I would recommend 4-semester hours each term, and would also prefer a return to the longer semester model of 16 or 17 weeks); barring those developments, a third 3-hr semester course should be added to complete the initial task (after which the now-required syntax/advanced grammar course would take place, thus filling out two full years of Greek, 12 semester hours).

Alan Bandy

> No. One year or 6hrs of Greek is only enough to give the student a basic knowledge of Greek morphology and syntax, but without further study they will (a) forget the majority of it in a year's time; or, (b) only use Greek superficially to give an appearance of knowledge while possibly misinterpreting the biblical text.
>
> However, I also understand that there are many other necessary courses to complete the degree requirements so that it is not really possible to require every student to have more credit hours in Greek. To require more Greek may not be as important as requiring them to learn Hebrew as well.

Mark Strauss

> It would be better to have more, but this is sufficient if the students are willing to continue on. Learning Greek is a lifelong process.

William Varner

> Absolutely not. They are reeling by the end of first year. They need additional time to process everything in first year Greek and then to build on that foundation.

James Voelz

> Probably, but I prefer a concentrated summer course. Immersion is really helpful, mainly to avoid distractions and the lure of other courses diluting focus.

Dan Wallace

> Yes, if it's rigorous enough. The great majority of first-year Greek instruction is not.

Anonymous 11

> Frankly, no. We require 12 hours. 2 semesters lays a fine foundation, but 'practice' in the real world of GNT translation, phrase diagramming, and basic exegetical methods all are needed to make that foundational knowledge more usable and solid . . . simply put, deeper understanding of grammatical matters and more substantial experience is invaluable.

A. Chadwick Thornhill

> Yes, it is sufficient to accomplish these objectives. The bigger question is if these are the correct objectives. Students have considerable grammatical skills with this model but do not yet acquire significant interpretive or exegetical skills until their third or fourth semester.

Danny Zacharias

> Yes and no. Yes in my context because I teach the upper elective New Testament courses at the college and so I expect/require them to make use of their Greek knowledge in their assignments. But no because on its own I'm not sure that just my textbook on its own could achieve the outcomes.

Delio DelRio

> It's possible, but proves difficult for most students in my experience. Most students struggle with the great amount of information that must be inductively learned (i.e., memorized) in such a short amount of time.

> **6**—Do you believe the majority of students look forward to taking biblical language classes? Why or why not?

Anonymous 7

> I think that most of my students in general are excited about the idea of knowing Greek, but most are afraid of passing through the process of learning Greek.

Anonymous 6

> No—poor teaching techniques; too much stress on great detail in too little time (i.e., accents)

Anonymous 3

> In general, no. For a variety of reasons, including stories about how difficult biblical language courses are, fear of learning a language based on past experience, lack of conviction about the usefulness of the languages, and the commonly-expressed opinion that "we have all the tools we need to do the job."

Michael Heiser

> I think the question is irrelevant, as they don't know what they're going to get. Probably most think that languages are very useful—and then we teach them to reproduce English translations we already have and never teach them to think exegetically. It's counter-productive and somewhat absurd.

Alan Bandy

> Yes, until they actually get into the work of learning Greek. I find that my classes lose a percentage of students each semester, but at the beginning of Elementary Greek 1 they are all excited, eager, and even brag to their friends that they know the Greek alphabet. By the middle of the semester, however, that excitement wanes as the reality sets in and some are doing extremely well while others are failing. Everyone who takes Greek wants to know it, but are not always successful because of what it takes to learn it.

Mark House

> It's a mix. Many students know from prior experience that they struggle with languages and thus dread taking Greek. However, I also hear from many who look forward to taking Greek. It's hard to say which group is in the majority.

Anonymous 1

> Not if it's simply a requirement to do what they otherwise want to do. But even so, in my personal experience of seminary, I took Greek (and Hebrew) only because it was required. But while taking it I fell in love with the languages and discovered I was relatively good at them. Had the biblical languages not been required by the seminary, I would likely have opted out of them, and consequently my life would have taken another path. I'm a believer that educational institutions should have required courses as specified by the expert faculty who know what it really takes to educate a student in a given field. Students have no idea about this until they've been educated. I know this runs counter to modern education models that allow students to have full choice and have no required courses.

Samuel Lamerson

> Most students enter first semester somewhat frightened. One of the problems is the saying "It is Greek to me." Others come to class having believed someone who told them that "they are just not good at languages." This causes students to think that Greek is much harder than it actually is and thus students come into the class with fear and trembling. I do my best to prove that Greek is not that difficult, but for some it is an uphill climb. I spend a good part of the first six to eight weeks "cheerleading" to let the class know that everyone has these kinds of difficulties and it will get easier.

Anonymous 4

> Depends on how it is taught. Our Hebrew program is an elective program (offering as much as 14 semester of Hebrew study) and consistently ranges between 15-25 students per year in our first-year courses. Our students love Hebrew and consider it their favorite class in college or seminary.

Delio DelRio

> To better understand the New Testament

Justin Langford

> The majority do not. Reasons for this could include difficulty, apprehension, and time.

Anonymous 2

> No, I would say about 25% are excited, another 25% are terrified, and other 50% are there because it is a requirement. Many have heard how difficult Greek is.

Anonymous 9

> I'm not sure what the majority's expectation is going in, although I know language courses cause more anxiety than most. I know that some students are excited (and nervous) at the prospects and others are more fearful.

Randall Buth

> Irrelevant, no opinion: Presently, there is no true incentive for students because they intuitively know that they are not going to learn the language to a level that we expect from interpreters of other literatures. People don't learn languages so that they can parse verbs.

Anonymous 5

> No. They have heard that the classes are hard, boring, and have very little pay-off.

Robert Plummer

> The majority of our students do. They are ravenous for the languages—for the most part. There are the occasional slackers.

Con Campbell

> Yes, but with some trepidation. It is daunting.

David Croteau

> No. They are scared. Many students tell "horror stories" of what taking language classes are like. Some of these are exaggerations. However, some biblical language professors use intimidation to motivate. I've heard countless stories of Greek professors kicking students out of the class if they don't seem fully prepared to translate. I don't think intimidation should have a place in theological education. I try to motivate through my excitement and passion for them to learn the language. I try to be gracious and merciful. But if you motivate by intimidation, of courses students will be reticent to take the courses.

Maurice Robinson

> I suspect they would if they were strongly encouraged and if the goals of such study were clearly explained. For the few who had no capacity in languages, I would recommend a Greek familiarity course only, to allow some use of lexicons, study aids, and commentaries. I also prefer that the biblical language courses be elective, so that those who have no inclination toward such will not be burdened nor a problem in the classroom such as to slow down the rate of instruction from what otherwise might occur.

Mark Strauss

> Yes, I think most do (at least they say so), although most all have a certain amount of fear and trepidation.

Anonymous 11

> No . . . not the 'majority.' It is known to be 'hard work' and some are just plain lazy . . . some other don't believe it's really needed . . . some are just afraid . . . some have had poor experience with other language study (high school or college modern language programs usually) . . . In our school, we try hard to have students in the MDiv or MABS programs (where Greek is required) who actually want to be there and study Greek . . . so in our school I think 60-75% do look forward to it, but I suspect we're an exception to what I've said above

A. Chadwick Thornhill

> I think most students are both excited and fearful. They understand the importance of the languages typically, but also are terrified about the process.

Anonymous 10

> Perhaps one half do, probably because they have a magical view of language (particularly Greek); the rest feel intimidated.

Mitzi Smith

> No. Not the way that we currently teach Greek. Most students that approach me want to take Greek alone without having to take other courses simultaneously but they don't want to take it in the summer as an intensive. At the same time there are the requirements of school loans that impact course load. Otherwise, students do want to take languages. Although most still have unrealistic expectations of the demands of language study, even when informed beforehand. When I first came to ATS students were required to take both Hebrew and Greek as part of the MDiv curriculum (that requirement was dropped), and I had to teach both as the only fulltime professor in Detroit. Some students were extremely hostile because of the pressure to do so and with two or three other courses, family responsibilities, work, and ministry!! It was very difficult. I gave a lot of motivational speeches J!

William Varner

> So they can get under the hood of the car and see the nuts and bolts of how the language works.

David Woodall

> If they are MDiv students, most of them do look forward to taking biblical language classes (although often with fear and trembling). Many of them, however, dread it after the first semester. They persevere because it is required or drop out because they realize that it is not for them.

Anonymous 8

> No, I don't believe that they do. The majority of students are not used to the rigors of what is required for study of languages, and their current lifestyles are not conducive to what is required to master a language.

Charles Quarles

> This depends largely on what their mentors and peers have communicated to them. Some mentors and peers who never learned Greek well themselves will insist the Greek is hard, a waste of time, and practically useless. But mentors and peers who were trained well encourage students to give their best to the study of Greek because of the exegetical insights made possible through language study.

Danny Zacharias

> No, it is the dreaded class and the main cause of anxiety. I will say, though, that this anxiety has been significantly reduced since our move to a single semester in the M.Div. And it has meant that those who move on to a second semester and beyond are those who love the language and are really motivated to learn.

James Voelz

> Some really do, but others are afraid, because they are make or break for a seminary career; if you cannot pass them, you cannot continue. But many are really anxious to open up the text.

Dan Wallace

> In my classes, yes. That's because I teach Honors Greek—the only Honors course ever offered at DTS. Students are self-selective based solely on desire.

Markus Klausli

> It's mixed. Some students see it as a hoop to jump through. Others are excited about engaging the Scriptures in the original languages.

7—In your opinion, what percentage of your students go on to study Greek beyond what their specific program requires (ex., Greek 3, exegetical courses, advanced degrees, etc.)?

Alan Bandy

> I would say as much as half of the students I have for Elementary Greek will take at least one semester of Intermediate Greek. About a third of those students will take both semesters of Intermediate Greek. About a half of that third will take Hellenistic Greek Readings.

David Croteau

> About 10%

Anonymous 6

> 10-15%

David Woodall

> Our program requires a Greek 3 (Syntax and Exegetical Method) course for all MDiv students. Pastoral Studies majors also need to take an exegesis course in either Greek or Hebrew. Only a small percent of students do work in biblical languages after the MDiv level.

Anonymous 9

> We have seen students purpose Greek exegetical options or continue with our Greek reading group, I'd say, at a percentage of about 10%.

Mark Strauss

> Maybe 10%

Anonymous 3

> Our program requires two full years of either Greek or Hebrew. About 35% add at least one year of a second language as part of their program. About 10% express an interest in taking one or more courses beyond the second year. About 10% pursue advanced degrees.

Michael Heiser

> Small percentage. Less than 5%.

Dan Wallace

> 90%

Samuel Lamerson

> I would guess less than 10%.

Justin Langford

> In my experience I would say 10-15%.

Anonymous 2

> 20%

Anonymous 5

> Almost none. Maybe 5%

Robert Plummer

> At least 50% take more classes

Charles Quarles

> In the past, probably 80%. Currently though I teach in an M.Div. program with a reduced number of hours that allots little time for more extensive study of the languages. Perhaps as few as 20% go on to study Greek at a more advanced level.

Anonymous 7

> I don't know about other programs, only about my own. In my setting, students are required to take 12 credit hours . . . .so all of them who continue pursuing their degree continue learning Greek.

Maurice Robinson

> I really have no idea on that issue. I know some of my students have done so in regard to advanced degree work, but how many proportionally remains unknown. Assuming that most of our students intend to go into pastoral or missionary work, probably only about 10-15% might go further academically—but that is only a guess.

Anonymous 8

> Our current requirement is four semesters of language for the MDiv degree. Perhaps 20% go on for more, but this is a guess only.

David Woodall

> Our program requires a Greek 3 (Syntax and Exegetical Method) course for all MDiv students. Pastoral Studies majors also need to take an exegesis course in either Greek or Hebrew. Only a small percent of students do work in biblical languages after the MDiv level.

Anonymous 10

> In our MA programs it is 100%; for people in our BA level Greek, perhaps half, but we are only now rolling it out and I do not have statistics.

Mitzi Smith

> Well, we used to require Greek 3. When we were on the quarter system, students were required to take Greek 1-3 and Hebrew 1-2 or vice versa. I have had maybe three or four students take further exegetical courses, but most did not feel confident in using their Greek in those courses, even when they had been excellent Greek students! It takes more time and we not make room for it in seminary. I'm not suggesting more courses in the overall MDiv program but more opportunities to design individualized and creative programs.

Anonymous 11

> Guess . . . 25%, though more would like to (time and money come into play) . . . I should say that in our seminary, third semester is required (syntax, grammar, translation focus . . . read Wallace cover to cover with exams; translate Mark and Philippians . . . intro to phrase diagramming, textual criticism, lexical analysis) and also a fourth semester (exegesis through Galatians)

A. Chadwick Thornhill

> I would estimate perhaps 10-15% go beyond the language requirements specified for their degree.

William Varner

> 20%

Randall Buth

> Probably the majority. They usually don't come to me until after they recognize that something is wrong with the field.

Con Campbell

> Our students must continue beyond the first year. Hard to estimate beyond that.

James Voelz

> At the seminary, all of them.

Delio DelRio

> it's very low, probably less than 10%

Danny Zacharias

> 10%

Markus Klausli

> Relatively few.

Anonymous 4

I do not have solid figures, but in our Hebrew program we consistently maintain large retention figures after first-year unless a majority of students enrolled in Hebrew late in their program and are graduating. The following table shows you the retention rates from semester to semester over the course of the last 8 years.

Mark House

All of our MDiv students are required to continue their Greek studies, but there is a growing trend for students directed toward ministry to get an MA degree with just enough Greek to get through the ordination process. I would guess that in our Reformed, Presbyterian context the majority of students go beyond first-year Greek.

Anonymous 1

An unfortunately small percentage, well less than 10%. But I don't follow my students in the years after graduation. Perhaps more of them do eventually go to seminary or into graduate school where they take more of the biblical languages.

8—Do you believe the majority of students go on to use their NT Greek training after graduation in their regular ministry? Why or why not?

Maurice Robinson

They should do so, but whether they do or not, I really have no idea. I know that the students who were my Greek graders all went on to either higher academic work or into a pastorate where exegetical expository preaching based on the original language texts was the norm; but these hardly represent the bulk of all the students I have taught.

Anonymous 10

Not adequately, no. The main reason is that they do not establish the regular discipline of reading the Greek NT.

Anonymous 9

While I don't think that a majority of students read Greek regularly after graduation, I do think (it has been my experience that) students use Greek in their teaching and preaching ministries routinely. Potentially more importantly, students have ideally learned good linguistic competency to avoid bad language preaching habits that have been problematic in the church

Anonymous 3

Yes, but they find their own level of comfort in doing so. Some continue doing their own work; others adopt a tools approach. The most commonly-expressed reason for the latter is the press of other ministerial responsibilities.

Michael Heiser

No. They don't have the time and don't see the value. They already have translations. Had they been taught to think exegetically about the text, they'd see the value.

James Voelz

I would figure about half and half. Here is where my answer in #2 is important. I want them to feel as if they should use it, even if they don't, and that if they don't they regret it.

Dan Wallace

Absolutely. Many of them go on to earn a PhD in NT and are now professors.

Randall Buth

I think that most students do not use Greek because they have not reached a level of reliably extracting information in Greek.

Mark House

My response here will be similar to my previous one. The majority of students who go on to pastoral careers or advanced theological studies will continue with their Greek, at least in the sense that they will used the tools and consult the Greek text related to their work with commentaries. Sadly, I would guess that only a minority of the students will attain anything approaching mastery.

Anonymous 1

Probably not as much they could, since they have minimal proficiency and it takes too much time to work through the Greek of a passage. But hopefully they have enough knowledge to read an exegetical commentary and follow the argument for one interpretation over another, and then form their own opinion. And of course, some students know just enough Greek to be dangerous, and make egregious mistakes if they try to display their knowledge of Greek in the pulpit.

Con Campbell

Mostly, yes. Anecdotal evidence.

Samuel Lamerson

I make special efforts to teach students why the language is important for their exegesis. I teach them not only the language but also how to use computer tools as an aid, not a substitute. I hope that this causes them to go on and use their Greek in regular ministry. I stress to them that learning to look up words is not really reading the language and that if they will simply commit to reading for 10-15 minutes a day their Greek will get better in small steps.

Justin Langford

The majority, no. Reasons for this could include time demands and ministry demands.

Anonymous 2

No. Most do not get enough Greek. Most students only take 2 semesters and at [my school] this often means only learning the basic grammar (and not syntax). Language cannot be properly understood or used without learning syntax. This is why we have started introducing syntax elements in Greek 2. Other are simply lazy and are not good stewards of what they have been entrusted with.

Anonymous 5

They don't. My evidence is anecdotal.

David Croteau

No. Many reasons. 1) Some seminaries require a minimal knowledge (1 year of just grammar) of either Greek or Hebrew. By doing this, students never reach the level of comfortability to continue their study on their own. 2) They get in to ministry and don't have the time to keep using it. 3) They were never taught how to actually use Greek in preparing sermons or teaching Bible studies. Greek professors typically teach Greek; homiletics professors teach preaching. If there is no integration between the two, most students won't be able to do this on their own.

Robert Plummer

Too many let their skills erode. That's why I started the Daily Dose of Greek.

Mitzi Smith

No. Not in helpful ways. Some students might throw out a Greek word here or there (whether they had Greek or not) in a sermon—for example "and Jesus ate bread. The Greek word for bread is artos". But how is this helpful? Anybody who has not taken a Greek course can find this out. But it is not theologically or hermeneutically insightful or helpful. It takes more opportunities for study, as Ph.D. students know.

A. Chadwick Thornhill

I think most students continue to use their skills, but probably not with the regularity I would hope. It generally seems to become a supplemental part of their teaching/sermon prep rather than a core or essential part of it.

Mark Strauss

I would expect that only a minority do.

Anonymous 11

> Probably not a 'majority' use it 'regularly' or in significant doses . . . but 30-40% use it in a 'strategic' way (key verses looked at closely when the need is felt by the pastor/teacher) . . . I suspect 70% don't use it much at all . . . I do hear pastors reference Greek but it's almost always to mention a word that "means this in the Greek" (usually not necessary in the sermon, adding little . . . one wonders why they do so . . .) Pastors/students I've known who do keep their Greek skills active always express deep appreciation for it and the impact it has on the quality of their interpretive labors as well as their homiletical outcomes

Delio DelRio

> No. After only two semesters, most students do not think themselves to be proficient enough, and the average church ministry doesn't require the skill of translating the Greek text. As a result, many lose the skill over time.

Anonymous 6

> No; those who are pastors have other duties than are more pressing, such as visitation; meetings, etc.

William Varner

> They were not taught well.

Markus Klausli

> This is also mixed. Some make it a regular part of the devotional/ministry life. Others never pick them up again.

David Woodall

> Most of them do not use it in the robust way that we would desire them to do. I think our (seminary students) use it more because we also incorporate the Logos Bible software into the training. This gives them greater tools to explore the use of Greek and Hebrew after graduation.

Anonymous 8

> I think that probably about 30% continue to use their Greek knowledge in ministry. Those who do so do so because they are convinced

of the value. Others fall victim to time pressures or environments where there is no reward or even disincentive to having and using such knowledge. This is probably a comment more on the modern church than it is on Greek.

Charles Quarles

Yes, but most only at a superficial level.

Danny Zacharias

No. But I do think it has increased with the prevalence of Bible Software.

Anonymous 4

Yes. Our alumni tell us they do.

Alan Bandy

Only those who continue on for a second year of Greek have the skills to use their Greek on a regular basis in ministry. Those with only one year of Greek will typically forget about 85-95% of what they learned, but will attempt to sound like they know Greek in their sermons by mentioning the meaning of a Greek word or case/tense. While this sounds like I am being negative, but I have been in ministry for 25 years and I have known a lot of pastors who don't know Greek although they had a year of it in seminary.

Anonymous 7

I think about half of my students go on to use their Greek in the future. But this is based only upon anecdotal remarks; I have never done a formal survey to find out whether this is correct or not.

9—Do you believe theological institutions should require more or less biblical language courses at the bachelors or masters levels? Please explain your reasoning.

Randall Buth

Obviously more is needed if we will treat the NT as God's Word, but qualitatively, this requires a new training paradigm, too.

David Croteau

> It's more complicated than a simple "more" or "less" answer, especially for the master's level. I wish every M.Div. student was required to take four semesters of each language. However, if my seminary did that, many students would avoid the M.Div. (just do an M.A.) or would go to another seminary to avoid that. So I wish we could require more, but without any students, it wouldn't matter what we required.

Alan Bandy

> Considering I teach Greek at an undergraduate university, I would say that they absolutely should require more pre-requisite Greek for an MDiv or MA. My students are able to go farther in Greek at the bachelors level then most students ever do at a seminary. My students who continue on to seminary often tell me how much easier the Greek classes are in seminary than my classes were. They excel in seminary and are well equipped for Ph.D. work down the road.

Anonymous 6

> More, but good luck with that since trend is toward reduction of units in MDiv

Anonymous 3

> I believe a reasonable objective should be proficiency in at least one biblical language beyond the tools level is the appropriate starting point. (In our seminary, that objective translates into two years of one language.) Ideally, I would like to see two years of one language and one year of the other (e.g., 2 years of Greek + 1 year of Hebrew).

> See the answer to 3.1 above. Both testaments are important, and proficiency in both Greek and Hebrew add value to the study of the text.

Danny Zacharias

> As a biblical scholar, I am always inclined to more language training :-) I am certainly opposed to wholesale removal of Greek and Hebrew, but beyond that I leave it to the discernment of the institution's leadership.

Michael Heiser

> See the above—a tools-based course should be required for everyone in every program. Same for Hebrew.

Mark House

> I took Greek on the college level at a Bible college, and I wish more students pursuing ministry had the opportunity to take biblical Greek on the college level as I did. This would make the demands of seminary much less daunting. The seminary I attended expected that students would have gotten their beginning Greek "out of the way" before beginning their seminary studies, and they offered intensive summer programs to that end. All that said, I think the competency required by our current curriculum is about all that can be expected, though I do wish the advanced New Testament courses would require Greek and a prerequisite and would incorporate more Greek translation and exegesis into their curriculum.

Anonymous 1

> I think at least three semesters of at least one of the biblical languages should be required for those majoring in Christian biblical studies or doing graduate work for professional biblical vocation. Students need to be introduced to the primary texts of their discipline, and to the ancient cultures that produced those texts. And the study of a language within a culture nurtures a mental discipline that few other courses do.

David Woodall

> There should be more at the seminary level where students get their professional degree.

Samuel Lamerson

> I believe that in a perfect world most schools (including my own) need more Greek training. I also believe that almost every department feels this way. Historians feel that there is not enough history, Hebrew scholars that there is not enough Hebrew, etc. Thus, everyone must be willing to compromise somewhat. I think that the cut-off line for me would be at least 3 semesters of Greek. Any less than this is, I feel, not enough to enable the student to make real use of the language.

Justin Langford

> As a Greek teacher, my initial answer is more, but this depends on the school and its language program. Here at my institution we have a good balance with our other courses in the degree program.

Anonymous 2

> More, at least at the masters level. As stated earlier, without an adequate knowledge of syntax, one cannot interpret the Scriptures and thus cannot properly use the Greek they have learned. If someone is planning to be a pastor or is planning to teach the Bible in various capacities, why wouldn't they want to read the Bible in the original languages?

Anonymous 5

> More courses are needed in order to read the GNT with comprehension.

James Voelz

> It is helpful if students have more than minimal competency at the bachelor's level, so that the hours spent teaching the languages can be spent on exegesis and hermeneutics.

Robert Plummer

> I'm biased, but at least one year of Greek and one year of Hebrew should be mandatory.

Anonymous 8

> I think that all levels of theological education should, in an ideal world, require more biblical language courses. I want my surgeon to know anatomy also. I think that decreasing language requirements is a way of undermining the foundations of ministry. However, I do not live in an ideal world, and the reality is that it is increasingly difficult to get students to take programs with language requirements. Churches and denominations do not require degrees with language requirements for ordination (some require no degrees whatsoever or require only minimal education), and students are increasingly aware of this.

Charles Quarles

> Absolutely. Most of first-year Greek is spent laying the essential foundation for Greek study through vocabulary acquisition and introduction of the grammatical system. Greek syntax is the most helpful aspect of Greek study for NT interpretation, but students are barely exposed to syntax. Students have too little opportunity to see the usefulness of Greek study for exegesis in just one year.

Anonymous 7

> I believe that seminaries should require 12 credit hours of Greek, including whatever amount of time it takes to accomplish elementary Greek proficiency (4-6 credit hours), a dedicated reading regiment (2-3 credit hours), and a dose of syntax and exegesis 3-6 credit hours). I won't comment on Hebrew.
>
> I think that undergraduate programs should include a biblical language option/track, but should also make a way for students to earn a degree in Bible somehow without any of the biblical languages. (Note that my school, [omitted], does not currently include that option. All Biblical & Theological Studies undergraduate students take 12 units of either Greek or Hebrew.)

Con Campbell

> More, not less. Standards are already slipping and this knowledge/skill is precious.

Anonymous 9

> I can speak to a master's level: I would love more space for languages, and we used to have more credits devoted to Greek. But I don't think that's very likely in a climate of decreased degree sizes. I feel fairly content still having 7.5 credits required and the options of teaching upper level independent studies and the more informal reading groups, as we offer at [my school]. More practice, whatever the method of learning, is always beneficial.

Maurice Robinson

> As noted above, I really prefer the biblical languages to be elective, but with more courses beyond the beginning level offered. If the languages are to be required, then no biblical book courses based on only the

English Bible should be permitted; the required languages should be prerequisite. If not, then there is less reason for students to continue using the language material that otherwise was imposed upon them.

Markus Klausli

Students who enter seminary with the languages behind them will be in a much better position to use the languages in exegesis. Given that, however, many people enter ministry training after completing a BA in another field, making a requirement is not realistic. That said, language courses could be counted as basic entrance requirements for MDiv work so that do not count toward the degree program. This is the model in German universities where students must pass exams in Greek, Hebrew, and Latin before they begin theological studies.

Anonymous 4

Again, if they are planning on going into teaching, they need to understand the issues as stake. That includes the complexities of the translation process as well as the skill set needed to evaluate or make sound exegetical decisions.

Mark Strauss

I think they should require more. But the direction of theological education toward programs that are shorter and cheaper will almost certainly move away from this. This is why learning how to use Greek and how not to use it is critically important. Teaching students linguistics is as important as teaching them Greek in this regard.

Mitzi Smith

It depends on a student's goals. Perhaps, students need one year of their study just to figure this out. We are so rigid in theological education. If students really want to use their Greek in meaningful ways in any space or ministry, they need more. But this needs to be an option and we need to find ways to help them figure this out. Not everybody can study a language and some don't know they can until they do.

A. Chadwick Thornhill

As a language teacher, I would say more, of course. In our MDiv program, we have a "tools" track and a grammar track. My preference would be to require languages for all students, but I also understand that some students are never quite able, regardless of how much tutoring they are given, to progress significantly in their language study. Some students seem more wired for it than others

Anonymous 10

> Our institution is heavy on languages, and I think that is about right. But institutions in general have been reducing or eliminating the topic, which is a mistake. First, because the interpretation of sacred texts is the church's main job; but negatively, because (especially with the misuse of Hebrew in Latin America), there is an apologetic function of biblical languages, to be able to defend against poor doctrine.

William Varner

> More. They learn pastoral theology and preaching by doing it or under the tutoring of a pastor. They must learn Greek in school.

Delio DelRio

> Ideally? . . . more at masters level, but that's difficult to accomplish given the current educational and student market climate

Anonymous 11

> 2 years seems a minimum for an MDiv or MA (Bib Studies) program

Dan Wallace

> Much more. This is the material foundation of our faith. We have been chipping away at the languages for a long time, in spite of what the Reformers stood for. The methodological battle cry of the Reformation—ad fontes!—and the formal battle cry—sola scriptura—are crucial for the evangelical faith. Second Timothy 4.2 comes to mind: "proclaim the word; be persistent whether it is convenient or inconvenient" (NAB).

10—If you could make ANY changes to the current pedagogical process of teaching Greek (ex., Grammar-Translation Method), what would they be and why?

Samuel Lamerson

> I wish that we had more time and could learn to write/speak as well as translate. However, given the pressures that the average student is under, this is just not possible at my school.

Randall Buth

> Teach Greek as a human language. Use what SLA knows will work for internalizing a language and avoid what SLA knows will hinder learning (e.g. GTM). Set the standard at a practical level: able to discuss letters of Paul in Greek, or able to discuss Josephus in Greek.

Anonymous 9

> As I've already mentioned a few times (and see link), I would wish all teachers of Greek to highlight solid linguistic principles so that Greek could be used more judiciously and with respect for its parameters in teaching and preaching. I refer to teaching Greek in ways that take seriously Barr's critique many years ago (see Moo's "We Still Don't Get It").

Alan Bandy

> I would include an immersive element of learning biblical Greek as a living language that is spoken. I have been experimenting with this and found that a reading only approach does not work well for language acquisition. When they can read, hear, and speak Greek they do much better.

Anonymous 6

> Medicate obsessive-compulsive teachers who love excruciating language details to the expense of good learning.

Anonymous 3

> None of which I am aware.

Michael Heiser

> See the above. We need to place thinking exegetically above memorization and translating. Even if students get A's in traditional courses and love those courses, they will never maintain that proficiency. Think about it. To really maintain that level, you'd need 10-12 hours

a week to keep reviewing vocab, reviewing forms, reviewing syntax categories you memorized. How many pastors even spend 10 hrs a week on sermons based on the ENGLISH Bible? Very few nowadays. Asking them to do this in Greek (And Hebrew, too - the OT is ¾ of the Bible) is delusional on our part. But we keep doing it because that's the way it's always been done.

Mark House

I feel that the 13-week semester is too compressed for most students. At one seminary where I teach, Greek is distributed over three 13-week semesters, and I like that better than trying to compress the same material into two 13-week semesters. I have no objection to the GTM approach as such, since I think that in addition to teaching Greek it gives students a better foundation in their understanding of language in general, which is no longer adequately taught in "grammar" school and high school.

Anonymous 1

a. That administrators would realize that classes in ancient languages will always be small relative to other courses, and not take that as a negative indicator.

b. That vocabulary learning be based more on semantic domains and less on the sheer frequency of occurrence.

c. That texts of biblical books and other contemporary Greek literature be produced with revisions to vocab and syntax appropriate to each level course, allowing students to read larger portions of text earlier in their studies.

David Croteau

A former student of mine did his Th.M. thesis at SEBTS (Shane Kraeger). He gave a compelling argument for starting with the infinitive and not the indicative. Many languages do this (Spanish, for example). I think if we started with the infinitive, it would help students grasp verbal aspect better and make more sense of different aorist forms. Unfortunately, BDAG (or something like it) would have to be re-written with the verbs listed in the infinitive form.

We need to do a better job of teaching students how to process through translating sentences.

Anonymous 8

> I think that current pedagogical processes of teaching Greek have accomplished an incredible amount. In a relatively short amount of time, the student moves from no knowledge of Greek to being able to perform the basic kinds of analysis that can provide value for teaching and ministry. However, the climate in which such work is being done has changed radically. Students are now already involved in ministry, have work and family responsibilities, and have often not learned to study in ways appropriate for learning Greek or seen its value in their own church contexts. The change needed would be either to change the environment of contemporary theological education—which is unreasonable, I realize—or find a way to convince students that they can and should study Greek—so far this has not worked—or find a way to accomplish the same goals in a different way with less required and less time commitment. However, I do now know what that pedagogical process is. I know that the immersion method is not the answer, as it requires a larger time commitment, an unreal environment, and does not produce the same tangible results for proportionate investment.

Con Campbell

> More Greek reading as soon as possible as this is key to enjoyment, inductive learning and consolidation.

Charles Quarles

> Introduce syntax along with grammar in the first year of study.

Anonymous 7

> If I could make any change to the current pedagogical process found at most schools, I would continue with the GTM, but would encourage people to use music to accomplish the large amount of grammar memorization that Greek requires. I have already made a way to accomplish this through [omitted]. My graduates will testify that even a decade out from school, they can still sing through all the basic Greek grammar they learned through music; that is, they have not forgotten it the way most students do. My former students still know their articles, noun endings, indicative verb endings, participles, infinitives, imperatives, etc., not to mention contract forms, forms of eimi, and the various meanings of the prepositions with their attendant cases.

Music employs parts of your brain to help you remember that other methods do not.

Maurice Robinson

Only as noted above: if possible, more hours per course, more weeks per semester, and certainly not allowing students to take over 12 sem. hrs. when a beginning language course is attempted.

Anonymous 10

It would be great to meet more often (we meet weekly) and study regularly and intensively together.

Mitzi Smith

I would write my own text. I have drawn from two or three in the past. Students learn differently texts don't account for this—those that I've used and seen. I would do what I mention in #9 above.

Justin Langford

I personally prefer mixing in some purely inductive approaches on occasion to give the students a different perspective on and exposure to the language.

Anonymous 2

Have a more stream-lined textbook that focused on the essentials.

Integrate more of the usage of tools and the interpretative process so that students become familiar with precisely how to use Greek in their ministries.

Danny Zacharias

Perhaps some more immersive methods and focus on pronunciation. Most intro grammars are also still locked in to the Erasmian pronunciation (myself included) but Reconstructed Koine pronunciation should probably be made more prevalent.

Anonymous 11

In 1st year Greek, the challenge is in finding a balance between the basic information one must know by memory to read with any level of joy and effectiveness . . . and having too much technical jargon (especially true in arcane and ultimately inexplicable matters of morphology) that will only be tangentially related to any preaching and teaching in the student's future . . . I work overtime to make the connection between a 'working knowledge' of Greek and the preaching teaching tasks students are truly passionate about pursuing with excellence. For instance, phrase diagramming can be clearly related to a sermon outline and key input in the sermon itself . . . .

Mark Strauss

Anything that would give students greater exposure to the text would be helpful. For example, Robert Plumber has a "daily dose of Greek" website which could be viewed daily by students. This kind of exposure will enable him to retain the languages.

Dan Wallace

I would like to have a more conversational approach to the language, which would require more class hours to accomplish.

A. Chadwick Thornhill

My main desire would be to see integration of larger reading/interpretation strategies as well as more inductive study of segments of scripture rather than single verses as most grammars seem to focus on. I haven't yet found a set of resources that accomplishes this. I would say current resources are fully adequate, but I think improvements could be made in these regards.

William Varner

Stop lecturing and model the translation and grammar by oral performance every day in class with prof supervision.

David Woodall

I would like for this method to incorporate more Bible software into the process. This would give the students the tools to continue their Greek studies with joy. It opens up works like BDAG to everyday use.

Anonymous 4

> Language is by nature a skill learned in community. Programs should consider better ways to get students to learn together. Most of our students do homework in groups and in addition we have a number of advanced students who serve as tutors every year (approximately 7-8 at a time). Faculty directly mentor these tutors and collectively our program creates a communal atmosphere that students regularly refer to as their Hebrew family. Community is one of the greatest facilitators of success.

Markus Klausli

> Given curriculum realities, I am pretty happy with our approach and text used for teaching Greek. In addition, a plethora of resources exist (in book and online formats) to help students with the languages.

James Voelz

> At CSL we have reduced the number of weeks and hours in the summer crash course—I designed this—to minimize what I talked about above, viz., "just in case" morphology. We have gone from 50 to 35 days/10 weeks to 7. I think that this is doable, given my experience in teaching in a different seminary setting with fewer hours (Kenrick-Glennon, the diocesan seminary of the Roman Catholic church in St. Louis).

Delio DelRio

> Stretch out the material that is usually taught in one semester into two semesters, thereby increasing Greek from 1 year to 2 years in length.

Bibliography

Adrados, Francisco Rodríguez. *A History of the Greek Language: From Its Origins to the Present.* Leiden; Boston: Brill, 2005.
Aland, Kurt, and Barbara Aland. *The Text of the New Testament: An Introduction to the Critical Editions and to the Theory and Practice of Modern Textual Criticism.* 2nd ed., rev. and enl. Grand Rapids: Eerdmans, 1995.
Anderson, Lorin. *A Taxonomy for Learning, Teaching, and Assessing: A Revision of Bloom's Taxonomy of Educational Objectives.* New York: Longman, 2001.
Angus, Samuel. "Modern Methods in New Testament Philology." *Harvard Theological Review* 4.2 (1909): 446–64.
Arndt, William, Frederick W Danker, and Walter Bauer. *A Greek-English Lexicon of the New Testament and Other Early Christian Literature.* 3rd ed. Chicago: University of Chicago, 2000.
Asher, James. "The Learning Strategy of the Total Physical Response: A Review." *Modern Language Journal* 50 (1966): 79–84.
———. "The Total Physical Response Approach to Second Language Learning." *Modern Language Journal* 53 (1969): 3–17.
Aubrey, Mike. "Daniel Streett on Learning Greek." *Koine Greek.* 28 May 2009. https://koine-greek.com/2009/05/28/daniel-streett-on-learning-greek/.
Baugh, S. M. *A New Testament Greek Primer.* Phillipsburg, NJ: P & R, 2012.
Beekes, R. S. P., and Lucien van Beek. *Etymological Dictionary of Greek.* Leiden: Brill, 2010.
Berding, Kenneth. *Sing and Learn New Testament Greek: The Easiest Way to Learn Greek Grammar.* Grand Rapids: Zondervan, 2008.
Berry, Tim. "What is a SWOT Analysis." *Bplans.* https://articles.bplans.com/how-to-perform-swot-analysis/.
Black, David A. *It's Still Greek to Me: An Easy-to-Understand Guide to Intermediate Greek.* Grand Rapids: Baker, 1998.
———. *Learn to Read New Testament Greek.* 3rd ed. Nashville: B&H, 2009.
———. *New Testament Textual Criticism: A Concise Guide.* Grand Rapids: Baker, 1994.
———. *Using New Testament Greek in Ministry: A Practical Guide for Students and Pastors.* Grand Rapids: Baker, 1993.
Bloom, Benjamin, Max Engelhart, Edward Furst, Walker Hill, and David Krathwohl. *Taxonomy of Educational Objectives: The Classification of Educational Goals.* Handbook I: Cognitive Domain. New York: David McKay Company, 1956.
Bluedorn, Harvey. *A Review of English Grammar for Students of Biblical Greek (and other Ancient Languages).* New Boston, IL: Trivium, 2008.
Boettcher, Judith V., and Rita-Marie Conrad. *The Online Teaching Survival Guide.* 2nd ed. Hoboken, NJ: Jossey-Bass, 2016.

Booth, Margaret Z., and Jean M. Gerard. "Self–Esteem and Academic Achievement: A Comparative Study of Adolescent Students in England and the United States." *Compare: A Journal of Comparative and International Education* 41.5 (2011): 629–48.

Brooks, James A., and Carlton L Winbery. *Syntax of New Testament Greek*. Washington, D.C.: University Press of America, 1978.

Brown, H. Douglas. *Principles of Language Learning and Teaching*. 5th ed. White Plains, NY: Pearson Longman, 2007.

Bruner, Jerome. *The Process of Education*. Cambridge, MA: Harvard University Press, 1960.

———. "The Role of Dialogue in Language Acquisition." In *The Child's Concept of Language*. Edited by A. Sinclair, R. J. Jarvelle, and W. J. M. Levelt. New York: Springer-Verlag, 1978.

Buth, Randall. "Eureka! I Found a New Approach to Greek." *Biblical Language Center*. 29 April 2012. https://www.biblicallanguagecenter.com/eureka-approach-greek/.

Campbell, Constantine. *Advances in the Study of Greek: New Insights for Reading the New Testament*. Grand Rapids: Zondervan, 2015.

———. *Basics of Verbal Aspect in Biblical Greek*. Grand Rapids: Zondervan, 2008.

———. *Keep your Greek: Strategies for Busy People*. Grand Rapids: Zondervan, 2010.

Caragounis, Chrys C. *The Development of Greek and the New Testament: Morphology, Syntax, Phonology, and Textual Transmission*. 1st pbk. ed., with corrections. Grand Rapids: Baker, 2006.

Carson, D. A. *Exegetical Fallacies*. 2nd ed. Carlisle, UK; Grand Rapids: Paternoster, 1996.

Christidēs, A.-F., Maria Arapopoulou, Maria Chritē, and Centre for the Greek Language. *A History of Ancient Greek: From the Beginnings to Late Antiquity*. Rev. & expanded translation of the Greek text. Cambridge, UK; New York: Cambridge University Press, 2007.

Coakley, James, and David Woodall. "Using Bible Software to Exegete the Text." Pages 389–406 in *The Moody Handbook of Preaching*. Edited by John Koessler. Chicago: Moody, 2008

Countryman, Louis William. *The New Testament is in Greek: A Short Course for Exegetes*. Grand Rapids: Eerdmans, 1993.

Croy, N. Clayton. *A Primer of Biblical Greek*. Grand Rapids: Eerdmans, 2011.

DeKeyser, Robert. "Beyond Explicit Rule Learning: Automatizing Second Language Morphosyntax." *Second Language Acquisition* 19 (1997): 195–221.

Dick, Walter, and Lou Carey. *The Systematic Design of Instruction*. 8th ed. New York: Harper Collins, 2014.

Doughty, Catherine., and Michael H. Long. *The Handbook of Second Language Acquisition*. Malden, MA: Blackwell, 2003.

Dunn, James D. G. *The Epistles to the Colossians and to Philemon: A Commentary on the Greek Text*. Grand Rapids: Eerdmans, 1996.

Duvall, J. Scott, and Verlyn Verbrugge. *Devotions on the Greek New Testament: 52 Reflections to Inspire and Instruct*. Grand Rapids: Zondervan, 2012.

Easley, Kendell H. *User–friendly Greek: A Common Sense Approach to the Greek New Testament*. Nashville: B & H, 1994.

Eckman, Fred R., and Linguistics Symposium of the University of Wisconsin–Milwaukee. *Second Language Acquisition: Theory and Pedagogy*. Mahwah, NJ: L. Erlbaum Associates, 1995.

Ellis, Rod, and Natsuko Shintani. *Exploring Language Pedagogy Through Second Language Acquisition Research*. New York: Routledge, 2014.

———. *Task-Based Language Learning and Teaching*. Oxford, New York: Oxford Applied Linguistics, 2003.

Erasmus, Desiderius. *Collected Works of Erasmus*. Edited by Richard Schoeck and Beatrice Corrigan. Toronto: University of Toronto, 1974.

Fairbairn, Donald. *Understanding Language: A Guide for Beginning Students of Greek and Latin*. Washington, D.C.: Catholic University of America Press, 2011.

Fasold, Ralph W., and Jeff Connor-Linton. *An Introduction to Language and Linguistics*. 2nd ed. Cambridge: Cambridge, 2014.

Fee, Gordon D. *New Testament Exegesis: A Handbook for Students and Pastors*. 3rd ed. Louisville, KY: John Knox, 2002.

Found, James, and Bruce Olson. *Basic Greek in 30 Minutes a Day: A Self-Study Introduction to New Testament Greek*. Bloomington, MN: Bethany House, 2012.

Fuller Theological Seminary. "Biblical Languages." http://www.fuller.global/biblicalstudies/.

Gass, Susan M., and Larry Selinker. *Second Language Acquisition: An Introductory Course*. 3rd ed. New York: Routledge/Taylor and Francis Group, 2008.

Gibson, Richard J., and Constantine R. Campbell. *Reading Biblical Greek: A Grammar for Students*. Grand Rapids: Zondervan, 2017.

Goodrich, Richard, and David Diewert. *A Summer Greek Reader: A Workbook for Maintaining Your Biblical Greek*. Grand Rapids: Zondervan, 2001.

Goodrick, Edward W. *Do It Yourself Hebrew and Greek: Everybody's Guide to the Language Tools*. 2nd ed. Grand Rapids: Zondervan, 1980.

Grattan, C. Hartley. *In Quest of Knowledge: A Historical Perspective on Adult Education*. New York: Association, 1955.

Groeling, Jeff, and Lester Ruth. "'The Times, They Are a-changin': How a Training Seminar for Online Education Changed a Seminary One Faculty Member at a Time." *Theological Education* 42.2 (2007): 57–66.

Guasti, Maria Teresa. *Language Acquisition: The Growth of Grammar*. Cambridge, MA: MIT Press, 2002.

Gupta, Nijay. *Prepare, Succeed, Advance: A Guidebook for Getting a PhD in Biblical Studies and Beyond*. Eugene, OR: Wipf and Stock, 2011.

Guthrie, George H., and J. Scott Duvall. *Biblical Greek Exegesis*. Grand Rapids: Zondervan, 1998.

Hansen, Hardy, and Gerald M Quinn. *Greek, an Intensive Course*. 2nd rev. ed. New York: Fordham University Press, 1992.

Harlow, Joel. "Successfully Teaching Biblical Languages Online at the Seminary Level: Guiding Principles of Course Design and Delivery." *Teaching Theology and Religion* 10.1 (2007): 13–24.

Harris, Murray J. *Colossians and Philemon*. B & H, 2013.

Hatch, Evelyn. *Second Language Acquisition: A Book of Readings*. Rowley, MA: Newbury House, 1978.

Hege, Brent A. R. "The Online Theology Classroom: Strategies for Engaging a Community of Distance Learners in a Hybrid Model of Online Education." *Teaching Theology & Religion* 14.1 (January 2011): 13–20.

Heiser, Michael. "Why Don't Scholars Understand Logos' Learn to Use Greek and Hebrew?" (sic). *NakedBible* 11 December 2012. http://drmsh.com/scholars-understand-logos-learn-greek-hebrew/.

Hillerbrand, Joachim. *The Reformation: A Narrative History Related by Contemporary Observers and Participants*. Grand Rapids: Baker, 1987.

Huffman, Douglas S. *The Handy Guide to New Testament Greek: Grammar, Syntax, and Diagramming*. Grand Rapids: Kregel, 2012.

Jackson, Paul Norman. *Devotions on the Greek New Testament, Volume Two: 52 Reflections to Inspire and Instruct*. Grand Rapids: Zondervan, 2017.

Jannaris, Anthony Nicholas. *An Historical Greek Grammar, Chiefly of the Attic Dialect as Written and Spoken from Classical Antiquity Down to the Present Time*. London; New York: Macmillan, 1897.

Kantenwein, Lee H. *Diagrammatical Analysis*. Winona Lake, IN: BMH Books, 1991.

Kemper, Jack. "Assessing the Response of Subject Matter Experts to a Limited Greek Grammar." DMin. diss., Oral Roberts University, 2011.

Kimak, Matthew. "A Relational Study of the Perceptions of the Students, Faculty, and Administration Concerning the Master of Divinity Program at Southeastern Baptist Theological Seminary from 2005–2009." EdD diss., Southeastern Baptist Theological Seminary, 2010.

King, Charles. "The Method of Teaching New Testament Greek." *Christian Perspectives of Education* 2.2 (2009): 1–12.

Köstenberger, Andreas, Benjamin Merkle, and Robert Plummer. *Going Deeper with New Testament Greek: An Intermediate Study of the Grammar and Syntax of the New Testament*. Nashville: B & H, 2016.

Kotter, John P. *A Sense of Urgency*. Boston: Harvard Business Press, 2008.

Koutropoulos, Apostolos. "Modernizing Classical Language Education: Communicative Language Teaching & Educational Technology Integration in Classical Greek." *Human Architecture: Journal of the Society of Self-Knowledge* 9.3 (2011): 55–69.

Krashen, Stephen D. *Principles and Practice in Second Language Acquisition*. New York; London: Phoenix ELT, 1995.

Kusurkar, R. A., Th. J. Ten Cate, C. M. P. Vos, P. Westers, and G. Croiset. "How Motivation Affects Academic Performance: A Structural Equation Modelling Analysis." *Advances in Health Science Education* 22 February 2012. https://www.ncbi.nlm.nih.gov/pmc/articles/PMC3569579/.

Lambert, William T. "Using an Adaptive–Mastery System to Teach Inductive Exegesis in the Greek–English New Testament: Description and Application." EdD diss., University of Arkansas, 1991.

Lamerson, Samuel. *English Grammar to Ace New Testament Greek*. Grand Rapids: Zondervan, 2004.

Larsen-Freeman, Diane, and Marti Anderson. *Techniques and Principles in Language Teaching*. 3rd ed. Oxford; New York: Oxford University Press, 2011.

Lehmann, Helmut T., and Walther I. Brandt, eds. *Luther's Works: The Christian in Society II*. Luther's Works. Philadelphia: Fortress, 1962.

Lightbown, Patsy, and Nina Margaret Spada. *How Languages are Learned*. 3rd ed. Oxford; New York: Oxford University Press, 2006.

Long, Mike. *Second Language Acquisition and Task-Based Language Teaching*. Oxford: Wiley-Blackwell, 2014.

Loschky, Lester, and Robert Bley-Vromon. "Grammar and Task-Based Methodology." Pages 123–67 in *Tasks and Language Learning*. Edited by Graham Crookes and Susan M. Gass. Bristol, UK: Multilingual Matters, 1993.

Louw, J. P., and Eugene A. Nida. *Greek-English Lexicon of the New Testament: Based on Semantic Domains*. 2nd ed. New York: United Bible Societies, 1989.

Major, Claire Howell. *Teaching Online: A Guide to Theory, Research, and Practice*. Baltimore: Johns Hopkins, 2015.

Marzano, Robert, Debra Pickering, and Jane Pollock. *Classroom Instruction that Works: Research-Based Strategies for Increasing Student Achievement*. Alexandria, VA: Association for Supervision and Curriculum Development, 2001.

———. *Designing a New Taxonomy of Educational Objectives*. Thousand Oaks, CA: Corwin, 2001.

McKeachie, Wilbert James. *McKeachie's Teaching Tips: Strategies, Research, and Theory for College and University Teachers*. 11th ed. College Teaching Series. Boston: Houghton Mifflin Co., 2002.

McLaughlin, Barry. "'Conscious' Verses 'Unconscious' Learning." *TESOL Quarterly* 24 (1990): 617–34.

McManis, Carolyn, Deborah Stollenwerk, Zheng-sheng Zhang, and The Ohio State University Dept. of Linguistics. *Language Files: Materials for an Introduction to Language*. 4th ed. Reynoldsburg, OH: Advocate Pub. Group, 1988.

Merkle, Benjamin, and Robert Plummer. *Greek for Life: Strategies for Learning, Retaining, and Reviving New Testament Greek*. Grand Rapids: Baker, 2017.

Miller, Rebecca. "Best Practices in Online Education." *American Theological Library Association Summary of Proceedings* 65 (2011): 113–21.

Mishra, Punya, and Matthew Koehler. "Technological Pedagogical Content Knowledge: A Framework for Integrating Technology in Teacher Knowledge." *Teachers College Record* 108.6 (2006): 1017–54.

Misut, Martin, and Katarina Pribilova. "Measuring Quality in Context of E-Learning." *Procedia – Social and Behavioral Sciences* 177 (2015): 312–19.

Moo, Douglas J. *The Letters to the Colossians and to Philemon*. Grand Rapids: Eerdmans, 2008.

Morris, Michael. *An Introduction to the Philosophy of Language*. Cambridge; New York: Cambridge University Press, 2007.

Morrison, Debbie. "How 'Good' is Your Online Course? Five Steps to Assess Course Quality." *Online Learning Insights* 26 May 2015. https://onlinelearninginsights.wordpress.com/2015/05/26/how-good-is-your-online-course-five-steps-to-assess-course-quality/.

Morse, MaryKate. "Enhancing the Learning and Retention of Biblical Languages for Adult Students." *Faculty Publications – George Fox Evangelical Seminary* 31 (2004): 45–50.

Moss, Connie, and Susan Brookhart. *Learning Targets: Helping Students Aim for Understanding in Today's Lesson*. Alexandria, VA: ASCD, 2012.

Mounce, William. *Basics of Biblical Greek Grammar*. 3rd ed. Grand Rapids: Zondervan, 2009.

———. *A Graded Reader of Biblical Greek*. Grand Rapids: Zondervan, 1996.

———. *Greek for the Rest of Us: Mastering Bible Study without Mastering Biblical Languages*. Grand Rapids: Zondervan, 2003.

Nam, Roger S. "Online Theological Education: Perspectives from First-Generation Asian-American Students." *Theological Education* 45.1 (2009): 59–69.

Nitz, Paul. "Communicative Greek.old. (sic.)" *Youtube.com* 14 June 2015. https://www.youtube.com/playlist?list=PLpxcmJ23ymcWixPoZUqggk-IztqZb57hG.

Nordling, John G. "Teaching Greek at the Seminary." *Logia* 21.2 (2012): 69–75.

Nunan, David. *Second Language Teaching & Learning*. Boston: Heinle, Cengage Learning, 1999.

———. *Task-Based Language Teaching*. Cambridge: Cambridge Language Teaching Library, 2004.

O'Donnell, Matthew Brook. *Corpus Linguistics and the Greek of the New Testament*. Sheffield: Sheffield Phoenix, 2005.

Okode, Enoch. "A Case for Biblical Languages: Are Hebrew and Greek Optional or Indispensable?" *African Journal for Evangelical Theology* 29.2 (2010): 91–106.

Overland, Paul. "Can Communicative Methods Enhance Ancient Language Acquisition?" *Teaching Theology and Religion* 7.1 (2004): 51–57.

Pao, David W. *Colossians & Philemon*. Zondervan Exegetical Commentary Series on the New Testament. Grand Rapids: Zondervan, 2012.

Perry, Peter S. *Brushing up English to Learn Greek*. Eugene, OR: Resource Publications, 2014.

Philonenko, Alexis. "Langue Morte et Langue Vivante." *Revue de Métaphysique et de Morale* 54.2 (2007): 157–78.

Plummer, Robert L. *40 Questions About Interpreting the Bible*. Grand Rapids: Kregel, 2010.

———. "Daily Dose of Greek." https://dailydoseofgreek.com/.

Porter, Stanley E. *Idioms of the Greek New Testament*. 2nd ed., with corrections. Sheffield: Sheffield Academic, 1999.

———. *Linguistic Analysis of the Greek New Testament: Studies in Tools, Methods, and Practice*. Sheffield: Sheffield Phoenix, 2015.

———. "The Usage-Based Approach to Teaching New Testament Greek." *Biblical and Ancient Greek Linguistics* 3 (2014): 120–40.

Porter, Stanley E., and Matthew Brook O'Donnell. *The Linguist as Pedagogue: Trends in the Teaching and Linguistic Analysis of the Greek New Testament*. Sheffield: Sheffield Phoenix, 2009.

Porter, Stanley E., Jeffrey Reed, and Matthew O'Donnell. *Fundamentals of New Testament Greek*. Grand Rapids: Eerdmans, 2010.

Prabhu, N. S. *Second Language Pedagogy*. Oxford: Oxford University Press, 1987.

Reformed Theological Seminary. "Summer Institute for Biblical Languages." http://www.rts.edu/site/rtsnearyou/jackson/mdiv/summerinstitute.aspx.

Reiner, Timon. "An Examination of the Basic Linguistic Structures of Biblical Hebrew and Koine Greek with the Purpose of Cross Cultural Communication for Modern Spanish Speakers." Unpublished senior thesis, Southeastern Baptist Theological Seminary, 2016.

Richards, Jack, and Theodore Rodgers. *Approaches and Methods in Language Teaching*. 2nd ed. Cambridge: Cambridge University, 2001.

Rico, Christophe. *Polis: Speaking Ancient Greek as a Living Language*. Jerusalem: Polis Institute Press, 2015.

Robertson, A. T. *The Minister and His Greek New Testament.* Pelham, AL: Solid Ground, 2008.

———. *Word Pictures in the New Testament.* Nashville: Sunday School Board of the Southern Baptist Convention, 1933.

Robinson, Thomas A. *Mastering New Testament Greek: Essential Tools for Students.* Peabody, MA: Hendrickson, 2007.

Rubin, Joan, and Irene Thompson. *How to Be a More Successful Language Learner: Toward Learner Autonomy.* 2nd ed. Boston: Heinle & Heinle, 1994.

Ruck, Carl A. P. *Ancient Greek, a New Approach.* 1st experimental ed. Cambridge, MA: MIT Press, 1968.

Ruijgh, Cornelis Jord, Brian E. Newton, Angeliki Malikouti-Drachman, and Michel Lejeune. "Greek Langugae." *Encylopedia Britannica* 31 January 2018. https://www.britannica.com/topic/Greek-language.

Sanders, Carl II. "Biblical Language Instruction by the Book: Rethinking the Status Quaestionis." *Teaching Theology & Religion* 20.3 (2017): 216–29.

Schmidt, Richard. "Deconstructing Consciousness in Search of Useful Definitions for Applied Linguistics." *AILA Review* 11 (1994): 11–26.

Schultz, Brian. "Why Fluency Workshops?" *Biblical Language Center.* https://www.biblicallanguagecenter.com/fluency-workshops/.

Scovel, Thomas. *Learning New Languages: A Guide to Second Language Acquisition.* Boston: Heinle & Heinle, 2001.

Seltzer, Rick. "Seminaries Squeezed." *Inside Higher Ed.* 27 May 2016. https://www.insidehighered.com/news/2016/05/27/traditional-theological-schools-explore-mergers-and-campus-sales-amid-financial.

Semenov, A. F. *The Greek Language in Its Evolution: An Introduction to Its Scientific Study.* London: G. Allen & Unwin, 1936.

Shulman, Lee. "Those Who Understand: Knowledge Growth in Teaching." *Educational Researcher* 15.2 (1986): 4–14.

Siefert, Thomas Raymond. "Translation in Foreign Language Pedagogy: The Rise and Fall of the Grammar Translation Method." PhD diss., Harvard University, 2013.

Silzer, Peter J., and Thomas John Finley. *How Biblical Languages Work. A Student's Guide to Learning Hebrew and Greek.* Grand Rapids: Kregel, 2004.

Simon, Marilyn, and Jacquelyn White. "Survey / Interview Validation Rubric for an Expert Panel." *Dissertation Recipes* 4 February 2016. http://www.dissertationrecipes.com/surveyinterview-validation-rubric-for-an-expert-panel/.

Smith, William Anton. *Ancient Education.* New York: Philosophical Library, 1955.

Spencer, James. "Online Education and Curricular Design." *Theological Education* 49.2 (2015): 19–31.

Stony Brook University. "Understanding the Difference Between Assessment and Testing." *The Faculty Center.* https://facultycenter.stonybrook.edu/articles/understanding-difference-between-assessment-and-testing.

Streett, Daniel. "Greek Immersion in the Seminary Curriculum–What's Needed to Make it Work? (Basics of Greek Pedagogy, pt. 7)." καὶ τὰ λοιπά 21 September 2011. https://danielstreett.com/2011/09/21/greek-immersion-in-the-seminary-curriculumwhats-needed-to-make-it-work-basics-of-greek-pedagogy-pt-7/.

Swain, Merrill, and Sharon Lapkin. "Problems in Output and the Cognitive Processes They Generate: A Step Towards Second Language Learning." *Applied Linguistics* 16 (1995): 371–91.

Terrell, Tracy. "A Natural Approach to Second Language Acquisition and Learning." *Modern Language Journal* 6 (1977): 325–37.
Thorne, James A. "Biblical Online Education: Contributions from Constructivism." *Christian Education Journal* 10.1 (2013): 99–109.
Thornhill, A. Chadwick. *Greek for Everyone: Introductory Greek for Bible Study and Application*. Grand Rapids: Baker, 2016.
Ulrich, Daniel W. "Could Theological Education be Better Online?" *Brethren Life and Thought* 55.3-4 (September 2010): 18–25.
Van Driel, Edwin Christiaan. "Online Theological Education: Three Undertheorized Issues." *Theological Education* 50.1 (2015): 69–79.
Van Voorst, Robert E. *Building Your New Testament Greek Vocabulary*. Grand Rapids: Eerdmans, 1990.
Via, Marjorie, and Kristen Sosulski. *Essentials of Online Course Design: A Standards-Based Guide*. New York: Routledge, 2016.
Vygotsky, Lev. S. *Mind in Society: The Development of Higher Psychological Processes*. Cambridge, MA: Harvard University Press, 1978.
Wallace, Daniel. *Greek Grammar Beyond the Basics: An Exegetical Syntax of the New Testament with Scripture, Subject, and Greek Word Indexes*. Grand Rapids: Zondervan, 1997.
Wasserman, Tommy, and Peter Gurry. *A New Approach to Textual Criticism: An Introduction to the Coherence-Based Genealogical Method*. Atlanta: SBL, 2017.
Webb, Joseph M., and Robert Kysar. *Greek for Preachers*. St. Louis: Chalice, 2002.
Wegner, Josiah. "The Application of Second Language Acquisition Theory to New Testament Greek Pedagogy." Unpublished senior thesis, Liberty University, 2013.
Weinreich, Harald, Hartmut Obendorf, Eelco Herder, and Matthias Mayer. "Not Quite the Average: An Empirical Study of Web Use." *ACM Transactions on the Web* 2.1 (February 2008).
Wheaton College Graduate School. "M.A. in Biblical Exegesis." https://www.wheaton.edu/graduate-school/degrees/ma-in-biblical-exegesis/.
Wheeler, Barbara G., and Anthony T. Ruger. "Sobering Figures Point to Overall Enrollment Decline: New Research from the Auburn Center for the Study of Theological Education." *In Trust* (Spring 2013): 5–11.
Whitacre, Rodney A. *Using and Enjoying Biblical Greek: Reading the New Testament with Fluency and Devotion*. Grand Rapids: Baker, 2015.
Wiggins, Grant, and Jay McTighe. *Understanding by Design*. Alexandria VA: ASCD, 2005.
Wilson, Mark. "Greek Vocabulary Acquisition Using Semantic Domains." *JETS* 46.2 (2003): 193–204.
Wood, David, Jerome Bruner, and Gail Ross. "The Role of Tutoring in Problem Solving." *Journal of Child Psychiatry and Psychology* 17 (1976): 89–100.
Wright, Roger V. "Greek Language: The Use of the Greek Language in the Pulpit and Classroom." Unpublished senior thesis, Southern Christian University, 2000.
ZA Blogs. "Interview with Ken Berding part 1 – 'Sing and Learn New Testament Greek.'" *Zondervan Academic*. 16 September 2008. http://zondervanacademic.com/blog/interview-with/.
———. "Interview with Ken Berding part 2 – 'Sing and Learn New Testament Greek.'" *Zondervan Academic*. 17 September 2008. http://zondervanacademic.com/blog/5-with-all-that/.

Zacharias, Daniel. *NT Greek Stripped Down: Mastering Greek Essentials in Conjunction with Bible Software.* Web–Based: Scholar's Publisher, 2012.

Zeps, Dainis. "The Learning of Ancient Languages as (Super) Human Effort." *Institute of Mathematics and Computer Science* 4 (2009): 1–8.

Zodhiates, Spiros. *The Complete Word Study Dictionary: New Testament.* Iowa Falls, IA: World Bible Publishers, 1992.

www.ingramcontent.com/pod-product-compliance
Lightning Source LLC
Chambersburg PA
CBHW050847230426
43667CB00012B/2184